D0998216

ICONS

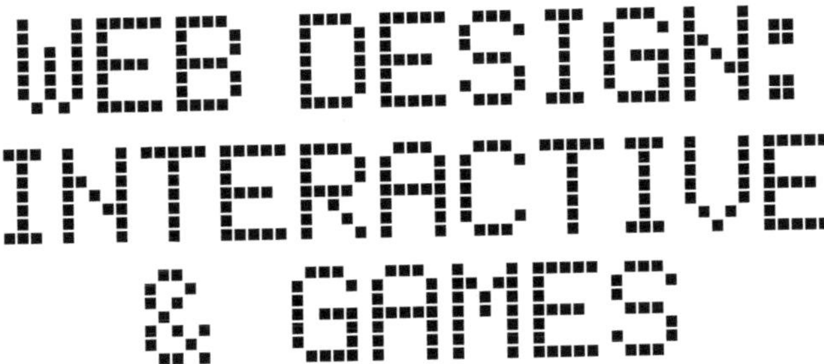

Ed. Julius Wiedemann

TASCHEN

HONG KONG KÖLN LONDON LOS ANGELES MADRID PARIS TOKYO

CONTENTS

INTRO by Mike John Otto. 4
CASE•01 by Sergio Mugnaine 16
CASE•02 by Jonathan Hills 22
CASE•03 by Partrick Gardner 28
30 Days of Night 34
A4 Global Drives 36
Absolut Disco 38
Adidas Game 40
Alive Is 42
Adidas Predator vs F50+ 44
Agile Crossfox 46
Allstate Garage 48
ATC-SIM 50
Bang on the Door 52
Barbie Hits. 53
Bean Boing Splash 54
Bau mit uns ein Flugzeug 56
Beboard 58
Berry Bones 60
Big Soil 62
Build Your Own Volvo V70 64
CDX 66
Choosing a Mortgage 68
Claus on Ice 70
Colour Your Music 72
Doctor in a Dash 73
Death in Sakkara 74
DELA Volleyball. 76
Doritos Collisions Mixer 78
Dylan Messaging 80
Edeka Lebensmitteldiplom 82
E-pousse (E-garden) 84
Exciting KIA 86
Fall Out Boy 88
Get The Glass 90
Get The Message 92
Guantánamo 94
Healthcare Mission 96
Het Huis Anubis 98

Howl-O-Scream 100
Hungry Suitcase 102
I'm a Cyborg, But That's OK 104
i-mode 106
Impossible Story 108
Jingle Along with Santa 110
Launchball 111
Juntos pela Natureza 112
Le petit oiseau va sortir 114
Level-up! 116
Lightning Game 117
Mencia Madness 118
Mencia Meltdown 119
Mini Swirlz 120
Monsters 122
Motocolors 124
Moving Day 126
Nokia 7500 Prism 127
Na Fogueira 128
Na Sniegu 130
Nike Windrunner Collectibles 132
One fine day in London 134
Peg Solitaire 136
Piggy Scope 137
Pepsi Roberto Carlos 138
Pepsi Twistão 140
Pharrell 142
Porsche Bloodlines 144
Reverze 146
Rubb-it for Healthy Eyes! 148
Starbucks Time 149
Saab Pilots Wanted 150
Sabrina Setlur - Rot.fm 152
Sarah Jane Adventures 154
Skatenis BIBI 156
Spooks 158
Starbucks Pass The Cheer 160
TDK WCA Challenge 162
The Coke Zero Game 164
The Grudge 2 166
The Pirates' Lair 168
Thyssen Gleistechnik 170
Toronto Tourism 172
Travel Finder 174
Trust the Man 176
Turner Road Show 178
VF Insider 180
Was auch kommt: HDI 182
Who is Doctor Who? 184
XM Wild Ride 186
Yaris vs. Yaris 188
CREDITS 191

INTRO

"We don't stop playing because we grow old; we grow old because we stop playing."
– G. Bernard Shaw

Introduction
Mike John Otto

Is this the reason for our increasing desire to play? And, above all, for the growing interest in digital games? Because, in this digital age, nobody wants to admit that he or she is getting old — or worse yet, already *is* old? Or perhaps we simply want to reawaken the child inside all of us. The fact is that our possibilities for play have never been as great and varied as they are today.

In the past, it was primarily younger children who messed about in front of computers and game consoles. Nowadays — thanks primarily to innovative, more intuitive and user-friendly hardware such as Nintendo Wii — digital games are becoming more and more attractive to the older generations amongst us as well. Our society is demanding increasingly active types of entertainment — forms of recreation which are both active and fun to interact with. Consumers ultimately want to participate in and influence their entertainment themselves, and not simply sit in front of the television set and passively absorb information from the media. As exemplified by the phenomenon of Web 2.0, many people have the desire to participate in the formation and development of recreational activities. A situation in which only a few people produce entertainment and many receive it no longer seems to function in our ever more individualized society.

Since this book is concerned with online games and advertainment, I do not wish to delve too deeply here into the world of game consoles such as PS2, Nintendo Wii, or Xbox. Nevertheless, it would be a mistake simply to ignore the enormous influence game consoles have had. It is only thanks to the game console boom and the ever-increasing interconnection between the newest console generation and the Internet that the demand for, and interest in online games has grown both amongst users and businesses. More and more businesses are using games as a further building-block in their brand communication strategies; there is an increasingly popular trend in marketing toward making brands tangibly accessible through the use of games.

Perhaps, however, at this point it would be better to speak of the growing trend toward so-called "advertainment" or "adgames" — that is, the area in which games are used as marketing tools and for product promotion. Along with classical online specials and microsites, the number of these adgames is constantly increasing since they allow the user to enjoy a playful experience of the brand in question — without too much blatant and annoying advertising. In this way, the brand and the product can be made accessible to a primarily young, flexible and very media-savvy target group, with no strings attached. An additional positive side-effect of this approach is that it lends the product a modern and very promising image: "We know what you want, and we can bring our products directly to you."

In contrast to TV commercials, print advertising, or online specials, in the case of adgames the product and its originator tend to have a more subliminal presence. The entertainment factor is predominant. Rather than being bombarded with information the way they are in classical forms of advertising, players receive the sender's message more casually and voluntarily. In general, such adgames should be quick and easy to consume. The goal should not be to imitate any elaborate and complex console games.

When an agency encourages its clients to develop an intricate online game for the product they wish to advertise — one that is comparable to a console game in its quality and complexity — the result is often nonsensical and misses out on the current trend. It is impossible to achieve the same quality found in a console game, since no customer is prepared to pay for the effort involved in developing it.

One should keep in mind that a high-quality racing game such as *Gran Turismo 4* for the PS2 has become nearly as expensive to produce as a feature film. The game that accompanied the movie *King Kong*, for example, was not much cheaper to produce than the film itself, and it was able to take advantage of synergy effects in the production process.

So, is it possible to compete with an online racing or adventure game?

You should always ask yourself, "Why should I put up with a long online waiting time in order actually to be able to play a game? Do I have the time and desire to do this at the office?" After all, very few people will play games like this at home in the evenings with a laptop on their laps; they would rather turn on the game console and use the controllers instead of wearing their fingers out playing with a mouse or on the arrow keys. Furthermore, users are likely to be skeptical if a game looks too much like advertising.

So is it better to forget about this approach completely? Not at all — because a good, simple idea is as important here as it is for classical forms of advertising or online campaigns.

BMW, for example, produced several high-quality driving simulation and racing games exclusively for the Internet. They are highly attractive visually, and the production quality is very good… so, did they do everything right? Not really. Because if it takes several minutes for the game to load even with a DSL connection, you have already gone beyond the reasonable scope of patience that you can expect from the user. In addition, the process of accessing the game is too complicated. It simply takes too long to get to the point where you can enjoy the well-produced driving segments. One has the impression that the makers conceived the games exactly according to the principles of a console game — apparently without taking the unique characteristics of the Internet medium into account, that is, to provide the user with information and entertainment that is accessible quickly.

Despite increasing online bandwidths, game concepts such as these are simply not appropriate for the medium, and certainly not user-friendly. It is better to design an online game that loads smoothly and is easy to understand and play but is clearly differentiated from high-tech consoles and the games that are produced for them. If the idea is funny and captivating, no user is likely to complain that "the racing game on my PS3 looks better." The user will know that there is no comparison between the two. But that's not the point.

Therefore, many clients such as BMW use a two-pronged approach. In addition to commissioning an elaborate online game, they pursue another strategy as well: integrating the company's new product range into a game like *Gran Turismo 4*. There, along with other car brands, the player can look at, configure and test-drive all of the BMW models. This is the result of a cooperation with the game manufacturer which allows BMW to score points with hardcore gamers as well.

So, is in-game advertising a more effective approach than that of advertainment using adgames? No, one can't say that across the board either. A great deal depends upon the product and the target group one wishes to reach. An opportunity to play at any time and which doesn't cost the user approximately € 60 is still a strong argument in favor of purely online games.

After all, just about everyone has the urge to play a quick game every now and then without having to read an entire manual in order to understand it. Here, you can simply play a straightforward little game for fun and relaxation without having to exert any extra effort during your already stressful day. Innovation is an important factor

— as it always is in advertising. After all, a funny TV spot doesn't need to have the production values of a blockbuster in order to sell the product and the message successfully.

And this brings us to the current trend in gaming. Why, for example, does the PS3 sell more poorly than the Wii? It is simply too complicated and overloaded. It can do more than what the majority of the target group demands. Instead of concentrating on a console that is easy to operate, the developers just continued to push the quality higher. The Wii, on the other hand, branched out in new directions. Here, a simpler, somewhat more primitive graphic quality was the trade-off for a revolutionary navigation principle.

So let's take a look at which gaming principles can make an adgame as successful in the field of advertainment as the Wii is in the world of console games.

Principle #1: Simply play!

The game *The Stuntman* is an example of a simple adgame that works. It carries Rexona's successful *Action City* campaign over into the Internet and has been thematically elaborated in a way that works well for the medium.

The instructions are as follows: "Throw a stuntman against everything in the room as many times as possible. Push him to his limits." The principle employed here is simple and fun to play. In addition, the visual quality is extremely high.

What does the game have to do with the product? Well... it extends the message of the campaign, "A body spray that can stand up to any challenge," in an entertaining way. Nothing more, but nothing less either.

Principle #2: Playful learning

Another possible approach for a good adgame is the principle of playful learning. Allowing the user to learn something about the product or the brand while he or she is playing is a very clever and subtle form of advertising.

A number of businesses are currently relying on games to educate their customers about their product or their company philosophy. Some examples of this are the milk campaign, *Get the Glass*, in which, through a playful and charming process, the user has to capture a glass of milk almost as if it were the Holy Grail, or the special site <www.wasauchkommt.de> ("no matter what happens"), from the HDI insurance company, where the player can personally experience how much damage he or she can do with just a few clicks. This experience is intended to teach the user why it is a better idea to make an appointment for a consultation at his nearest HDI branch. In both of these cases, an already successful television campaign was expanded upon in a self-contained, Internet-appropriate format.

Perhaps these adgames work so well because, in addition to the high fun factor, users find them original and return to them repeatedly, perhaps even passing the link on to their friends. In other words, people spend a relatively long time with them. They become a little bit addicted. And as we all know, it is always the simplest things that are the most addictive.

Principle #3: Unexpectedly addictive

I recently discovered a website for the band Krezip. Along with a visually attractive and very pared-down site, I found the idea of allowing visitors to listen to a song both simple and original. The user is instructed to use circular motions of the mouse to move a disc depicting the band the way a vinyl record would spin on a turntable. If the user manages to turn the "record" long enough at a correct and constant speed, he or she can win various prizes. One finds oneself trying the game again and again, hoping to improve one's result.

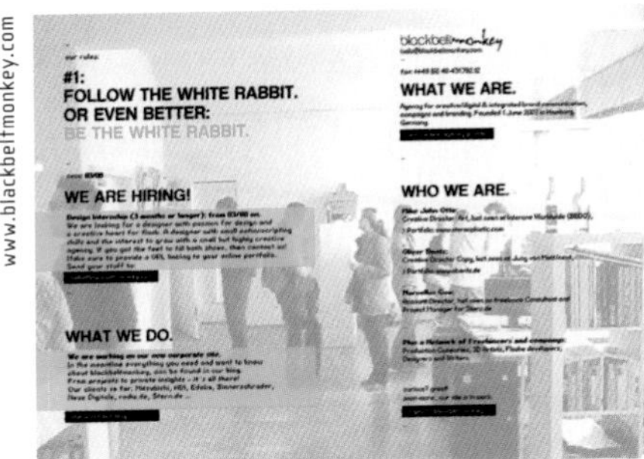

www.blackbeltmonkey.com

If people write and talk so much about a certain phenomenon, we can definitely call it a successful form of advertising because the target group has been reached. Almost as a side-effect the product in question is given a higher profile and may even win over new fans who were not interested in it or the brand before. Here, the point is not only to sell a lot more of the product, but also to make its positive recognition factor as strong and widespread as possible. After that, sales usually follow automatically.

Let's stay on the subject of music for a moment. I was amused by a passage of text I heard on the new album "The Black and White Album" by The Hives, which contains the line: "A definition of madness is doing the same thing again and expecting a different result."

So are the users crazy? Do games make us crazy? A little bit, certainly. Because games can make us addicted in the sense that we keep doing the same thing over and over again in the hope of improving our results — in the hope of getting better at the game or simply reaching the next level. This is OK in moderation; after all, it's also fun. In recent years, digital games have had an enormous influence on our society. They have become more and more sophisticated and the story lines have become better and better. The film industry alone has experienced a surge thanks to the filming of game story-lines such as *Resident Evil* or more recently, *Hitman*, or through games accompanying films.

We can no longer imagine our modern society without electronic games. You have to know something about them in order to talk about them and have an opinion about them. So if anyone tells you that games are bad for you, simply answer in a paraphrase of Shigeru Miyamoto (inventor of *Mario* and *Donkey Kong*): "Games are bad for you? That's what they said about Rock'n' Roll, too."

So, Dear Reader... LET'S PLAY!

Mike John Otto is the co-founder and Creative Director of the Hamburg-based agency **blackbeltmonkey**. After completing his studies in Visual Communication in 2000, he worked as a freelancer in London before assuming the position of Senior Designer at the Razorfish Agency in 2001. After two years at Razorfish, he took over the post of Art Director at Elephant Seven in Hamburg; in early 2002, he moved to INTERONE (an agency of BBDO). He worked as Senior Art Director for such companies as BMW and later as Creative Director for the o2 and MINI brands. For his work for BMW and MINI, he received numerous awards both at Cannes and from the Art Directors Club, as well as many additional awards such as the Clio, Cresta, New York Festivals and EFFIE. Together with two of his former colleagues from INTERONE, he founded the blackbeltmonkey Agency in 2007. **<www.blackbeltmonkey.com>**

INTRO

„Wir hören nicht auf zu spielen, weil wir alt werden, sondern wir werden alt, weil wir aufhören zu spielen." – G. Bernard Shaw

Einführung

Mike John Otto

Ist das also der Grund für die steigende Lust am Spielen? Und vor allem das steigende Interesse an digitalen Spielen? Weil im digitalen Zeitalter keiner gerne zugibt, alt zu werden oder gar alt zu sein? Vielleicht möchte man auch nur gerne wieder das Kind in sich wecken. Fakt ist, dass die Möglichkeiten zum Spielen noch nie so groß und vielfältig waren wie heute.

Früher waren es vor allem die jüngeren Kids, die sich vor dem Rechner und den Konsolen tummelten. Heute sind es, besonders geprägt durch innovative, intuitivere und einfacher zu bedienende Hardware wie die Nintendo Wii, in steigendem Maße auch die Älteren unter uns, die Gefallen an digitalen Spielen finden. Die Gesellschaft verlangt immer mehr aktive Unterhaltungsformen — aktive Freizeitgestaltung, die Spaß macht. Die Verbraucher wollen endlich selbst handeln, selbst Einfluss nehmen und nicht nur vor dem Fernseher sitzen und passiv Informationen von den Medien aufnehmen. So wie beim Phänomen Web 2.0 wünschen sich viele, auch bei der Freizeitgestaltung selbst mitmachen zu können. Dass einige produzieren und viele empfangen, scheint in einer immer individuelleren Gesellschaft nicht mehr zu funktionieren.

Da sich dieses Buch mit Online-Games und Advertainment beschäftigt, möchte ich nicht zur sehr in die Welt der Konsolen wie PS2, Nintendo Wii, oder Xbox einsteigen. Jedoch wäre es ein Fehler, den enormen Einfluss der Konsolen einfach unter den Teppich zu kehren. Denn erst durch den Boom der Spielkonsolen sowie der immer größeren Vernetzung der neuesten Konsolen-Generation mit dem Internet ist der Anspruch und das Interesse an Online-Games gestiegen, und zwar sowohl beim User als auch bei den Unternehmen. Immer mehr Unternehmen nutzen Spiele als einen weiteren Baustein der Markenkommunikation. Der Trend, die Marke auch spielerisch erlebbar zu machen, findet im Marketing immer mehr Gefallen.

Doch vielleicht sollten wir an dieser Stelle besser vom Trend des sogenannten „Advertainments" oder von den „Adgames" sprechen, also dem Bereich, in dem Spiele als Marketing-Tool und zur Produktunterstützung genutzt werden. Diese Adgames nehmen neben den klassischen Online-Specials und Microsites ständig zu, weil der User damit die Marke spielerisch erleben kann — ohne zuviel offensichtliche und nervende Werbung. Damit können die Marke und das Produkt einer meist jungen, flexiblen und sehr medienaffinen Zielgruppe unverbindlich näher gebracht werden. Ein positiver Nebeneffekt ist zudem, der Marke ein modernes Image zu geben — ein viel versprechendes Image: „Wir wissen, was ihr wollt, und kommen mit unseren Produkten direkt zu euch."

In der Regel treten das Produkt und der Absender bei den Adgames im Gegensatz zum TV-Spot, dem Plakat oder dem Online-Special eher unterschwellig auf. Der Entertainment-Faktor überwiegt. Statt wie bei klassischen Werbeformen mit Informationen bombardiert zu werden, ruft der Spieler die zu vermittelnde Botschaft freiwillig und nebenbei ab. Solche Adgames sollten in der Regel einfach und schnell zu konsumieren sein. Das Ziel darf nicht sein, die aufwendigen und komplexen Konsolen-Spiele zu imitieren.

Wenn Agenturen ihren Kunden vorschlagen, ein aufwendiges Online-Game für das zu bewerbende Produkt zu entwickeln, welches qualitativ und von der Komplexität her mit einem Konsolen-Spiel vergleichbar sein soll, ist das oft unsinnig und geht am Trend vorbei. Die gleiche Qualität wird man nie erreichen, da kein Kunde bereit ist, den benötigten Aufwand zu bezahlen.

Man beachte, dass ein gutes Rennspiel wie *Gran Turismo 4* für die PS2 mittlerweile fast so teuer zu produzieren ist wie ein Spielfilm. Das Spiel zum Film *King Kong* war beispielsweise nicht viel billiger als der Film selbst und nutzte Synergie-Effekte bei der Produktion.

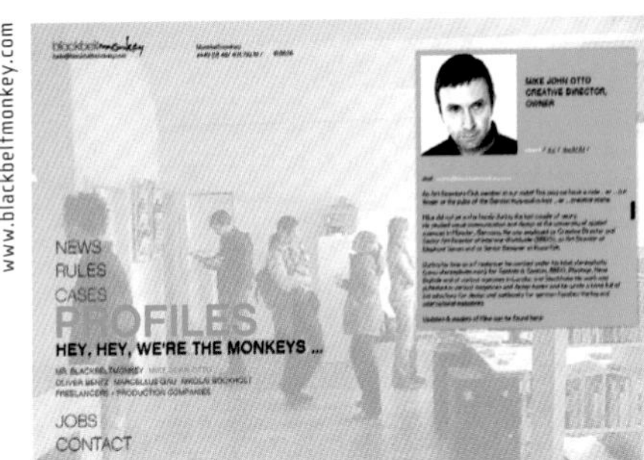

www.blackbeltmonkey.com

Kann man da mit einem Online-Rennspiel oder einem Online-Adventure mithalten?

Man wird sich immer fragen: „Warum soll ich online lange Wartezeiten in Kauf nehmen, um endlich spielen zu können? Habe ich Zeit und Lust, das im Büro zu tun?" Denn kaum jemand spielt solche Spiele abends zuhause mit dem Laptop auf dem Schoß. Dann doch lieber schnell mal die Konsole anwerfen und sich mit Controllern statt der Maus zu vergnügen oder sich mit den Cursor-Tasten beim Spielen die Finger zu brechen.

Zudem ist der User oft eher skeptisch, wenn etwas zu stark nach Werbung riecht. Also doch eher die Finger davon lassen? Keineswegs, denn eine gute und einfache Idee ist hier genauso wichtig wie bei den klassischen Werbeformen oder bei Online-Kampagnen.

Für BMW wurden z.B. rein für das Internet einige Online-Fahrsimulationen und Rennspiele auf hohem Niveau produziert. Diese sehen optisch schick aus und sind auch aufwendig erstellt worden ... also alles richtig gemacht? Nicht wirklich. Denn wenn man trotz DSL-Verbindung erst einmal einige Minuten warten muss, damit das Spiel endlich geladen ist, sprengt das den zumutbaren Rahmen. Zudem ist der Einstieg zum Spiel zu komplex. Es dauert einfach zu lange, bis man in den Genuss der gut gemachten Fahrsequenzen kommt. Es wirkt, als ob man die Spiele 1:1 nach dem Prinzip von Konsolengames konzipiert hat (ohne anscheinend die Eigenart des Mediums Internet zu berücksichtigen — nämlich dem User schnell aufrufbare Informationen und Unterhaltung zu bieten).

Solche Spielkonzepte sind trotz steigender Online-Bandbreite einfach nicht mediengerecht, geschweige denn anwenderfreundlich. Besser ist es, wenn ein Online-Game flüssig lädt und einfach zu verstehen sowie zu spielen ist, aber sich klar von den High-Tech-Konsolen und den dafür produzierten Spielen abgrenzt. Ist die Idee witzig und fesselnd, wird kaum ein User sagen: „Das sieht aber in dem Rennspiel auf meiner PS3 besser aus." Der User weiß selbst, dass man das nicht vergleichen kann. Darum geht es gar nicht.

Viele Kunden wie BMW fahren daher zweigleisig. Neben dem Auftrag für ein aufwendiges Online-Game ist man zusätzlich einen anderen Weg gegangen: die Einbindung der neuen Produktpalette in Spiele wie *Gran Turismo 4*. Der Spieler kann dort neben anderen Marken alle BMWs anschauen, konfigurieren und Probe fahren. Das ist das Ergebnis der Kooperation mit dem Spielehersteller, was BMW auch bei den Hardcore-Gamern Punkte bringt.

Ist also der Weg des Ingame Advertisings effektiver als der des Advertainments mit den Adgames? Das kann man pauschal nicht sagen. Es hängt viel von dem Produkt und der umworbenen Zielgruppe ab. Ein jederzeit verfügbares Spielvergnügen, für das man nicht knapp 60 € ausgeben muss, ist immer noch ein starkes Argument, das für reine Online-Games spricht.

Schließlich hat ja jeder auch mal Lust, schnell mal etwas zu spielen, ohne gleich ein ganzes Handbuch für das Spiel lesen zu müssen. Hier kann man einfach mal ganz banal etwas spielen, das einen entspannt und Freude macht, ohne dass man neben dem stressigen Alltag schon wieder gefordert wird. Innovation ist gefragt, wie in der Werbung schon immer. Ein witziger TV-Spot muss auch nicht immer wie ein Blockbuster aussehen, um die Botschaft und das Produkt erfolgreich zu verkaufen.

Und damit wären wir auch beim aktuellen Trend angekommen. Warum verkauft sich die PS3 z.B. schlechter als die Wii? Sie ist schlicht zu komplex und überladen. Sie kann mehr, als die breite Zielgruppe verlangt. Statt über eine einfach zu bedienende Konsole nachzudenken, wurde nur die Qualität hochgeschraubt. Die Wii ging stattdessen neue Wege. Bei ihr wurde eine einfachere, etwas primitivere Grafikqualität zugunsten eines revolutionären Navigationsprinzips in Kauf genommen.

Schauen wir uns also an, welche Spielprinzipien beim Advertainment ein Adgame so erfolgreich werden lassen, wie es die Wii beim Konsolenvergleich ist.

Prinzip #1: Einfach spielen

Das Spiel *The Stuntman* ist ein gelungenes Beispiel für ein einfaches Adgame. Es setzt die erfolgreiche Kampagne *Action City* von Rexona im Internet fort und ist thematisch für das Medium Internet gut weitergedacht.

Die Aufgabe lautet: „Werfe einen Stuntman so oft wie möglich gegen alles, was sich im Raum befindet. Bring ihn an seine Grenzen." Das angewandte Prinzip ist einfach und macht Spaß. Dabei ist es zudem visuell extrem gut gemacht.

Was hat das mit dem Produkt zu tun? Na ja … es setzt die Kampagne mit der Message „Ein Körperspray, das alle Belastungen aushält" unterhaltsam fort. Nicht mehr, aber auch nicht weniger.

Prinzip #2: Spielerisch lernen

Eine weitere Möglichkeit für ein gutes Adgame ist das Prinzip des spielerischen Lernens. Beim Spielen etwas über das Produkt oder die Marke zu erfahren, ist sehr schlaue und subtile Werbung.

Mehrere Unternehmen setzen derzeit darauf, ihre Firmenphilosophie oder ihr Produkt dem Kunden durch ein Spiel näherzubringen. Sei es wie bei der Milchkampagne *Get the Glass*, bei der ein Glas Milch schon fast wie der Heilige Gral spielerisch und sehr charmant erobert werden muss, oder bei dem Special <wasauchkommt.de> der Versicherungsgesellschaft HDI, bei der man online am eigenen Leib erfährt, was man mit wenigen Klicks alles anrichten kann. Eine Erfahrung, die einem zeigen soll, warum man lieber einen Beratungstermin bei der nächsten HDI-Filiale vereinbaren sollte. In beiden Beispielen wurde die erfolgreiche TV-Kampagne sehr mediengerecht und eigenständig fortgeführt.

Diese Adgames funktionieren vielleicht so gut, weil man neben dem hohen Spaßfaktor diese auch originell findet und sich öfter anschaut, den Link sogar an Freunde versendet — sich also verhältnismäßig lange damit beschäftigt. Man wird etwas süchtig. Und süchtig machen ja bekanntlich die einfachsten Dinge.

Prinzip #3: Überraschend süchtig

Neulich habe ich eine Seite für die Band Krezip entdeckt. Neben einer optisch schönen und sehr reduzierten Seite fand ich die Idee, wie man sich den Song anhören kann, so überraschend wie einfach zugleich. Der User wird aufgefordert, mit kreisförmigen Mausbewegungen den Drehteller mit der Band darauf wie bei einem Schallplattenteller in einer konstanten Bewegung zum Drehen zu bringen. Tut der User das lange genug in der richtigen und gleichen Geschwindigkeit, kann er verschiedene Preise gewinnen. Dabei ertappt man sich, es immer wieder neu zu probieren, um es immer besser hinzubekommen.

Wenn über etwas soviel geschrieben und gesprochen wird, kann man ruhig von einer erfolgreichen Werbeform sprechen, denn man hat die Zielgruppe erreicht. Das beworbene Produkt wird ganz nebenbei gestärkt und findet eventuell sogar neue Fans, die sich vorher für die Marke oder das Produkt nicht interessierten. Es geht dabei gar nicht allein darum, ob dadurch viel mehr verkauft wurde, sondern um eine möglichst große und positive Bekanntheit und Verbreitung. Das Verkaufen kommt dann meistens ganz von selbst.

Bleiben wir doch kurz beim Thema Musik. Lustig fand ich eine Textpassage, die ich im neuen Album „The Black

www.blackbeltmonkey.com

and White Album" von The Hives gehört habe. Darin kommt die Zeile vor: „A definition of madness is doing the same thing again and expecting a different result" („Eine Definition von Wahnsinn ist, dass man das Gleiche noch einmal tut und ein anderes Ergebnis erwartet").

Ist der User also verrückt? Machen Spiele verrückt? Ein bisschen bestimmt. Denn Games können süchtig machen, indem man das Gleiche immer wieder tut, um das Ergebnis zu verbessern, um immer besser zu werden oder um einfach nur weiterzukommen. Das ist in Maßen aber okay, denn es macht ja auch Spaß. Digitale Games haben in den letzten Jahren einen riesigen Einfluss auf die Gesellschaft gehabt. Sie wurden immer raffinierter und bekamen immer bessere Handlungen. Allein die Filmindustrie erlebte einen wahren Schub durch Verfilmungen von Spielehandlungen wie *Resident Evil* oder jüngst *Hitman* oder durch begleitende Games zum Film.

E-Games sind aus der modernen Gesellschaft nicht mehr wegzudenken. Man sollte sich auskennen, um mitreden zu können und eine Meinung zu haben. Solltet ihr also von jemandem hören, dass Games schlecht für euch sind, dann antwortet einfach im Sinne von Shigeru Miyamoto (dem Erfinder von *Mario* und *Donkey Kong*): „Games are bad for you? That's what they said about Rock 'n' Roll, too."

Also, liebe Leser... LET'S PLAY!

Mike John Otto ist Creative Director und Mitbegründer der Hamburger Agentur **blackbeltmonkey**. Nach dem Studium der visuellen Kommunikation im Jahr 2000 arbeitete er zunächst frei in London, bis er dann 2001 als Senior Designer bei der Agentur Razorfish begann. Nach zwei Jahren bei Razorfish startete er als Art Director bei Elephant Seven in Hamburg, bis er Anfang 2002 zu INTERONE (Agency of BBDO) ging. Dort war er zunächst als Senior Art Director unter anderem für die Marke BMW und später als Creative Director für die Marken o2 und MINI tätig. Seine Arbeiten für BMW und MINI wurden mehrmals sowohl in Cannes als auch vom ADC ausgezeichnet und bekamen viele weitere Awards wie Clio, Cresta, New York Festivals und EFFIE. Mitte 2007 gründete er zusammen mit zwei ehemaligen INTERONE-Kollegen die Agentur blackbeltmonkey. **<www.blackbeltmonkey.com>**

« Nous n'arrêtons pas de jouer parce que nous vieillissons ; nous vieillissons parce que nous arrêtons de jouer. »
– G. Bernard Shaw

Introduction
Mike John Otto

Est-ce la raison de notre désir grandissant de jouer ? Et avant tout de notre intérêt croissant pour les jeux numériques ? À l'ère du numérique, personne ne veut admettre qu'il vieillit, ou pire encore, qu'il *est* déjà vieux. Peut-être s'agit-il simplement de faire renaître l'enfant qui sommeille en nous. Le fait est que nos chances de jouer n'ont jamais été aussi grandes et variées qu'aujourd'hui.

Avant, c'était surtout les enfants qui prenaient du bon temps devant des ordinateurs et des consoles de jeux. À l'heure actuelle, et grâce notamment à des équipements innovateurs, plus intuitifs et conviviaux comme la Nintendo Wii, les jeux numériques attirent aussi de plus en plus les générations plus âgées. Notre société est demandeuse de divertissements chaque fois plus actifs, des formes de jeu à la fois actives et amusantes. Les consommateurs veulent enfin prendre part à leur divertissement et l'influencer, plutôt que de rester assis devant la télévision et d'absorber passivement des informations des médias. Comme l'a montré le phénomène du Web 2.0, de nombreuses personnes souhaitent participer à la création d'activités ludiques. Le schéma dans lequel seules quelques personnes sont à l'origine de distractions et un grand nombre en profitent ne semble plus fonctionner dans notre société de plus en plus individualisée.

Comme cet ouvrage s'attache aux jeux et à l'advertainment en ligne, je ne souhaite pas approfondir dans ces pages le monde des consoles vidéo comme PS2, Nintendo Wii et Xbox. Néanmoins, il serait une erreur d'ignorer l'énorme influence qu'elles ont exercée. C'est à leur boom et à l'interconnexion croissante entre la dernière génération de consoles et Internet que l'on doit une demande et un intérêt pour les jeux en ligne chaque fois plus importants parmi les utilisateurs et les entreprises. Celles-ci ont de plus en plus recours aux jeux comme pièce clé de leurs stratégies de communication de marque. Il existe une tendance marketing chaque fois plus répandue visant à rendre les marques accessibles de façon tangible via des jeux.

Il serait toutefois peut-être préférable à ce stade de mentionner la place croissante de l'« advertainment » ou des « adgames » : dans ce domaine, des jeux servent d'outils marketing et de promotion pour des produits. À part les jeux et les mini-sites en ligne classiques, le nombre d'adgames ne cesse d'augmenter, car ils offrent à l'utilisateur une expérience amusante de la marque en question sans trop de publicité flagrante et ennuyante. De cette façon, la marque et le produit deviennent accessibles pour un groupe cible principalement jeune, flexible et très calé en médias, sans compromis. Autre conséquence positive de cette approche : elle dote le produit d'une image moderne et très prometteuse, de type « Nous savons ce que vous voulez et nous pouvons vous fournir directement nos produits ».

Par rapport aux spots télévisés, à la publicité sur papier ou en ligne, le produit et la marque exercent dans le cas des adgames une présence plus subliminale, le divertissement étant prédominant. Au lieu de se faire bombarder d'informations comme dans les formes classiques de publicité, les joueurs reçoivent le message de l'émetteur de façon plus fortuite et volontaire. En général, ces adgames sont courts et faciles. L'objectif ne doit pas être d'imiter des jeux vidéo élaborés et complexes.

Lorsqu'une agence encourage ses clients à développer un jeu en ligne compliqué pour le produit à promouvoir, du niveau d'un jeu vidéo en termes de qualité et de difficulté, le résultat est souvent inepte et passe à côté de la tendance actuelle. Il est impossible d'obtenir la même qualité qu'un jeu vidéo, sachant que le consommateur n'est pas prêt à payer l'effort investi dans son développement.

www.blackbeltmonkey.com

Il faut bien penser qu'un jeu de course de haute qualité comme *Gran Turismo 4* pour la PS2 a coûté presque autant que la production d'un film. Par exemple, la production du jeu qui accompagnait le film *King Kong* n'a pas été meilleur marché que le film en soi, alors qu'il était possible de profiter de la synergie lors du processus de production.

Peut-on alors faire de l'ombre à un jeu en ligne de course ou d'aventure ?

La question à toujours se poser est : « Pourquoi devrais-je tolérer une longue attente pour jouer à un jeu en ligne ? Ai-je le temps et l'envie de le faire au bureau ? » Car en fin de compte, rares sont les personnes qui joueront à ce type de jeu chez elles le soir, avec un portable sur les genoux. Elles préféreront dans ce cas allumer la console de jeux et se servir des manettes au lieu de se fatiguer avec la souris ou les touches fléchées du clavier. En outre, les utilisateurs risquent d'être sceptiques si un jeu ressemble trop à une publicité.

Vaut-il donc mieux oublier totalement cette approche ? Pas du tout, puisqu'une idée bonne et simple compte autant que dans les formes classiques de publicité ou de campagnes en ligne.

Par exemple, BMW a produit plusieurs jeux de simulation et de course de haute qualité exclusivement pour Internet. Ces jeux sont visuellement très attirants et la qualité de production est excellente. Ont-ils donc eu raison ? Pas vraiment : il faut plusieurs minutes pour que le jeu se charge, même avec une connexion haut débit, et les limites raisonnables de la patience de l'utilisateur sont alors déjà dépassées. Par ailleurs, l'accès au jeu est trop compliqué. Il faut trop de temps avant d'arriver au point où vous pouvez apprécier les segments de conduite si bien faits. Il donne l'impression que les développeurs ont conçu le jeu exactement comme un jeu vidéo (sans prendre visiblement en compte les caractéristiques d'Internet), pour fournir à l'utilisateur des informations et une distraction rapidement accessibles.

Malgré les largeurs de bande croissantes, les concepts des jeux de ce type ne sont pas adaptés au support et encore moins conviviaux. Il est préférable de concevoir un jeu en ligne se chargeant facilement et simple à comprendre et à suivre, tout en se démarquant clairement des consoles high-tech et des jeux conçus pour elles. Si l'idée est drôle et captivante, aucun utilisateur ne risque de se plaindre que « le jeu de course sur ma PS3 est mieux ». L'utilisateur saura qu'il n'y a pas de place à la comparaison entre les deux. Mais là n'est pas la question.

Par conséquent, beaucoup de clients comme BMW suivent une approche sur deux fronts. En plus de commander un jeu en ligne élaboré, ils appliquent une autre stratégie : l'intégration de la nouvelle gamme de produits de la marque à un jeu comme *Gran Turismo 4*. Parmi d'autres marques de véhicules, le joueur peut observer, configurer et tester tous les modèles BMW. Grâce à la coopération avec le fabricant du jeu, BMW peut aussi marquer des points avec des joueurs avertis.

L'approche consistant à insérer de la publicité dans des jeux est-elle alors plus efficace que celle de l'advertainment à base d'adgames ? Non, personne ne peut non plus faire une telle affirmation, tout dépend surtout du produit et du groupe cible à atteindre. Un jeu disponible à tout moment et qui ne coûte pas quelque 60 € à l'utilisateur est toujours un argument de poids en faveur des jeux exclusivement en ligne.

Après tout, tout le monde a besoin de jouer à un jeu rapide de temps à autre sans devoir lire un manuel entier pour le comprendre. Vous pouvez ainsi jouer à un petit jeu banal pour vous amuser et vous détendre, sans effort supplémentaire au cours de votre journée déjà stressante. L'innovation est un facteur clé, comme elle l'est aussi toujours en publicité. Un spot drôle à la télévision n'a en effet pas besoin d'un budget aussi élevé qu'une superproduction pour réussir à vendre le produit et faire passer le message.

Tout ceci nous amène à la tendance actuelle en matière de jeux. Pourquoi par exemple la PS3 se vend-elle moins que la Wii ? Tout simplement parce qu'elle est plus compliquée et surchargée. Les fonctions qu'elle offre dépassent la majorité des demandes du groupe cible. Au lieu de se concentrer sur une console facile d'emploi, les développeurs n'ont cessé de mettre la barre toujours plus haut pour la qualité. La Wii s'est en revanche orientée vers d'autres directions. Dans son cas, une qualité graphique un peu plus primitive a été acceptée en échange d'un principe de navigation révolutionnaire.

Observons donc les principes des jeux qui peuvent rendre un adgame aussi célèbre dans le domaine de l'advertainment que la Wii dans le monde des jeux vidéo.

Principe #1 : Rien que du jeu

Le jeu *The Stuntman* est un exemple d'adgame simple et qui fonctionne. Il diffuse la campagne réussie *Action City* de Rexona sur Internet et a été conçu de façon thématique selon une approche adaptée au support.

Les instructions sont les suivantes : « Lancez un cascadeur contre tout ce qui se trouve dans la pièce autant de fois que possible. Poussez-le à ses limites. » Le principe employé ici est simple et amusant. Par ailleurs, la qualité visuelle est excellente.

Quel est le rapport entre le jeu et le produit ? Disons qu'il étend le message de la campagne « Un spray corporel qui résiste à tous les défis », et ce d'une façon amusante. Rien de plus, mais rien de moins non plus.

Principe #2 : Apprentissage amusant

Une autre approche possible pour un bon adgame consiste à offrir un apprentissage amusant. Le fait de permettre à l'utilisateur d'apprendre quelque chose sur le produit ou la marque tout en jouant est une forme de publicité très intelligente et subtile.

Plusieurs entreprises ont actuellement recours à des jeux pour éduquer leurs clients à propos de leur produit ou de leur philosophie ; par exemple, la campagne pour le lait *Get the Glass*, dans laquelle, de façon drôle et plaisante, l'utilisateur doit attraper un verre de lait comme s'il s'agissait du Saint Graal, ou encore le site spécial <wasauchkommt.de> (« quoi qu'il se passe ») de la compagnie d'assurance HDI, où le joueur peut connaître en personne les dommages qu'il peut causer en quelques clics. Cette expérience vise à lui apprendre pourquoi il est préférable de prendre rendez-vous chez la succursale HDI la plus proche pour s'informer. Dans les deux cas, une campagne publicitaire déjà réussie à la télévision s'est étendue dans un format indépendant approprié pour Internet.

Il se peut que ces adgames fonctionnent si bien car, à part le facteur ludique, les utilisateurs les trouvent originaux et y reviennent plusieurs fois, et envoient parfois le lien à des amis. En d'autres termes, les gens passent beaucoup de temps à y jouer et en deviennent un peu accrocs. C'est bien connu, c'est toujours les choses les plus simples qui sont les plus prenantes.

Principe #3 : Étonnamment prenant

J'ai récemment découvert un site Web pour le groupe Krezip. En plus d'être visuellement attirante et très minimaliste, j'ai trouvé à la fois simple et originale l'idée de permettre aux visiteurs d'écouter un titre. Des instructions expliquent à l'utilisateur comment décrire des

www.blackbeltmonkey.com

mouvements circulaires avec la souris pour faire tourner le disque, tout comme un vinyle sur une platine. Si l'utilisateur réussit à faire tourner le « disque » suffisamment longtemps à une vitesse correcte et constante, il remporte plusieurs prix. On finit par essayer le jeu encore et encore, dans l'espoir d'améliorer ses résultats.

Si des gens écrivent et parlent autant d'un phénomène particulier, nous pouvons sans conteste le qualifier de forme prospère de publicité puisque le groupe cible a été atteint. Comme conséquence, le produit en question en ressort plus fort et peut même faire de nouveaux adeptes qui ne s'intéressaient pas à lui ou à la marque auparavant. Ici, le but va au-delà d'accroître les ventes : il consiste à renforcer et amplifier autant que possible son facteur de reconnaissance positive. En fin de compte, les ventes se font normalement de façon automatique.

Restons dans le domaine de la musique pour un instant. J'ai bien aimé des paroles sur le nouvel album « The Black and White Album » de The Hives : « A definition of madness is doing the same thing again and expecting a different result » (Une définition de la folie est la répétition de la même chose en espérant un résultat différent).

Les utilisateurs sont-ils donc fous ? Les jeux nous font-ils perdre la raison ? Certainement un peu. Les jeux peuvent être prenants dans le sens où nous répétons la même chose en boucle dans l'espoir d'améliorer nos résultats (être plus performant dans le jeu ou simplement atteindre le niveau supérieur). De façon modérée, pas de problème, car tout est ludique. Ces dernières années, les jeux numériques ont eu une énorme influence sur notre société et sont devenus de plus en plus sophistiqués, avec des intrigues chaque fois meilleures. L'industrie du cinéma a fait un bond en avant grâce à la mise en scène d'actions de jeux comme *Resident Evil* ou, plus récemment, *Hitman*, et aux jeux accompagnant la sortie de films.

Nous ne pouvons plus imaginer notre société moderne sans jeux électroniques. Vous devez en connaître quelque chose pour en parler et vous faire une opinion sur le sujet. Si quelqu'un vous dit que les jeux sont mauvais pour vous, rétorquez simplement en paraphrasant Shigeru Miyamoto (inventeur de *Mario* et de *Donkey Kong*) : « Les jeux sont mauvais pour vous ? C'est aussi ce que l'on avait dit du Rock'n'Roll. »

Alors cher lecteur, PLACE AU JEU !

Mike John Otto est le cofondateur et le directeur de la création de l'agence **blackbeltmonkey** installée à Hambourg. Au terme de ses études en communication visuelle en 2000, il a travaillé comme freelancer à Londres, avant d'occuper le poste de designer en chef au sein de l'agence Razorfish en 2001. Au bout de deux ans, il a assumé les fonctions de directeur artistique chez Elephant Seven à Hambourg. Début 2002, il est passé chez INTERONE (agence de BBDO). Il a travaillé comme directeur artistique en chef pour plusieurs marques comme BMW, puis comme directeur de la création pour les marques o2 et MINI. Pour son travail pour BMW et MINI, il a reçu de nombreuses récompenses à Cannes et de l'ADC, ainsi que d'autres prix comme Clio, Cresta, des festivals à New York et EFFIE. Avec deux de ses anciens collègues d'INTERONE, il a fondé l'agence blackbeltmonkey en 2007. **<www.blackbeltmonkey.com>**

CASE:01

The Pleasure of Driving

Sergio Mugnaini

Perhaps the best creative opportunities arise when you are faced with a major challenge. The challenge takes on even more importance when the client in question is Volkswagen. Internationally renowned for its excellent ad campaigns, the company was about to launch the new Golf, the updated version of the German firm's best-loved car.

In the automobile sector it is extremely hard to come up with a truly original idea for a campaign. All cars today advertise themselves as the "most modern" or as having the "best technology". Design has become more important than the structure of the vehicle itself and Japanese, Chinese, and US car-makers have already won the trust of drivers. In other words, it is increasingly difficult to come up with an ad concept that stands out from the crowd and which only promotes one particular vehicle.

The brief was prepared and the ad team began to explore different paths in the search for ideas. They cruised the roads of inspiration, enjoying the simple pleasure of trying out different possibilities. Eventually, after a great deal of work, considerable time and with various kilometers behind them, they came up with the concept of "the pleasure of driving" — something easily attributable to the Golf, a car that enables the driver to floor it on the highway or cruise the streets in pursuit of the basic enjoyment of driving. The team decided that the best way to get the "pure driving pleasure" idea across would be to let users get a true appreciation of the car and have fun with it. In other words, to let them test-drive it in a recreational, experimental fashion.

We started looking into ways to demonstrate the concept as best as possible. Eventually we came across Andreas Gysin <www.ertdfgcvb.ch>, an extraordinary Swiss programmer whose personal website featured many interactive experiments including a simple car in Shockwave which was just sensational. He sounded like the perfect person to produce this interactive experience. From the first contact, Andreas was on board and proved there were no barriers to him, even though he was halfway around the world, running the service directly from Switzerland to São Paulo.

The project got the go-ahead at the first presentation to the client. In fact, the hardest task in the process may well have been prising the keypad from the client's hands. We then went ahead with the production and execution of the work, which was to be done in phases. The first involved making the 3-D model of the Golf, which was done by the production company Sumatra <www.sumatravfx.com.br>. For this it was necessary to use a Shockwave plug-in because back in the days before Papervision, the technology that enables the website to run on Flash today, this was the only platform for an interactive 3-D object.

This involved a small risk: Shockwave technology is still not as popular as Flash Player is today, and at the time there was concern about how many people would use it. However, because the advertising for the car was directed at a fairly specific target (people who really love driving) we insisted from the start that people would use Shockwave in return for surfing a site they enjoyed so much. Aware that all innovation involves a risk, the agency and client decided to step up to the challenge and go ahead with this groundbreaking project.

With the 3-D model completed and approved, the material was sent to Andreas Gysin to program the website. A few days later we received the first beta-test and it was clear we were on to an extremely original idea. All the other phases and approvals were done by email and slowly but surely, with tests and new beta versions, the bugs were eliminated.

But there was still something missing. We felt there must be another way to enhance the feeling of driving a Golf still further and to make the experience even more

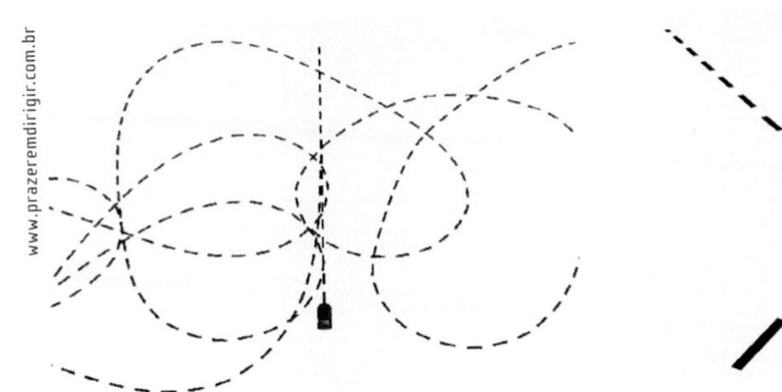

interactive — and we found the answer in music. A score was composed which worked like a soundtrack to boost the feeling of freedom and pleasure that comes from driving a Golf.

The result owes its success to a fantastic combination of the creation of the work itself, the fundamental execution of the project, and the integration of the music with the interactive experience, all brought together in a simple fashion while preserving the essence of the initial concept, i.e., the simple pleasure of driving.

Sergio Mugnaini is an art director at **AlmapBBDO** (São Paulo, Brazil). Originally trained in Communication, he went on to complete his studies at the School of Visual Arts in New York and worked at Ogilvy Interactive, J. Walter Thompson and DM9DDB before accepting his current position. His work has garnered awards from Cannes, the Art Directors Club, One Show Interactive, D&AD, and the New York Festival. He has also been a member of the jury at Design & Advertising, the London International Advertising Festival, and El Ojo Interactivo. In 2005 he was voted Art Director of the Year and his campaigns have included work for IBM, Volkswagen, Pepsi, Havaianas, Renault, Unilever, Honda, Philips and Greenpeace. **<www.mug9.com>**

Fahrvergnügen

Sergio Mugnaini

Die besten kreativen Möglichkeiten ergeben sich manchmal aus den größten Herausforderungen. Vor allem, wenn der Kunde Volkswagen heißt. Das Unternehmen, das international für seine hervorragenden Werbekampagnen bekannt ist, wollte den neuen Golf lancieren – die neueste Version seines beliebtesten Autos.

In der Automobilbranche ist es extrem schwierig, eine originelle Idee für eine Werbekampagne zu finden. Alle Autos werden als „supermodern" oder „technisch überragend" beworben. Deshalb ist das Design der Werbung inzwischen oft wichtiger als das Auto selbst. Hinzu kommt, dass japanische, chinesische und US-amerikanische Hersteller bei Autofahrern bereits einen Vertrauensvorsprung aufbauen konnten. Es wird also zunehmend schwieriger, ein Werbekonzept zu entwickeln, das sich von den anderen abhebt und nur einen einzigen Autotyp vorstellt.

Das Briefing kam, und das Werbeteam machte sich auf Ideensuche. Sie befuhren unterschiedlichste Inspirationswege und vergnügten sich damit, verschiedene Möglichkeiten durchzuspielen. Schließlich wurde nach viel Arbeit, Zeit und etlichen Kilometern das Konzept des „Fahrvergnügens" geboren. Ein Konzept, das zum Golf passt: ein Auto, mit dem man sowohl über die Autobahn brettern als auch durch die Stadt kurven kann und sich dabei auf die Suche nach der ursprünglichen Freude am Autofahren macht. Das Team beschloss, dass diese Idee des „reinen Fahrvergnügens" am einfachsten zu vermitteln ist, wenn man den Benutzern die Möglichkeit gibt, das Auto selbst auszuprobieren. Mit anderen Worten: sie auf vergnügliche und spannende Testfahrten zu schicken.

Auf der Suche nach der bestmöglichen Art und Weise, dieses Konzept zu realisieren, stießen wir auf Andreas Gysin <www.ertdfgcvb.ch>, einen außergewöhnlichen Programmierer aus der Schweiz, dessen eigene Website voller interaktiver Experimente steckt, einschließlich eines sensationell einfachen, mit Shockwave umgesetzten Autos. Er schien die ideale Person zu sein, um unser interaktives Experiment zu produzieren. Andreas war sofort begeistert und bewies, dass er das Projekt auch auf der anderen Seite des Erdballs, von der Schweiz nach São Paulo, würde pflegen können.

Das Konzept erhielt schon bei der ersten Präsentation die Zustimmung des Kunden. Die schwerste Aufgabe war dabei, ihm anschließend die Tastatur wieder zu entreißen. Dann ging die eigentliche Produktion los, die in verschiedene Phasen unterteilt wurde. Phase Eins bestand aus der Konstruktion des 3-D-Modells für den Golf, die von der Produktionsfirma Sumatra <www.sumatravfx.com.br> übernommen wurde. Dafür war die Verwendung eines Shockwave-Plugins notwendig, denn vor Papervision, der Technologie, die die Website heute mit Flash abspielbar macht, war dies die einzige Plattform für ein interaktives 3-D-Objekt.

Dies barg ein gewisses Risiko: Shockwave ist auch heute noch nicht so beliebt wie der Flash Player, und es wurden Bedenken geäußert, ob genug Menschen es einsetzen würden. Da die Kampagne jedoch an eine ganz spezielle Zielgruppe gerichtet war (Menschen, die wirklich gerne Auto fahren), bestanden wir bei ihnen von Anfang an auf dem Einsatz von Shockwave, wenn sie mit einer Site belohnt werden wollten, auf der man richtig Spaß haben konnte. Im vollen Bewusstsein, dass Innovationen immer mit Risiken verbunden sind, beschlossen Agentur und Kunde, die Herausforderung anzunehmen und mit diesem bahnbrechenden Projekt fortzufahren.

Nachdem das 3-D-Modell fertiggestellt und abgesegnet war, schickten wir Andreas Gysin das Material, um die Website zu programmieren. Ein paar Tage später erhielten wir den ersten Betatest, und allen war klar, dass wir es mit einem äußerst originellen Konzept zu tun hatten. Alle

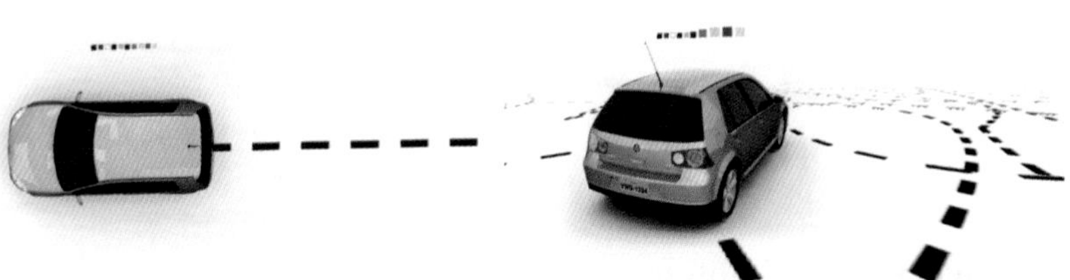

weiteren Phasen und Abnahmen erfolgten per E-Mail, und langsam, aber sicher wurden nach weiteren Tests und neuen Betaversionen alle Schwachstellen ausgemerzt.

Aber irgendetwas fehlte noch. Es musste noch eine weitere Möglichkeit geben, das Gefühl des Golf-Fahrens zu vermitteln und das Erlebnis noch interaktiver zu gestalten. Die Antwort war Musik. So wurde ein Soundtrack komponiert, der das Gefühl von Freiheit und Vergnügen beim Fahren eines Golfs intensivierte.

Das Endergebnis ist also eine unschlagbare Kombination aus der Grundidee, der technischen Ausführung und der Integration von Musik in das interaktive Erleben, das auf einfache Weise die Essenz des Konzepts, nämlich ein simples und reines Fahrvergnügen, vermittelt.

Sergio Mugnaini ist Art Director bei **AlmapBBDO** (São Paulo, Brasilien). Ursprünglich als Kommunikationsfachmann ausgebildet, beendete er sein Studium an der School of Visual Arts in New York und arbeitete danach bei Ogilvy Interactive, J. Walter Thompson und DM9DDB, bevor er seine jetzige Stelle antrat. Für seine Arbeit wurde er in Cannes und beim New York Festival sowie vom Art Directors Club, von One Show Interactive und D&AD ausgezeichnet. Er war Jurymitglied bei Design & Advertising, dem London International Advertising Festival und El Ojo Interactivo. 2005 wurde er zum „Art Director of the Year" gewählt. Er hat unter anderem Kampagnen für IBM, Volkswagen, Pepsi, Havaianas, Renault, Unilever, Honda, Philips und Greenpeace entworfen. <www.mug9.com>

CASE:02

Rush Hour 3 Game

Jonathan Hills

Part of the appeal of interactive executions, for clients and agencies, is reach. We want as many people in our target audience to notice, engage and re-engage with a brand experience. If that brand experience is a billboard, with a few exceptions getting the message in front of lots of people is time-consuming and expensive. One exception is when that billboard is so good, or horrendous, that some picture-happy citizen snaps a shot and posts it in all the right places online. When a noteworthy experience lives online, word of its existence spreads faster than the flu on mass transit. The result is reach with little or no additional investment beyond the creation of the experience.

The challenge for us is to create a brand experience that is so good that it naturally spreads with positive fanfare. That's where smart interactivity, knowing your audience and being keyed into the latest technologies, come into play. Today, gaming consoles and popular games incorporate or tap into web-based features. This phenomenon leaves the door wide open for interactive developers. With a little ingenuity and planning, new technologies enable us to extend our reach into exciting new realms without overextending our budgets or staff. We're able to re-skin experiences and make them accessible both online and through gaming consoles.

The promotional game that we created for New Line Cinema's *Rush Hour 3* is a good example of smart interactivity advancing reach by bridging the online and gaming console screens. Because of budget and timing, we focused on creating a microsite experience that lived off the official movie website and developing a comparable game for the popular Nintendo Wii gaming console.

In one month we created "Rush for Shy Shen," a multilevel game that played off the movie's plot. In our game, you fight off Triads and save Shy Shen. Shy Shen, the big secret of the movie, is still kept secret. Your reward is a movie trailer. Since the turnaround was quick, and the budget limited, we held our own photo shoot in-house. Colleagues were shot on greenscreen in staged progressive poses. Each character was cut out and stitched together to make the animations.

Working within Flash 7, the version supported by the Wii's exclusive web browser Opera, presented a layer of programming limitations. We made sure to make these limitations part of the character of the throwback game. We then reworked the game in Flash 8 for the online execution.

Without any promotion, and thanks to online social networks, word of the game spread across various gaming, Wii and movie fan sites. The game appealed to the *Rush Hour* target audience. We were able to extend our reach because our online world has collided nicely with the once exclusive gaming kingdom.

www.rushhourmovie.com/game

Jonathan Hills started Domani Studios, a high-end, interactive design studio in Brooklyn, where he is creative director. **Domani Studios** creates top-shelf interactive environments and viral marketing experiences for clients such as Volkswagen, Anheuser-Busch, Gucci, and W Hotels. **<www.domanistudios.com>**

CASE.02

Rush Hour 3 Game

Jonathan Hills

Ein Großteil des Reizes interaktiver Werbemaßnahmen besteht darin, dass sie einen hohen Verbreitungsgrad haben. Unser Ziel ist es, so viele Menschen aus der Zielgruppe wie möglich in ein Markenerlebnis einzubinden. Wenn es sich dabei um ein Plakat handelt, so ist es, von wenigen Ausnahmen abgesehen, sehr zeitaufwendig und teuer, vielen Menschen die Botschaft zu vermitteln. Eine Ausnahme entsteht dann, wenn das Plakat entweder so gut oder so scheußlich ist, dass irgendein fotografierfreudiger Mensch es knipst und online an den richtigen Stellen platziert. Wenn ein denkwürdiges Erlebnis erst einmal online ist, verbreitet sich die Kunde seiner Existenz schneller als ein Schnupfen im öffentlichen Nahverkehr. Das Ergebnis ist ein hoher Verbreitungsgrad, der wenige oder gar keine zusätzlichen Investitionen über die Produktion des eigentlichen Erlebnisses hinaus erfordert.

Die Herausforderung besteht darin, ein so gutes Markenerlebnis zu schaffen, dass es sich ganz von allein und mit positivem Feedback verbreitet. Dabei sind clevere Interaktivität, Kenntnis der Zielgruppe und das neueste technische Know-how gefragt. Heutzutage beinhalten Spielkonsolen und beliebte Spiele meist Online-Elemente oder verweisen darauf. Damit steht die Tür sperrangelweit offen für die Entwicklung interaktiver Elemente. Mit etwas Kreativität und Planung erlauben uns die neuen Technologien, unsere Reichweite in ungeahnte neue Gefilde auszudehnen, ohne Budget oder Personal überzustrapazieren. Wir können unsere Erlebnisse sowohl online als auch über Spielkonsolen zugänglich machen.

Das Promotionsspiel, das wir für New Line Cinemas Rush Hour 3 entwickelten, ist ein Beispiel dafür, wie clevere Interaktivität die Reichweite erhöht, indem eine Brücke zwischen Websites und Spielkonsolen geschaffen wird. Um Kosten und Zeitaufwand niedrig zu halten, konzentrierten wir uns darauf, ein Microsite-Erlebnis zu schaffen, das sich aus der offiziellen Filmwebsite speiste, und entwickelten ein vergleichbares Spiel für die beliebte Spielkonsole Nintendo Wii.

Innerhalb eines Monats entstand „Rush for Shy Shen", ein Spiel mit mehreren Levels, das sich auf den Filmplot bezieht. Die Spieler kämpfen darin gegen Triaden und retten Shy Shen (das Geheimnis von Shy Shen wird nicht gelüftet). Als Belohnung gibt es einen Filmtrailer. Da Zeit und Geld begrenzt waren, veranstalteten wir ein Inhouse-Fotoshooting. Kollegen wurden mittels Greenscreen-Technik bei verschiedenen Bewegungsabläufen fotografiert, und daraus entstanden die Animationen.

Weil wir mit Flash 7 arbeiteten, der von Wiis exklusivem Webbrowser Opera unterstützten Version, waren unseren Programmiermöglichkeiten klare Grenzen gesetzt. Wir bauten diese Grenzen jedoch bewusst in das Spiel ein. Für die Online-Version überarbeiteten wir das Spiel dann in Flash 8.

Ohne PR-Aktionen verbreitete sich die Kunde von unserem Spiel nur durch das soziale Netzwerk des Webs auf verschiedenen Spiel-, Wii- und Film- Fansites. Es gefiel der „Rush Hour"-Zielgruppe. Wir konnten also unsere Reichweite expandieren, weil unsere Online-Welt sich gut mit der einst exklusiven Spielewelt ergänzte.

www.rushhourmovie.com/game

Jonathan Hills ist Gründer und Creative Director von Domani Studios, einem in Brooklyn ansässigen interaktiven Designstudio auf höchstem technischen Niveau. **Domani Studios** entwickelt hochkarätige interaktive und virale Marketingevents für Kunden wie Volkswagen, Anheuser-Busch, Gucci und W Hotels. **<www.domanistudios.com>**

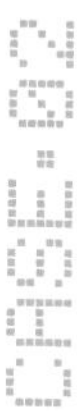

Rush Hour 3 Game

Jonathan Hills

Pour les clients comme pour les agences, partie de l'intérêt des créations interactives est leur portée. Nous voulons que le plus de personnes possible de notre public cible remarquent une expérience de marque, y participent et la renouvellent. Si cette expérience est un panneau d'affichage, la diffusion du message à un grand nombre de personnes demande beaucoup de temps et d'argent. Sauf rares exceptions. Sauf quand le panneau est tellement beau ou tellement horrible et qu'une personne fan d'images décide de le prendre en photo et de le publier partout où il se doit sur Internet. Lorsqu'une expérience de choix est disponible en ligne, la nouvelle se répand plus vite que la grippe dans les transports en commun. Résultat : une portée avec peu ou pas d'investissement supplémentaire au-delà de celui pour la création.

Notre défi consiste à créer une expérience de marque d'une telle qualité que sa promotion se fait tout naturellement. C'est là qu'intervient l'interactivité intelligente, en connaissant le public et en maîtrisant les dernières technologies. Aujourd'hui, les consoles et les jeux populaires incorporent ou utilisent des fonctions basées sur le Web, un phénomène qui laisse la porte ouverte aux développeurs interactifs. Avec un peu d'ingéniosité et d'organisation, les nouvelles technologies nous permettent d'étendre notre portée à des domaines passionnants, sans augmenter de façon démesurée le budget ou le personnel nécessaires. Nous pouvons ainsi modifier complètement les expériences et les rendre accessibles à la fois en ligne et sur des consoles de jeu.

Le jeu promotionnel que nous avons créé pour le film Rush Hour 3 de New Line Cinema illustre parfaitement comment l'interactivité intelligente étend la portée en mettant en relation la navigation en ligne et les consoles. En raison du budget et des délais, nous avons privilégié la création d'un mini-site alimenté par le site Web officiel du film et le développement d'un jeu similaire pour la célèbre console vidéo Nintendo Wii.

En l'espace d'un mois, nous avons créé « Rush for Shy Shen », un jeu multiniveau qui suit l'intrigue du film. Dans ce jeu, vous combattez les Triads et sauvez Shy Shen, grande énigme du film qui est tenue secrète ; votre récompense est une bande-annonce du film. Comme le temps de réalisation était court et le budget limité, nous avons effectué notre propre séance photos en interne. Des collègues ont été photographiés devant un fond vert dans des poses progressives. Chaque personnage a été ensuite découpé et recomposé pour créer les animations.

L'utilisation de Flash 7, la version prise en charge par le navigateur Web Opera exclusif de la Wii, a supposé des limitations en matière de programmation. Nous avons veillé à faire de ces limitations la caractéristique du jeu d'affrontement. Nous l'avons ensuite converti à Flash 8 pour l'exécution en ligne.

Sans aucune promotion et grâce aux réseaux sociaux sur Internet, le jeu a été annoncé sur plusieurs sites de jeux, de la Wii et du film, et il a plu au public cible de Rush Hour. Nous avons pu étendre notre portée, notre monde en ligne ayant gentiment pénétré dans le royaume exclusif des jeux.

www.rushhourmovie.com/game

Jonathan Hills a créé Domani Studios, un studio de design interactif de pointe à Brooklyn, dont il est directeur de la création. **Domani Studios** crée ses propres environnements interactifs de haut niveau pour des clients comme Volkswagen, Anheuser-Busch, Gucci et W Hotels. **<www.domanistudios.com>**

CASE·03

K•SWISS Free Running

Patrick Gardner

What makes one site more interactive than another? No easy question since interactivity can mean so many different things. When it came to the K-Swiss *Free Running* campaign, all we knew was that we were launching a new shoe for a brand with a long and rich history, but limited name recognition, in a market flooded with big players. If we wanted to make any headway then a glossy online brochure just wasn't going to do it. What we needed was an experience that could capture the target audience's attention and motivate them to create their own conversations with friends about this interesting brand.

When Creative Social founder Mark Chalmers and his partner James Goode first brought this campaign to Perfect Fools in early fall 2007, the brief was relatively open. K-Swiss was launching the Ariake, the world's first sneaker designed especially for free running, which they had developed together with the sport's creator Sébastien Foucan. Known for his role as a villain in the James Bond movie *Casino Royale*, and performances with Madonna, Foucan was K-Swiss' Free Running spokesperson and would be central to the upcoming integrated launch campaign.

Foucan's free running philosophy — all about simplicity, elegant movement, athleticism and following your own way — became the cornerstone for our brainstorming together with Mark. Parkour, free running and even Foucan had already been exposed in popular TV shows and major ad campaigns, so it was important to find a visual style and environment that felt new and original. Free running in a city setting was discarded in favor of something cleaner and more stylized. Foucan's gravity-defying moves are so amazing we knew they would look great on film, especially in slow motion. We wanted the site to offer the visual richness and quality of a high-end TV commercial while still using the interactive potential of the Web.

Two reference cases were given particular consideration: Nike's *Tiger Woods Swing Portrait* and our own *Saab Pilots Wanted*. An initial idea emerged, involving Foucan free running a vertical 360 circle in slow motion, but it was quickly abandoned as not interactive enough and worse, too similar to *Swing Portrait*. Finally, Karl Nord, a twenty-one-year old intern fresh out of the Swedish digital school Hyper Island, leaned forward and said, "I've got an idea…", and proceeded to describe the campaign mechanic essentially as it went live. Foucan would be filmed in a minimalistic studio vaulting over, under and through prop versions of each alphabet letter. Site visitors could type a message and would then be treated to an apparently edited film of Foucan free running the words they had just written, after which they would be able to pass their message on to friends.

The idea showcased Foucan's acrobatics in an attractive new setting; it gave plenty of opportunities to feature the Ariakes doing their high-tech stuff; it embodied Foucan's philosophy of "expressing yourself"; and it spread itself naturally by promoting conversations between friends. Now that's interactive. Also attractive were the concept's simplicity and the fact that visitors wouldn't have a complete picture of the interactivity until they tried it all the way through. The surprise would be fun. We were sold.

Getting it built was another matter. Some team members thought it couldn't be done, at least not within the budget and schedule. We were allotted only two days to film Foucan and the math was daunting. Twenty-six letters plus… and a payoff shot meant no less than thirty setups. To minimize the risks we hired Acne Film to shoot the video and booked a large studio nearby in Sweden. Video was shot with the amazing Phantom high speed DV camera. Originally developed for the military, it clocks up to 1000 fps at HD quality. Against all odds the prop letters

www.kswissfreerunning.com

(including a looming four meter 'T') were all built and delivered on time and Foucan, the consummate professional, performed thirty unique and fantastic moves, none of which were faked or stunt-doubled in any way.

Surprisingly, the ensuing site production passed with many ups and few downs. Subtle refinements were incorporated, like a message entry tool that dynamically realigns itself as the message gets longer, whilst at the same time serving as a smart loader for the films. There were also the requisite shoe 360s and a competition to attract further traffic. But at its heart, the site that went live on launch day remained very straightforward, built around a simple and elegant interactivity designed to spark a brand conversation between friends.

The Team

Client: K-Swiss Europe. Creative Agency: Mark Chalmers (Creative Director) and James Goode (Account Lead). Perfect Fools: Christian Mezöfi (Lead Art Director), Oscar Asmoarp (Art Director), Björn Kummeneje (Lead Tech), David Genelid (Tech), Karl Nord (Genius Intern), Fredrik Heghammar and Kathrin Spaak (Producers), Christian Johansson and Vinh Kha (Design Concept), Tony Högqvist (Creative Director), Patrick Gardner (Account Lead and Copy). Acne Film: Pål Åsberg (Producer). Ensrette: Linnéa Bergman Sjöstrand and Daniel Skoglund (Film Directors).

Patrick Gardner started his career as an assistant speechwriter to the US Vice-President in 1990 and 1992. During the mid-nineties he worked for the global language education group EF Education on business development and marketing projects in Indonesia, Mexico, China, Russia, Sweden, the UK and the United States. He has been focused on Internet advertising since 1995, and co-founded Stockholm-based Houdini Digital Creations in 1999 and Perfect Fools in 2002. Gardner is currently a partner at **Perfect Fools**, where he continues to write for client campaigns, mainly from the company's Stockholm office. His articles on digital media have appeared in magazines such as *Computer Arts Special* and *Cre@teOnline*. **<www.perfectfools.com>**

CASE·03

K•SWISS Free Running

Patrick Gardner

Was macht eine Website interaktiver als eine andere? Keine einfache Fragen, denn Interaktivität kann vieles bedeuten. Bei der Free Running-Kampagne von K-Swiss wussten wir zunächst nur, dass ein neuer Schuh für eine Marke lanciert werden sollte, die zwar alteingesessen und erfolgreich war, in einem Markt voller Big Player jedoch nur einen begrenzten Bekanntheitsgrad besaß. Eine Online-Hochglanzbroschüre würde uns hier nicht weiterhelfen. Wir brauchten vielmehr ein Erlebnis, das die Aufmerksamkeit der Zielgruppe erregen und sie dazu anregen würde, sich kreativ mit Freunden über diese interessante Marke auszutauschen.

Als Mark Chalmers, der Gründer von Creative Social, und sein Partner James Goode die Kampagne im Herbst 2007 an Perfect Fools herantrugen, war das Briefing relativ offen. K-Swiss wollte Ariake lancieren, den ersten Turnschuh, der speziell für Free Running entworfen wurde – zusammen mit Sébastien Foucan, dem Erfinder dieser Sportart. Foucan, der für seine Schurkenrolle im James-Bond-Film *Casino Royale* sowie Auftritten mit Madonna bekannt ist, war das Aushängeschild von K-Swiss für Free Running und würde eine zentrale Figur in der anstehenden Werbekampagne sein.

Foucans Free Running-Philosophie mit seiner Einfachheit, den eleganten Bewegungen, der Athletik und Selbstfindung wurde der Ausgangspunkt unseres Brainstormings mit Mark. Parkour, Free Running und auch Foucan selber waren schon in beliebten TV-Shows präsentiert und für große Werbekampagnen eingesetzt worden. Wir mussten also einen visuellen Stil und ein Umfeld finden, die neu und originell waren. Anstelle einer urbanen Umgebung wollten wir etwas Schlichteres und Stilisierteres. Wir wussten, dass Foucans erstaunliche, die Schwerkraft überwindenden Bewegungen im Film wunderbar wirken würden, vor allem in Zeitlupe. Die Website sollte den visuellen Reichtum und die hohe Qualität eines TV-Werbespots bieten, aber gleichzeitig das interaktive Potenzial des Webs nutzen.

Zwei Beispiele nahmen wir besonders unter die Lupe: Nikes Spot „Tiger Woods Swing Portrait" und unseren eigenen Spot „Pilots Wanted" für Saab. Eine erste Idee sah Foucan beim Free Running mit 360-Grad-Umdrehung in Zeitlupe vor. Doch sie wurde schnell verworfen, weil sie zum einen nicht interaktiv genug war und zum anderen dem Woods-Spot zu sehr ähnelte. Schließlich beugte sich Karl Nord, ein 21-jähriger Azubi frisch von der schwedischen Digitalschule Hyper Island, vor und sagte: „Ich habe eine Idee ..." Er beschrieb die Kampagne dann im Wesentlichen so, wie sie schließlich realisiert wurde. Foucan sollte in einem minimalistischen Studio gefilmt werden, wie er riesige Buchstaben überspringt. Sitebesucher könnten eine Nachricht eintippen und bekämen dann einen Film zu sehen, in dem Foucan im Free Running-Stil die Buchstaben der eingetippten Nachricht athletisch überwindet. Den Film könnte man dann an Freunde verschicken.

Das Konzept präsentierte Foucans Akrobatik in einem attraktiven neuen Umfeld, es bot ausreichend Gelegenheit, die High-Tech-Performance des Ariake-Schuhs zu zeigen, es verkörperte Foucans Philosophie des „Express yourself" und konnte kommunikativ weiterverbreitet werden. Nun handelte es sich um eine wirklich interaktive Kampagne. Ebenfalls attraktiv waren die Einfachheit der Idee und die Tatsache, dass Benutzer erst zum Schluss das gesamte Ausmaß der Interaktivität erfassen würden – eine Überraschung mit Spaßfaktor. Wir hatten das Ding in der Tasche.

Das Konzept in die Tat umzusetzen, war eine andere Sache. Einige aus dem Team glaubten, dass es nicht möglich wäre, zumindest nicht innerhalb des vorgegebenen Budgets und Terminplans. Uns standen nur zwei Drehtage mit Foucan zur Verfügung, in denen mehr als 26

www.kswissfreerunning.com

Buchstaben gefilmt werden mussten (und das bedeutete mindestens 30 Einstellungen). Um die Risiken zu minimieren, engagierten wir Acne Film für das Video und mieteten ein großes Studio in der Nähe. Das Video wurde mit der erstaunlichen Highspeed-Kamera Phantom gedreht, die ursprünglich für militärische Zwecke entwickelt wurde und bis zu 1000 Bilder pro Sekunde in HD-Qualität produziert. Entgegen allen Befürchtungen wurden alle Buchstaben (inklusive eines 4 Meter hohen „T") rechtzeitig fertig, und Foucan, ganz Profi, führte 30 einzigartige Moves aus, bei denen weder getrickst noch gedoubelt wurde.

Erstaunlicherweise gab es bei der Erstellung der Website viele Hochs und nur wenige Tiefs. Es wurden einige Kleinigkeiten hinzugefügt wie zum Beispiel eine Texteingabeleiste, die sich dynamisch der Textlänge anpasst und gleichzeitig als Smartloader für die Filme dient. Ergänzt wurden auch eine 360-Grad-Präsentation der Schuhe sowie ein Wettbewerb, der mehr Besucher anlocken soll. Doch im Kern blieb es eine sehr gradlinige Website, um ein simples und elegantes interaktives Element herum aufgebaut, die eine markengestützte Unterhaltung zwischen Freunden anregen sollte.

Das Team:

Kunde: K-Swiss Europe. Agentur: Mark Chalmers (Creative Director) und James Goode (Account Lead). Perfect Fools: Christian Mezöfi (Lead Art Director), Oscar Asmoarp (Art Director), Björn Kummeneje (Lead Tech), David Genelid (Tech), Karl Nord (genialer Auszubildender), Fredrik Heghammar und Kathrin Spaak (Producers), Christian Johansson und Vinh Kha (Designkonzept), Tony Högqvist (Creative Director), Patrick Gardner (Account Lead und Lektorat). Acne Film: Pål Åsberg (Producer). Ensrette: Linnéa Bergman Sjöstrand und Daniel Skoglund (Regisseure).

Patrick Gardner begann seine berufliche Laufbahn als stellvertretender Redenschreiber für den US-amerikanischen Vizepräsidenten in den Jahren 1990 und 1992. Mitte der 90er-Jahre arbeitete er für die internationale Sprachschule EF Education, bei der er mit Projekten in Indonesien, Mexiko, China, Russland, Schweden, Großbritannien und den USA befasst war. Seit 1995 liegt sein Schwerpunkt auf Internetwerbung. 1999 war er Mitbegründer der Stockholmer Agentur Houdini Digital Creations und 2002 der Agentur Perfect Fools. Gardner ist zurzeit Teilhaber von **Perfect Fools**, wo er, vorwiegend vom Stockholmer Büro aus, weiterhin für Kundenkampagnen schreibt. Seine Artikel über digitale Medien sind in Zeitschriften wie *Computer Arts Special* und *Cre@teOnline* erschienen. **<www.perfectfools.com>**

CASE:03

K•SWISS Free Running

Patrick Gardner

Pourquoi un site résulte-t-il plus interactif qu'un autre ? La question n'est pas simple, l'interactivité faisant référence à une variété de choses. Pour la campagne K-Swiss Free Running, nous savions uniquement que nous lancions une nouvelle chaussure pour une marque forte d'une histoire longue et riche, mais avec une reconnaissance limitée de son nom, sur un marché submergé de grosses pointures. Pour marquer un pas en avant, une brochure de luxe en ligne n'allait pas suffire. Il nous fallait une expérience capable d'attirer l'attention du public cible et de l'inciter à parler entre amis de cette marque intéressante.

Lorsque le fondateur de Creative Social, Mark Chalmers, et son partenaire James Goode, ont présenté pour la première fois la campagne à Perfect Fools au début de l'automne 2007, le brief était relativement ouvert. K-Swiss lançait Ariake, la première chaussure de sport au monde conçue spécialement pour le free running, dont le créateur de la discipline Sébastien Foucan a participé au développement. Connu pour son rôle de méchant dans le film de James Bond Casino Royale, ainsi que pour ses performances avec Madonna, Foucan était le porte-parole du free running de K-Swiss et allait jouer un rôle clé dans la campagne qui s'annonçait.

La philosophie du free running de Foucan, qui repose sur la simplicité, des mouvements élégants, l'athlétisme et le fait de suivre sa voie, est devenue la pierre angulaire de notre brainstorming avec Mark. Le parkour, le free running et même Foucan étaient déjà apparus dans des émissions TV populaires et de grandes campagnes publicitaires ; il était donc important de trouver un style visuel et un environnement inédit et original. Le free running dans un cadre urbain a été éliminé pour préférer quelque chose de plus propre et de plus stylisé. Les mouvements de Foucan, un défi aux lois de la gravité, sont tellement impressionnants qu'ils allaient forcément bien rendre en vidéo, notamment au ralenti. Nous voulions que le site offre la richesse visuelle et la qualité d'un spot TV haut de gamme, tout en exploitant le potentiel interactif du Web.

Deux cas de référence ont reçu une attention particulière : la décomposition du swing de Tiger Woods par Nike et notre propre opération « Pilots Wanted » pour Saab. La première idée à surgir était le free running de Foucan d'un cercle vertical à 360° au ralenti. Elle a toutefois été rapidement rejetée, car pas assez interactive et, pire encore, trop semblable au film du swing. Finalement, Karl Nord, un stagiaire de 21 ans fraîchement sorti de l'école de design suédoise Hyper Island, s'est penché, a dit « J'ai une idée... » et a décrit la mécanique de la campagne comme elle s'est finalement réalisée. Foucan serait filmé dans un studio minimaliste en train de sauter par dessus, en dessous et dans des versions de chaque lettre de l'alphabet comme appuis. Les visiteurs du site pourraient taper un message et verraient un film monté de Foucan faisant un free running des mots saisis ; ils pourraient ensuite envoyer le message à leurs amis.

L'idée mettait en scène les acrobaties de Foucan d'une façon attirante et nouvelle, offrait plein d'occasions de montrer les Ariake en pleine action high tech, incarnait la philosophie de Foucan de l'« expression de soi » et se répandait naturellement en incitant les conversations entre amis. Elle est désormais interactive. Tout aussi attirants étaient la simplicité du concept et le fait que les visiteurs n'obtiendraient pas une vision complète de l'interactivité avant la fin de l'expérience. La surprise serait amusante. Nous étions emballés.

La mettre en pratique était une autre histoire. Certains membres de l'équipe voyaient l'opération impossible, du moins avec le budget et le planning établis. Nous ne disposions que de deux jours pour filmer Foucan et les calculs étaient décourageants. Vingt-six lettres et..., plus

www.kswissfreerunning.com

une prise finale, soit pas moins de trente montages. Pour limiter les risques, nous avons engagé Acne Film pour le tournage et réservé un grand studio en Suède. La vidéo a été réalisée avec l'incroyable caméra numérique Phantom ultra rapide. À l'origine conçue pour l'armée, elle prend jusqu'à 1 000 ips à une qualité haute définition. Contrairement à toute attente, les lettres d'appui (y compris un imposant T de quatre mètres) ont toutes été fabriquées et livrées dans les temps et Foucan, en professionnel accompli, a réalisé trente fantastiques mouvements uniques, aucun n'ayant demandé de trucage ou une doublure.

Ensuite, la production du site a par surprise connu beaucoup de hauts et peu de bas. De subtils perfectionnements ont été intégrés, comme un outil de saisie de messages qui conserve son alignement de façon dynamique selon la longueur du message, tout en servant de chargeur intelligent pour les films. Sans oublier le modèle 360s demandé et un concours pour augmenter le trafic. Mais au fond, le site publié le jour du lancement est resté très simple, avec une interactivité élégante pensée pour déclencher une conversation d'amis sur la marque.

L'équipe :

Client : K-Swiss Europe. Agence de création : Mark Chalmers (directeur de la création) et James Goode (responsables des comptes). Perfect Fools : Christian Mezöfi (directeur artistique en chef), Oscar Asmoarp (directeur artistique), Björn Kummeneje (technicien en chef), David Genelid (technicien), Karl Nord (stagiaire de génie), Fredrik Heghammar et Kathrin Spaak (producteurs), Christian Johansson et Vinh Kha (conception du design), Tony Högqvist (directeur de la création), Patrick Gardner (responsable des comptes et des copies). Acne Film : Pål Åsberg (producteur). Ensrette : Linnéa Bergman Sjöstrand et Daniel Skoglund (réalisateurs du film).

Patrick Gardner a débuté sa carrière comme rédacteur assistant des discours du vice-président des États-Unis en 1990 et 1992. Au milieu des années 90, il a travaillé pour le groupe d'enseignement linguistique mondial EF Education sur le développement commercial et des projets marketing en Indonésie, au Mexique, en Chine, en Russie, en Suède, au Royaume-Uni et aux États-Unis. Depuis 1995, ses activités se centrent sur la publicité sur Internet ; il a co-fondé en 1999 Houdini Digital Creations, installé à Stockholm, puis Perfect Fools en 2002. Actuellement partenaire de **Perfect Fools**, Gardner continue à écrire des campagnes pour les clients, surtout depuis le bureau de Stockholm. Ses articles sur des supports multimédia ont été publiés dans des magazines comme *Computer Arts Special* et *Cre@teOnline*. <www.perfectfools.com>

30 DAYS OF NIGHT

USA

www.sonypictures.com/movies/30daysofnight

2007

Concept

To set the mood for the players of the movie console game *30 Days of Night*, an online game was created with a fullscreen environment made up of high impacting graphics and animation. /// Um Spieler auf das Konsolenspiel zum Film *30 Days of Night* einzustimmen, wurde ein Online-Spiel mit Fullscreen-Szenerie und hochwertigen Grafiken und Animationen entwickelt. /// Pour motiver les joueurs du jeu vidéo *30 Days of Night*, un jeu en ligne a été créé avec un environnement plein écran doté d'impressionnants effets graphiques et animations.

Info

Design: Big Spaceship <www.bigspaceship.com>. /// **Programming:** Big Spaceship. /// **Tools:** Adobe Photoshop, Flash, After Effects.

ABOUT
CAST
FILMMAKERS
GRAPHIC NOVEL
DOWNLOADS
GAME
2690
100%
GAME
OVER
11890
86%

A4 GLOBAL DRIVES

GERMANY

www.neue-digitale.de/projects/audi_A4_globaldrives

2007

Concept

Users are able to map their most enjoyable driving routes, customised with their preferred A4 model. Moreover, they can add images and set numerous parameters for the journey. /// Benutzer können ihre Lieblingsfahrstrecken angeben und einen Audi A4 ihrer Wahl einsetzten. Sie können zudem Bilder hinzufügen und verschiedene Parameter für die Fahrt wählen. /// Les utilisateurs peuvent configurer les itinéraires de leur prédilection en les personnalisant avec leur modèle Audi A4 préféré. Ils peuvent aussi ajouter des images et définir de nombreux paramètres pour le voyage.

Info

Design: Neue Digitale <www.neue-digitale.de>, Sven Küster, Oliver Hinrichs, Stefan Schuster, Florian Uihlein. /// **Programming:** Adalbert Sohns, Dorian Roy, Heiko Schweickhardt, Marius Bulla, Andreas Diwisch, Kay Wiegand, Manuel Roraius, Jens Steffen. /// **Tools:** Adobe Photoshop, Flash. /// **Awards:** Adobe Best Customer Site Award 2007 (First Prize). /// **Others:** Silke Zielhofer, Robert Woloschanowski (Concept); Mathias Sinn (Account Management); Jana Wardag (Project Management).

A4 Global Drives
Routen entdecken
Routen einstellen
Gewinnerrouten
Voting
Über A4 Global Drives
St Moritz
Chiavenna
71.1 km
Bellinzona
155.7 km
St Moritz - Monza
4.75
Zurück
Ton aus
Sprache
Kontakt
Impressum
Datenschutz
Weiterempfehlen
Login/Registrierung
A4 Global Drives
Routen entdecken
Routen einstellen
Gewinnerrouten
Voting
Über A4 Global Drives
Top 10 - die besten Bewertungen
1
Erik Lykke O. , 55
Washington - Baltimore
5.00
Route ansehen
2
Christian T. , 30
Sydney - Port Macquari...
4.90
Route ansehen
3
VICTOR FERNANDO C. , 21
Conchucos - Santa
4.80
Route ansehen
4
Bernd B. , 53
St Moritz - Monza
4.75
Route ansehen
5
Anders Å. , 33
Geilo - Bergen
4.75
Route ansehen
6
Christopher E. , 47
Kenmare - Dingle
4.75
Route ansehen
Asia
Australia
Ton aus
Sprache
Kontakt
Impressum
Datenschutz
Weiterempfehlen
Login/Registrierung

ABSOLUT DISCO

INTERNATIONAL
2007

www2.absolut.com/disco

Concept

Special packaging turns the Absolut bottle into a disco ball. It's all part of a newly integrated campaign with a microsite produced by Perfect Fools for Great Works. Create your own disco films, either with your keyboard or a webcam. /// Durch spezielle Verpackung verwandelt sich die Absolut-Flasche in eine Discokugel. Dies ist Teil einer neuen Kampagne mit einer von Perfekt Fools für Great Works produzierten Microsite. Benutzer können entweder mit der Tastatur oder einer Webcam ihre eigenen Discofilme erzeugen. /// L'emballage spécial transforme la bouteille d'Absolut en boule à facettes. Il s'inscrit dans le cadre d'une nouvelle campagne, avec un mini-site créé par Perfect Fools pour Great Works. Créez vos propres films disco à l'aide du clavier ou d'une webcam.

Info

Design: Perfect Fools <www.perfectfools.com>, Perfect Fools: Vinh Kha (Creative Director), Christian Mezöfi, Fredrik Stutterheim (Art Director); Great Works: Mathias Päres (Art Director). /// **Programming:** Perfect Fools: Björn Kummeneje (Technical Director), Jonathan Pettersson (Tech); Great Works: Jocke Wissing (Lead Tech). /// **Tools:** Adobe Photoshop, Flash, After Effects, Eclipse. /// **Others:** Kathrin Spaak (Producer Perfect Fools); Great Works: Charlotta Rydholm (Account Lead), Linn Tornéhielm (PL), Sofie Vestergren (PL).

ABSOLUT CARS
COME ON LET'S DANCE!

ABSOLUT ORIENTAL BREEZE
OOOOH YEEAAH!

GET OUT ON THE DANCE FLOOR!

ABSOLUT DISCO DRINKS
GET OUT ON THE DANCE FLOOR!

BACK TO ABSOLUT.COM
ABSOLUTDRINKS.COM
ABSOLUT DISCO
PUT YOUR HAND IN THE AIR AND WAVE IT LIKE YOU JUST DON'T CARE!
SHOW US YOUR HAND MOVES! (WITH WEBCAM)
SHOW US YOUR LIGHTNING SKILLS! (WITHOUT WEBCAM)
USE YOUR KEYBOARD TO CREATE DISCO MAGIC
PRESS HERE TO RECORD YOUR MOVES
ABSOLUT DISCO GIFT PACK
ABSOLUT DISCO DRINKS
DOWNLOADS
SOUND OFF
TERMS & CONDITIONS
PRIVACY POLICY
SEND TO A FRIEND

ADIDAS GAME

FRANCE

www.leschinois.com/adidasgame

2004

Concept

A running game for sports material and apparel brand Adidas, with an urban graphics-like visual language. /// Ein Laufspiel für den Sportausstatter Adidas mit visueller Sprache im Urban-Stil. /// Jeu de course pour la marque d'équipements et de vêtements de sport Adidas, avec un langage visuel aux allures de graphisme urbain.

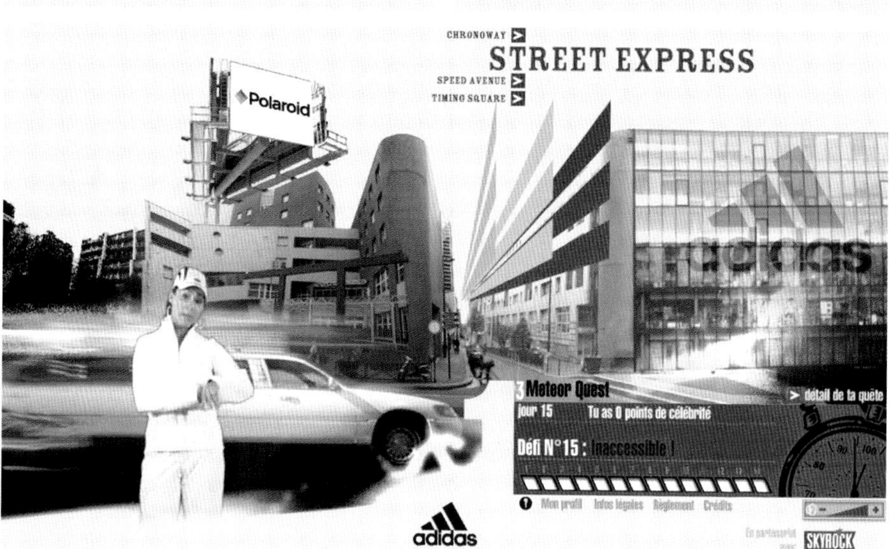

Info

DESIGN: LES CHINOIS <www.leschinois.com>, Ludovic Roudy. /// PROGRAMMING: Julien Bennamias. /// TOOLS: Adobe Photoshop, Flash. /// AWARDS: Clics d'Or Awards Winner (Bronze). /// COST: 4 months.

Results

Over 100,000 unique visitors. Website activity growth equals over 25% for each new quest. /// Über 100.000 Unique User. Website-Wachstumsrate von über 25% bei jedem Spiel. /// Plus de 100 000 visiteurs uniques. La croissance de l'activité du site Web représente plus de 25 % à chaque nouvelle course.

ALIVE IS

UK

http://aliveis.preloaded.com

2005

Concept

This fruit drink portal chose to offer a number of simple games and allow users to choose the ones they want to pay, enabling them to save the scores and to see a video demo before they start to interact. /// Auf der Website dieses Fruchtgetränks stehen eine Reihe von einfachen Spielen zur Auswahl, inklusive Videodemos und Punktesicherung. /// Ce portail pour une boisson aux fruits offre une série de jeux simples et permet aux utilisateurs de sélectionner ceux qu'ils souhaitent payer, afin d'enregistrer leurs scores et de voir une vidéo de démonstration avant de commencer.

Info

Design: Preloaded <www.preloaded.com>. /// **Programming:** Preloaded. /// **Tools:** Adobe Photoshop, Flash. /// **Awards:** SXSW, BIMA, FlashForward, Macromedia (Site of the Day).

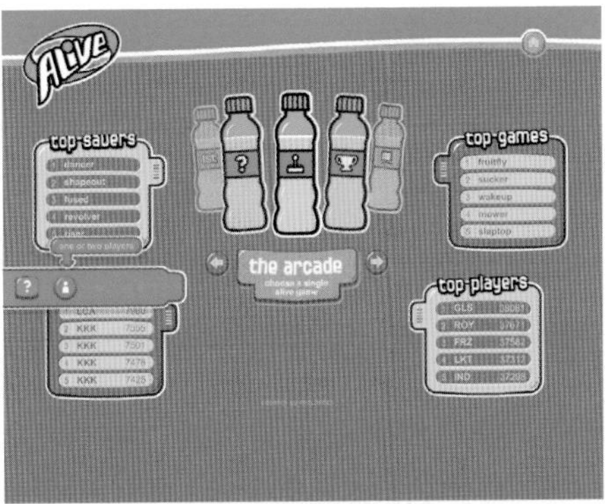

Alive
top-savers
1 dancer
2 shapeout
3 fused
4 revolver
one or two players
the arcade
choose a single alive game
top-games
1 fruitfly
2 sucker
3 wakeup
4 mower
5 slaptop
top-players

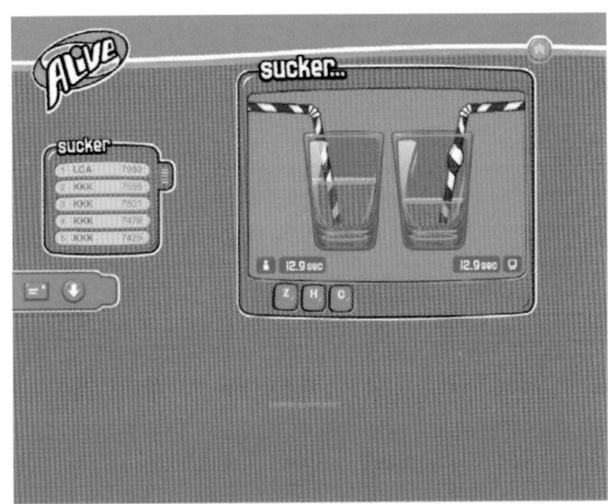

Alive
sucker...
sucker
1 LCA 7980
2 KKK 7555
3 KKK 7501
4 KKK 7476
5 KKK 7425
12.9sec
12.9sec
Z
H
C

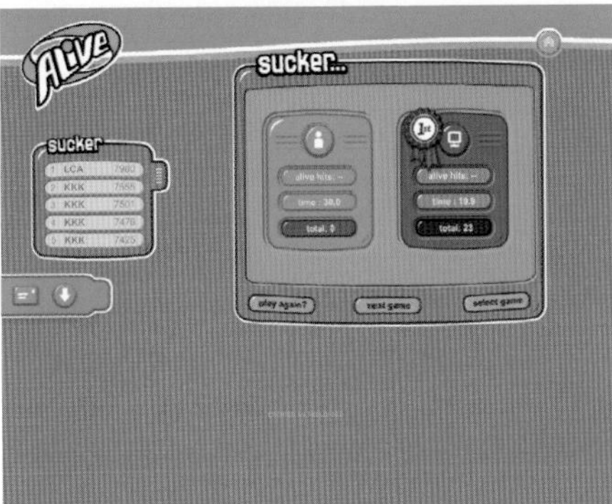

Alive
sucker...
sucker
1 LCA 7980
2 KKK 7555
3 KKK 7501
4 KKK 7476
5 KKK 7425
total: 0
total: 23
play again?
next game
select game

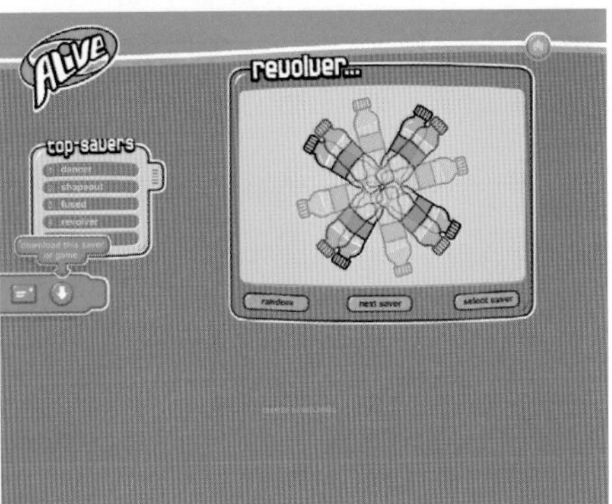

Alive
revolver...
top-savers
1 dancer
2 shapeout
3 fused
4 revolver
random
next saver
select saver

Alive
bowler...
top-savers
1 dancer
2 shapeout
3 fused
4 revolver
download this saver or game
random
next saver
select saver

ADIDAS PREDATOR VS F50+

HONG KONG

www.rice5.com/r5_adShowCase/adidas/bannerAd/football07/msnGame/msnGame.html

2007

Concept

A brand new and innovative digital advertising campaign through MSN Messenger. The overall campaign drove impressive results and audience interaction through brilliant design, strategic media execution and negotiation. /// Eine brandneue und innovative digitale Werbekampagne, die über MSN Messenger läuft. Die übergeordnete Kampagne erzielte eindrucksvolle Resultate und Besucherinteraktion aufgrund eines brillanten Designs, einer strategischen Medienausnutzung und aufgrund von geschickten Verhandlungen. /// **Campagne publicitaire numérique inédite et innovante via MSN Messenger. Elle a donné des résultats exceptionnels et entraîné l'interaction du public, grâce à un design brillant, une exploitation stratégique des supports et une bonne négociation.**

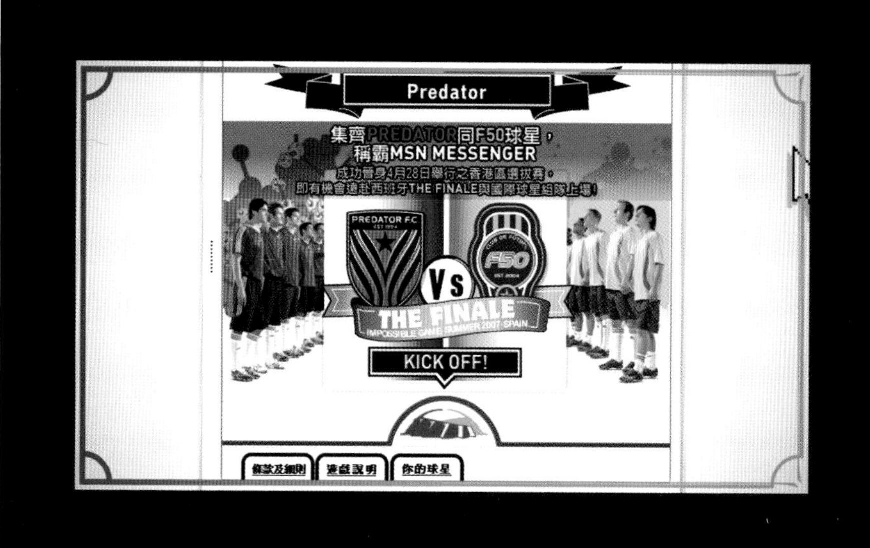

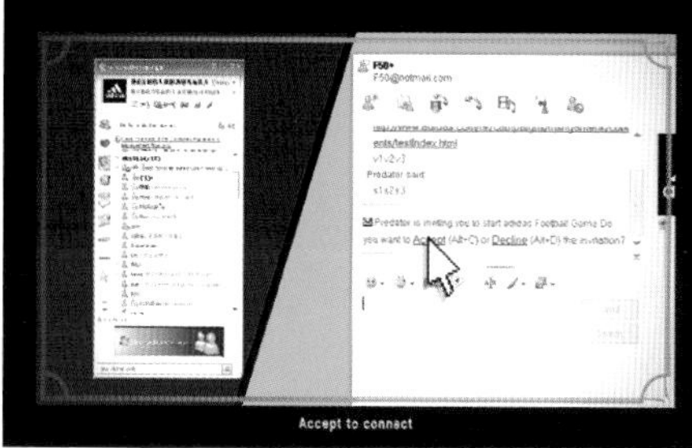
Accept to connect

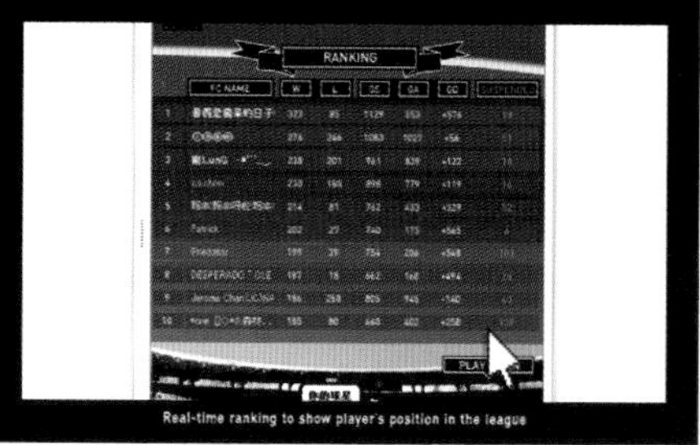

Real-time ranking to show player's position in the league

Info

DESIGN: Rice 5 <www.rice5.com>, Snowman Tsang. /// PROGRAMMING: Rex Chan, Eric Ho, Mike Li. /// TOOLS: Adobe Photoshop, Flash, Fireworks. /// AWARDS: 2007 HK4As Interactive & Direct Awards (Viral Marketing, Bronze); 2007 HK4As Interactive & Direct Awards (Gaming, Silver).

To collect over 100 types of famous adidas football stars

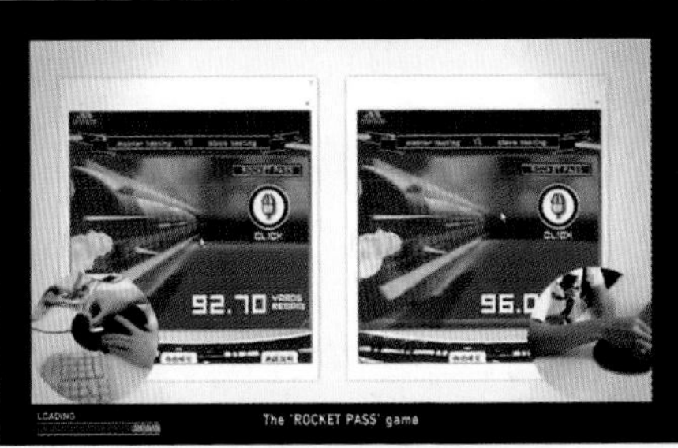

The 'ROCKET PASS' game

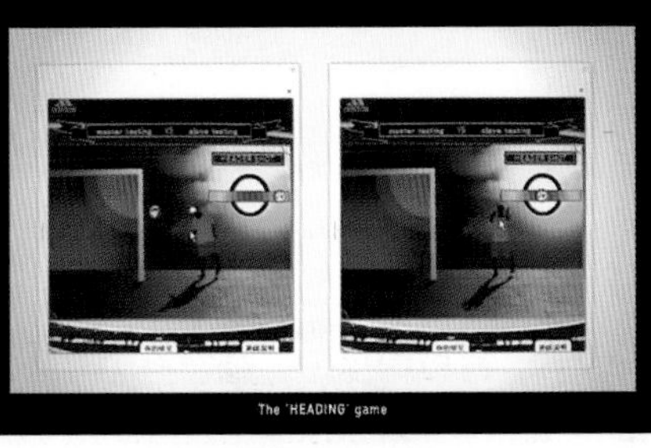

The 'HEADING' game

The winner will be awarded a new card from the card pool

The stars were divided into 2 teams - Predator and F50-

AGILE CROSSFOX

BRAZIL

http://200.186.92.250/awards/2007/vw/crossfox_case/eng

2006

Concept

The Volkswagen CrossFox car was about to be launched, and to complement the campaign, ALMAP developed a game for mobile and online play, which consisted of an offroad car race. /// Als Ergänzung zur Werbekampagne des neuen VW-Modells Cross Fox entwickelte ALMAP ein Geländewagenrennen als Online- und Handyspiel. /// Le modèle Cross Fox de Volkswagen était sur le point de sortir sur le marché. En plus de la campagne, ALMAP a mis au point un jeu de course de véhicules tout-terrain pour portable.

Info

Design: AlmapBBDO <www.almapbbdo.com.br>, Sergio Mugnaini (Creative/Art Director), Luciana Haguiara (Copywriter). /// **Programming:** Raphael H. de Carvalho (Flash Developer), Yves Apsi. /// **Tools:** Adobe Photoshop, Flash, After Effects, Illustrator, Java (Mobile Version).

Results

Unique users: 378,000 (month); 105,000 mobile downloads (3 months). /// Unique User: 378.000 (1 Monat) 105.000 Handy-Downloads (3 Monate). /// Utilisateurs uniques : 378 000 (mois) 105 000 téléchargements sur portables (3 mois).

ALLSTATE GARAGE

USA

www.allstategarage.com

2008

Concept

The website is the online side of a garage business, which allows users to navigate in a very playful way. The site also contains a game to build a motorbike. /// Die Website einer Kfz-Werkstatt. Benutzer können spielerisch darin herumnavigieren. Die Site enthält außerdem ein Spiel, bei dem man sein eigenes Motorrad bauen kann. /// Le site Web montre le coin de mécanique d'un garage et permet aux utilisateurs de naviguer d'une façon très amusante. Il inclut aussi un jeu pour fabriquer une moto.

Info

DESIGN: Domani Studios <www.domanistudios.com>. /// **PROGRAMMING:** Domani Studios. /// **TOOLS:** Adobe Photoshop, Flash, Illustrator, XML, HTML, After Effects, 3D Modeling, Ruby On Rails, RubyAMF. /// **COST:** 4 months. /// **CLIENT:** Leo Burnett.

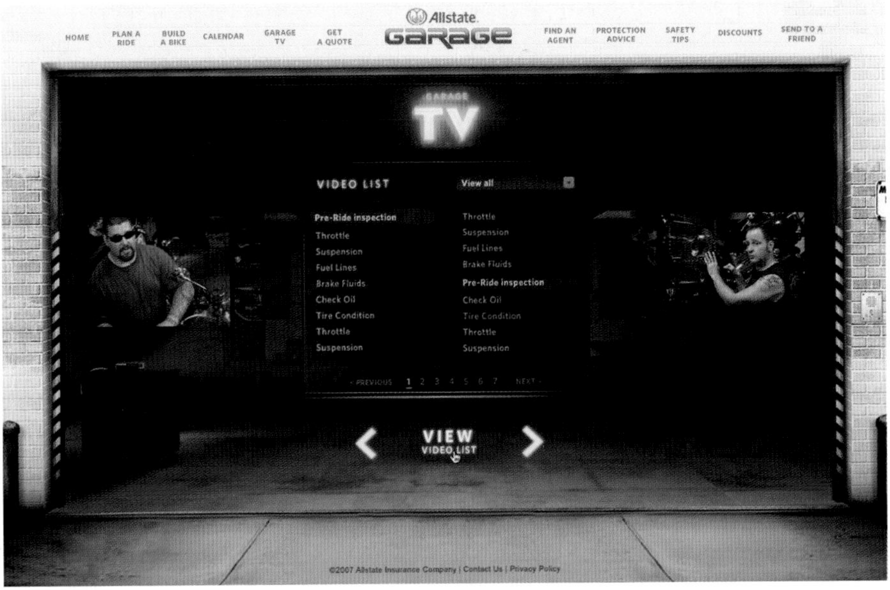

HOME
PLAN A RIDE
BUILD A BIKE
CALENDAR
GARAGE TV
GET A QUOTE
Allstate
GARAGE
FIND AN AGENT
PROTECTION ADVICE
SAFETY TIPS
DISCOUNTS
SEND TO A FRIEND
TV
VIDEO LIST
View all
Pre-Ride inspection
Throttle
Suspension
Fuel Lines
Brake Fluids
Check Oil
Tire Condition
Throttle
Suspension
Throttle
Suspension
Fuel Lines
Brake Fluids
Pre-Ride inspection
Check Oil
Tire Condition
Throttle
Suspension
1 2 3 4 5 6 7
VIEW
VIDEO LIST
©2007 Allstate Insurance Company | Contact Us | Privacy Policy

HOME
PLAN A RIDE
BUILD A BIKE
CALENDAR
GARAGE TV
GET A QUOTE
Allstate
GARAGE
FIND AN AGENT
PROTECTION ADVICE
SAFETY TIPS
DISCOUNTS
SEND TO A FRIEND
CLOSE X
MOBILE GARAGE
CALENDAR
Allstate's Mobile Garage will be at all the major bike rallies this year. It's your chance to meet Tommy "Clutch" Creal and learn how to build your own bike at his chopper college.
Get a sneak peek in the Mobile Garage Photo Gallery.
> VIEW GALLERY
> SIGN UP FOR UPDATES
> GET A QUOTE
< SEPT
OCTOBER 2007
NOV >
1 2 3 4 5 6
7 8 9 10 11 12 13
14 15 16 17 18 19 20
21 22 23 24 25 26 27
28 29 30 31

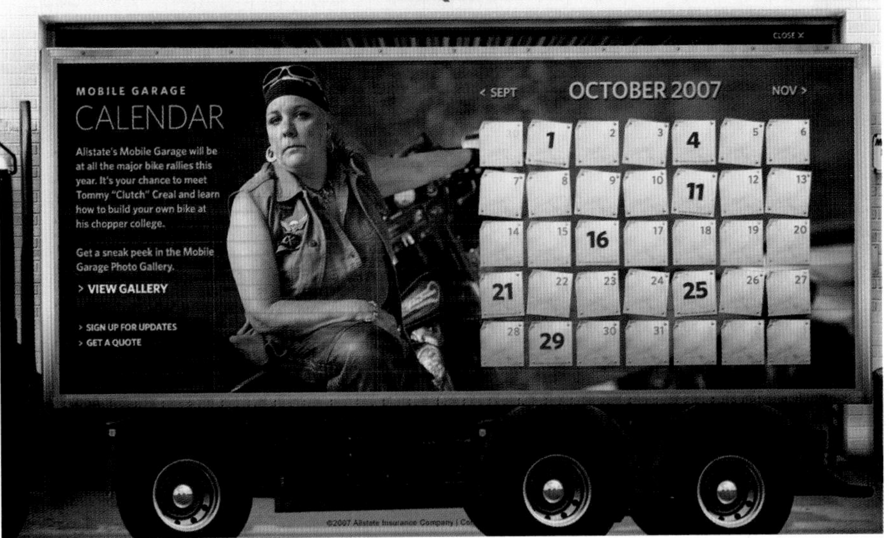

ATC-SIM

USA

www.atc-sim.com

2006

Concept

A complex air traffic control game that simulates real professional challenges and situations. /// Ein komplexes Luftverkehrskontroll-Spiel, das echte Situationen und Herausforderungen simuliert. /// Jeu de contrôle aérien complexe qui simule des difficultés et les situations professionnelles réelles.

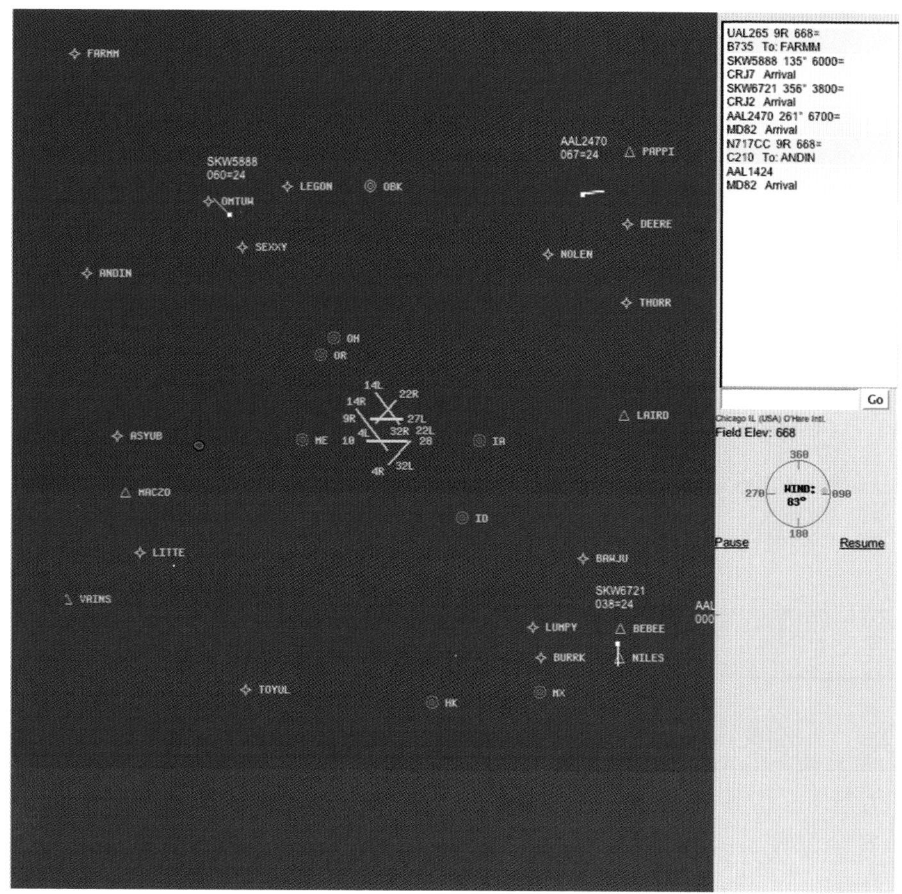

Info

Design: Jay Link <www.jaylink.name>, Jay Link, Eddy van de Winckel. /// **Programming:** Jay Link. /// **Tools:** Zend Studio, PHP, HTML, Javascript, MySQL. /// **Awards:** NATCA (National Air Traffic Controllers Association) <www.natca.net>. /// **Cost:** 200 hours.

Begin simulation

Airport

Chicago O'Hare (ORD)

Need more airports? Login here

Airline Codes

Regional Preferences

ICAO (3-digit) IATA (2-digit)

Wind Direction

Frequency of change

Wind will not change

Realism

Level of difficulty

Normal

* If you select anything other than "normal", you will not qualify for the high score table.

Map Scale Markers

Customize the Scale command

Circles

Performance Options

Enhancements for older PCs

Plane trails on Plane trails off

Begin simulation

Instructions

ATC-SIM is a web-based air traffic control simulator. No plug-ins or additional software are required to play.

Objective

Controllers must route arriving and departing aircraft both safely and accurately.

Safe Separation Standards

Your job is to ensure that aircraft are separated by either of the following criteria:
Laterally — 5 miles
Vertically — 1,000 feet

Commands

All commands are in the format:
FlightID + Command + [Command String].

Takeoff

Questions? Comments? Need help? Email: info (at) atc-sim.com

View site news & recent additions

See the Top 100 Controllers!

Ready for a break? Here are some suggested links and the ATC Webring.

BANG ON THE DOOR

UK

www.bangonthedoor.com

2007

Concept

FRONT was asked to create a vibrant, immersive and playful world for the international brand Groovy Chick and her companion characters. The site needed to be captivating and memorable for a young audience. /// FRONT wurde gebeten, für die Figuren der internationalen Marke Groovy Chick eine lebhafte, verspielte und liebenswerte Welt zu erschaffen. Die Website sollte ein junges Publikum ansprechen. /// FRONT a reçu la commande d'un monde passionnant, attirant et amusant pour la marque internationale Groovy Chick et les personnages qui l'accompagnent. Le site devait être à la fois captivant et inoubliable pour un public jeune.

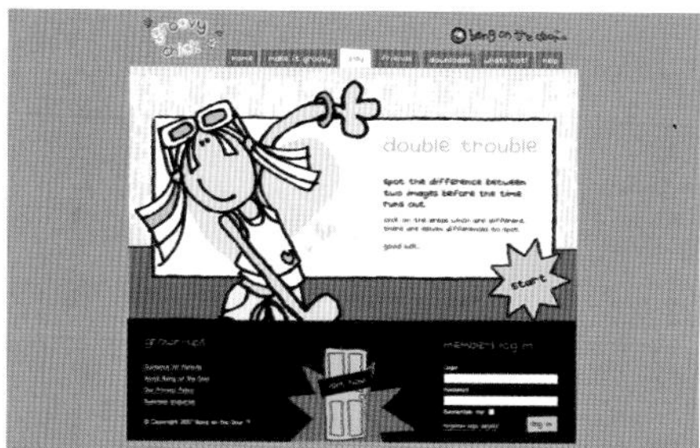

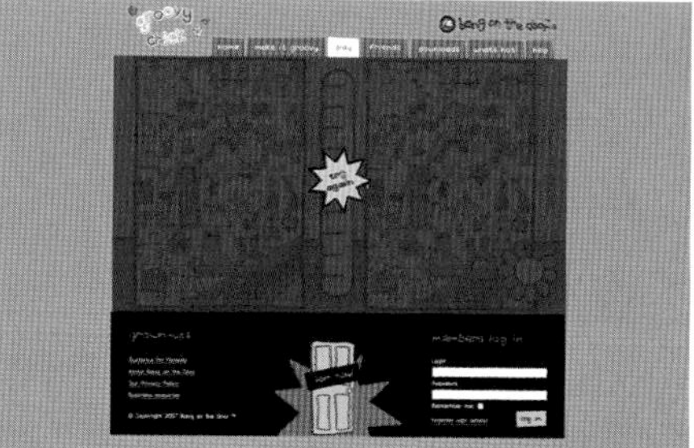

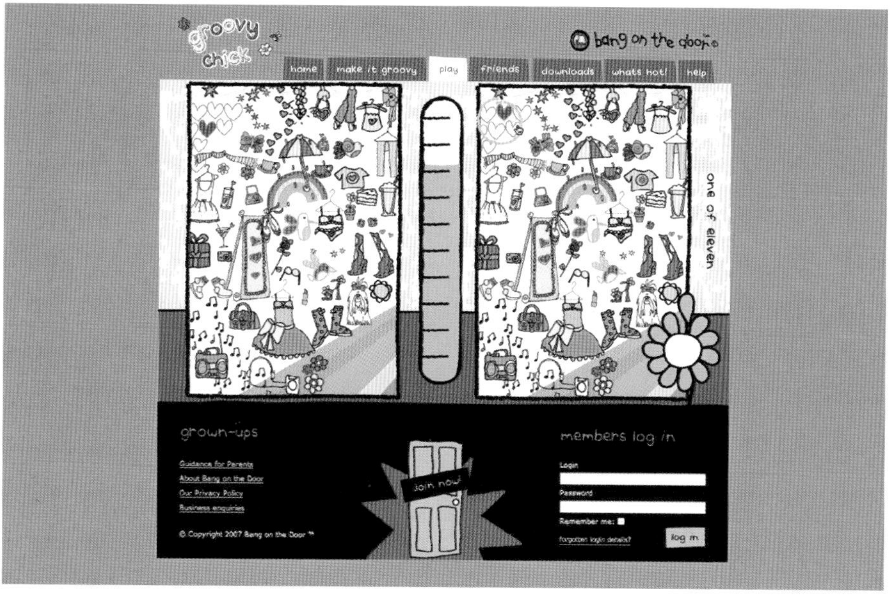

Info

Design: FRONT <www.designbyfront.com>, Jamie Neely, Eamonn Murphy. /// **Programming:** Stephen Rushe, Michal Wronka, Warren Sangster, Charlie Neely. /// **Tools:** Flash, Ruby on Rails content management system. /// **Results:** The site has been a huge success since its launch, already attracting tens of thousands of new and regular users.

BARBIE HITS

BRAZIL

www.grendene.com.br/www/barbiehits/intro

2006

Concept

Totally musical, the website's lead tool is its virtual Karaoke, where girls can sing and record musical webcards that can be sent to their friends. /// Das Haupttool der Website ist ein virtuelles Karaokespiel, bei dem Mädchen musikalische Webcards singen und aufnehmen und sie anschließend an ihre Freunde verschicken können. /// Entièrement musical, l'outil principal du site Web est un karaoké virtuel, dans lequel les petites filles peuvent chanter et enregistrer des cartes Web musicales à envoyer à leurs amies.

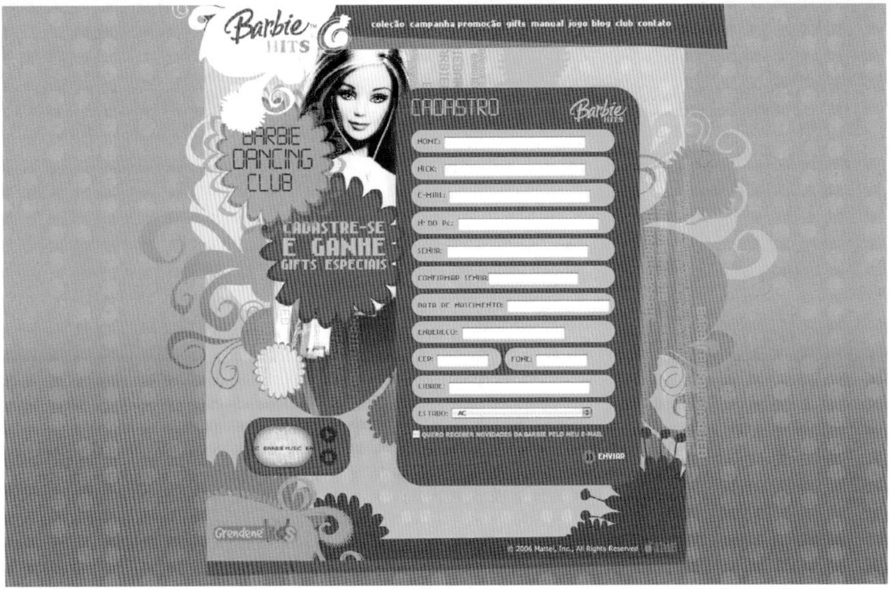

Info

Design: W3Haus <www.w3haus.com.br>, Chico Baldini, Diego Chiarelli. /// **Programming:** Carolina Sebben, Alessandro Cauduro. /// **Tools:** Adobe Photoshop, Flash, ASP.net, HTML, XML. /// **Cost:** 800 hours. /// **Others:** Diego Grandi (Project Manager).

BEAN BOING SPLASH

NEW ZEALAND

http://play.resn.co.nz/beanboing

2007

Concept

Drag bubbles for Beanie to bounce off. The aim is to get him into the coffee cup high up in the clouds. The longer the line of bubbles the higher he bounces. /// Ziehe Bläschen auf das Bild, mit deren Hilfe Beanie hochhüpfen kann. Sein Ziel ist es, in den Kaffeebecher hoch oben in den Wolken zu gelangen. Je länger die Bläschenreihe, desto höher kann er hüpfen. /// Faites glisser des bulles pour que Beanie rebondisse dessus et atteigne la tasse de café dans les nuages. Plus la ligne de bulles est longue, plus il rebondit haut.

Info

DESIGN: Resn <www.resn.co.nz>. /// PROGRAMMING: Resn. /// TOOLS: Adobe Photoshop, Flash. /// COST: 4 weeks.

Results

Visitors and customers of coffeesupreme.com enjoyed the game and provided great feedback. The game has also received tens of thousands of visitors worldwide, redirecting thousands to the *Coffee Supreme* site. /// Besuchern und Kunden von coffeesupreme.com gefiel das Spiel, wie ihrem Feedback zu entnehmen war. Das Spiel hatte Zehntausende Besucher weltweit und verwies davon Tausende auf die Website von *Coffee Supreme*. /// Les visiteurs et les clients de coffeesupreme.com ont aimé le jeu et renvoyé des commentaires positifs. Le jeu a aussi reçu des dizaines de milliers de visiteurs dans le monde entier, dont des milliers ont été redirigés vers le site de *Coffee Supreme*.

BAU MIT UNS EIN FLUGZEUG

GERMANY

http://wysiwyg.de/garage/tks_spiel

2006

Concept

On-stage dual player game setup for Ideenpark Expo 2006 by ThyssenKrupp. Using airplane production logistics as (the client's) backdrop, the game uses three simple but different concepts so kids with different skill sets can compete. /// Ein Online-Spiel für zwei Spieler, entworfen für ThyssenKrupp anlässlich der Ideenpark Expo 2006. Es geht um die Logistik einer Flugzeugproduktion. Das Spiel bietet drei verschiedene Schwierigkeitsstufen, sodass es von Kinder mit unterschiedlichen Fähigkeiten gespielt werden kann. /// Jeu à deux joueurs mis au point pour Ideenpark Expo 2006 par ThyssenKrupp. En prenant la logistique de fabrication des avions comme toile de fond (du client), le jeu fait appel à trois concepts simples pour que des enfants aux compétences diverses puissent s'affronter.

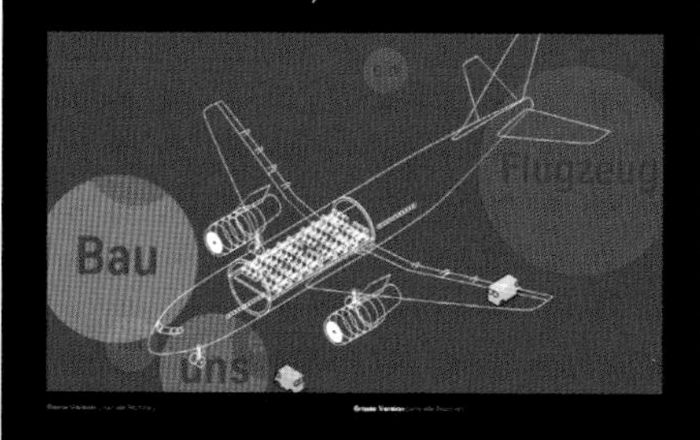

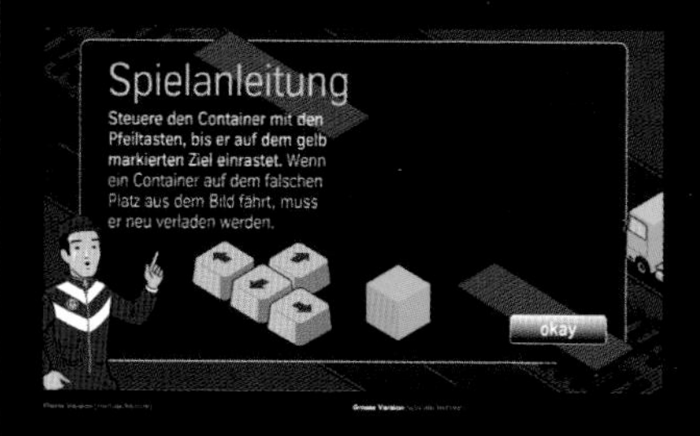

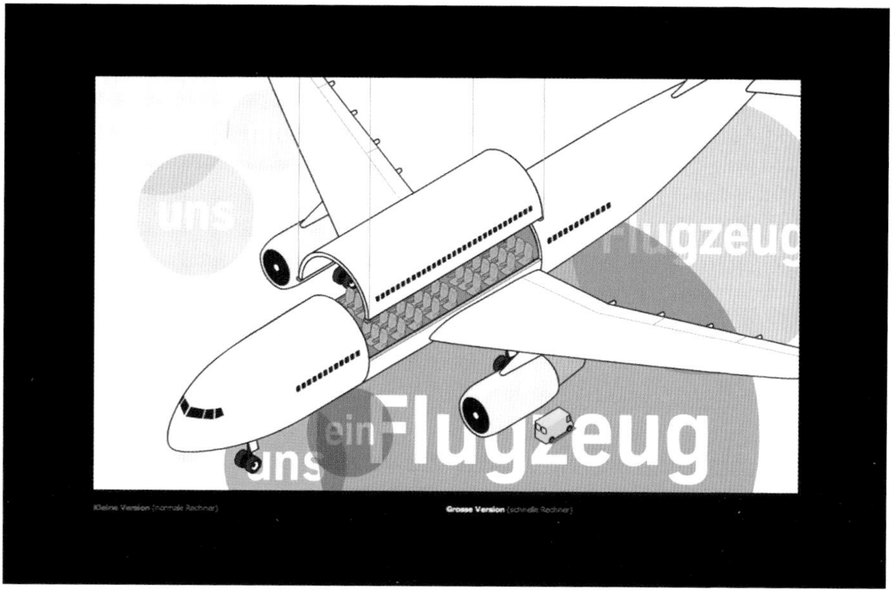

Info

DESIGN: wysiwyg* software design <www.wysiwyg.de>, Alexander Koch, Pattrick Kreutzer. /// PROGRAMMING: Pattrick Kreutzer. /// TOOLS: Flash, Illustrator, Java Server. /// AWARDS: Designpreis Bundesrepublik Deutschland Nominee, Red Dot Award, Jahrbuch der Werbung 2007, Part of the permanent exhibiton of Deutsches Museum in Munich. /// OTHERS: Dirk Rittberger – hippielook, Berlin (Illustration).

airlebnis
L.U.F.T
airholung
okay
hotline
ChickenWings
Kleine Version (normale Rechner)
Grosse Version (schnelle Rechner)

Spieler
Dein Name:
TASCHEN
Dein Alter:
9–12
13–16
16+
Los geht's!

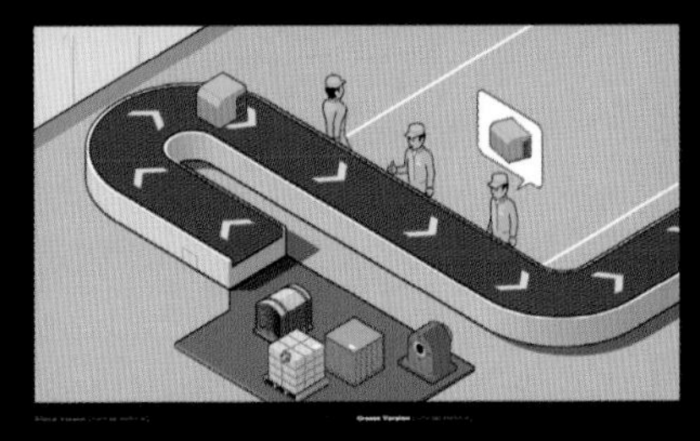

0:20

Gut. 300 Punkte
Du hast 2 Container verladen
okay

BEBOARD

ITALY

www.beboard.net

2007

Concept

The configurator is very simple and usable, the target is using it and producing thousands of boards. The project was also bought by MTV Italy to make an online graphic contest. /// Der Konfigurator ist sehr einfach zu bedienen. Ziel ist es, damit Tausende von Boards zu entwerfen. Das Projekt wurde von MTV Italien für einen Online-Grafikwettbewerb gekauft. /// Le configurateur est très simple d'emploi, l'objectif étant de créer des milliers de planches. Le projet a aussi été présenté par MTV Italie pour organiser un concours graphique en ligne.

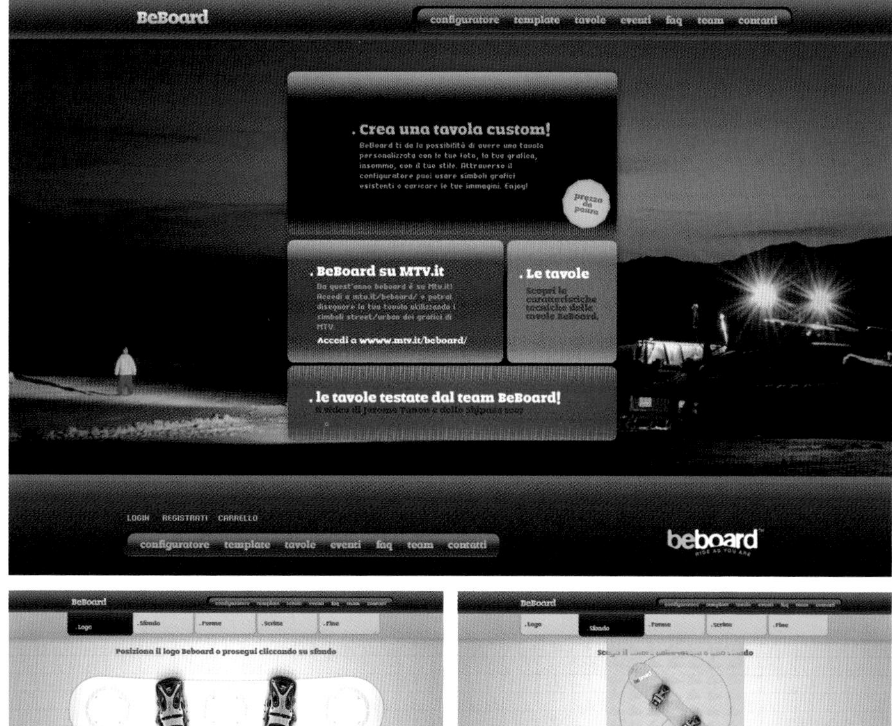

Info

DESIGN: vanGoGh <www.vangogh-creative.it/interactive>, Enrico Penzo, Arnaldo Boico. /// **PROGRAMMING:** Enrico Penzo. /// **TOOLS:** Adobe Photoshop, Flash, Illustrator.

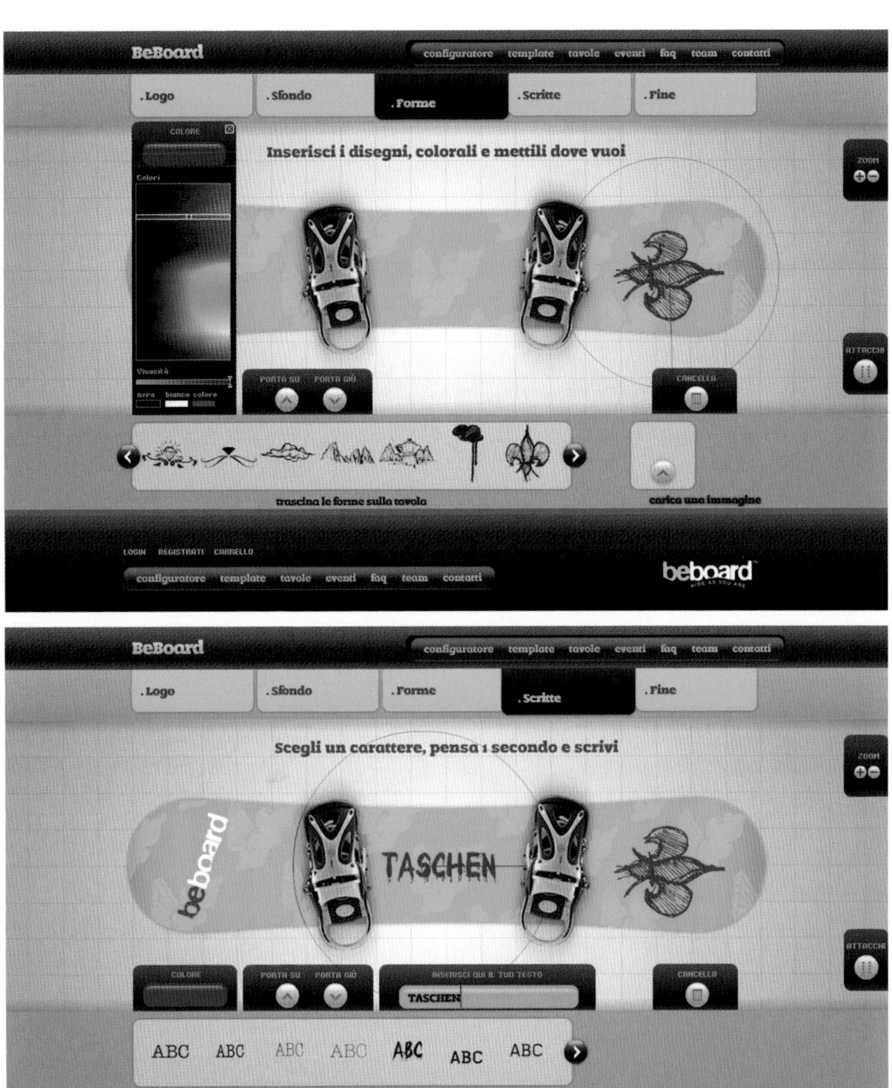

Results

The Beboard site sold 200 customised boards. /// Die Website verkaufte 200 maßgefertigte Boards. /// Le site Beboard a vendu 200 planches personnalisées.

BERRY BONES

USA

www.BerryBones.com

2005

Concept

As part of the promotional campaign for Scooby Doo's cereal, this inventive online game requires players to click on the monsters trying to steal Scooby Doo's food from the cereal box. /// Dieses einfallsreiche Online-Spiel ist Teil einer Werbekampagne für Scooby Doos Frühstückscerealien. Die Spieler müssen auf Monster klicken, die versuchen, Scooby Doos Essen aus der Cerealienpackung zu stehlen. /// Dans le cadre d'une campagne promotionnelle pour les céréales Scooby Doo, ce jeu en ligne inventif demande aux joueurs de cliquer sur les monstres qui essayent de voler la nourriture de Scooby Doo dans la boîte de céréales.

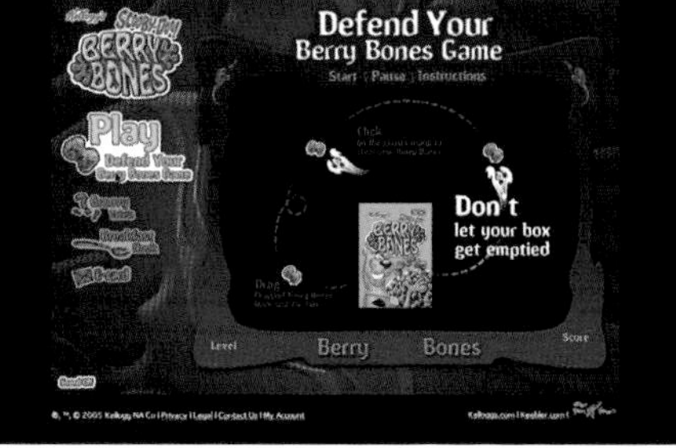

Info

Design: Freedom Interactive Design <www.freedominteractivedesign.com>. /// **Programming:** Freedom Interactive Design. /// **Tools:** Game uses Flash's local shared object functionality to store high scores, encouraging repeat visits and plays. Fans can tell friends about the site with CGI-driven e-card function.

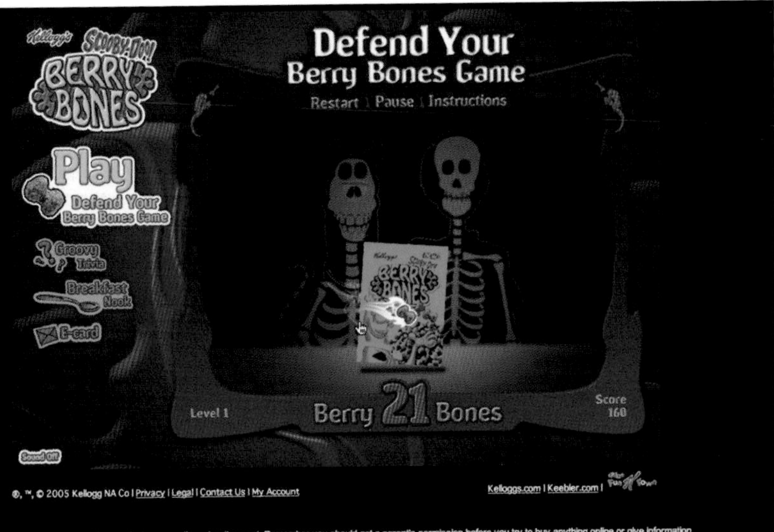
Kellogg's
Scooby-Doo!
Berry Bones
Play
Defend Your Berry Bones Game
Groovy Trivia
Breakfast Nook
E-card
Defend Your
Berry Bones Game
Restart | Pause | Instructions
Level 1
Berry 21 Bones
Score 160
Sound Off
®, ™, © 2005 Kellogg NA Co | Privacy | Legal | Contact Us | My Account
Kelloggs.com | Keebler.com |
KIDS: This page may contain a product or promotion advertisement. Remember you should get a parent's permission before you try to buy anything online or give information about yourself.

Defend Your
Berry Bones Game
Restart | Pause | Instructions
Level 1
Berry 24 Bones

Defend Your
Berry Bones Game
Restart | Pause | Instructions
Level 1
Berry 13 Bones

Breakfast Nook
Eat Kellogg's Ready-to-Eat Cereal
to Promote a Healthy Body Weight

Dig This
Groovy Trivia!
Did You Know...

BIG SOIL

www.bigsoil.com

HONG KONG

2006

Concept

An official website for a local illustrator named Big Soil. The entire site showcases Big Soil's illustrations to create his world, in which visitors can experience a journey with Big Soil when browsing around the website. /// Die offizielle Website für einen lokalen Künstler namens Big Soil. Die Site präsentiert Big Soils Illustrationen und schickt den Besucher beim Navigieren auf eine Reise durch die Welt des Künstlers. /// **Site Web officiel pour un illustrateur local nommé Big Soil. Tout le site présente ses illustrations pour recréer son monde, dans lequel les visiteurs peuvent naviguer pour l'accompagner dans un voyage.**

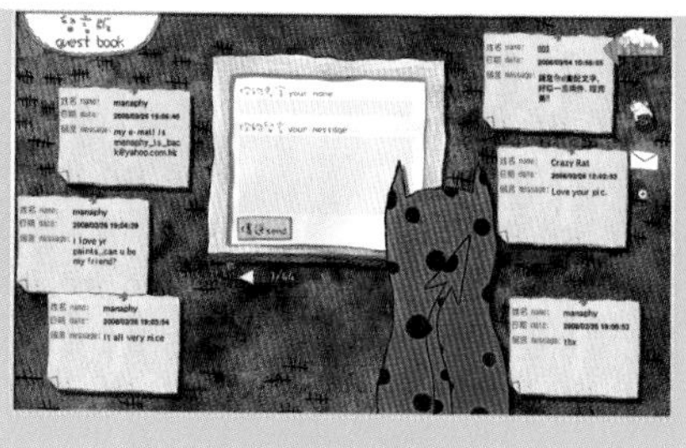

Info

DESIGN: Rice 5 <www.rice5.com>, Tom Shum, Celine Leung. /// **PROGRAMMING:** Mike Li. /// **TOOLS:** Adobe Photoshop, Flash, Fireworks. /// **AWARDS:** 2006 HK4As Interactive & Direct Awards (Corporate Website, Silver).

近期展出
Event

home

off

飛得起

飛得起，大泥作品展於阿貓地攤 03.12.2003 至 14.02.2004
First exhibition at Cat’s Café in 03.12.2003 to 14.02.2004

近期展出
Event

home

off

漫有引力

香港藝術節漫有引力於香港藝術中心 10.03.2006 至 15.04.2006
Comix magneto of Hong Kong Art Festival at Hong Kong Art Centre in 10.03.2006 to 15.04.2006

BUILD YOUR OWN VOLVO V70

SWEDEN

http://demo.fb.se/e/volvo/v70/buildyourown

2007

Concept

Why should the task of styling your new car (and see how much it will cost) be boring and complex? Why not make a site where every option is just one click away? /// Warum sollte die Entscheidung über die Ausstattung Ihres neuen Autos (und das Ausrechnen der Kosten) langweilig und langwierig sein? Warum nicht eine Website entwickeln, wo jede Option nicht mehr ist als ein Klick? /// Pourquoi la personnalisation de votre nouvelle voiture (et le calcul de son coût) devrait-elle être ennuyeuse et compliquée ? Pourquoi ne pas faire une site dans lequel toutes les options sont accessibles en un clic ?

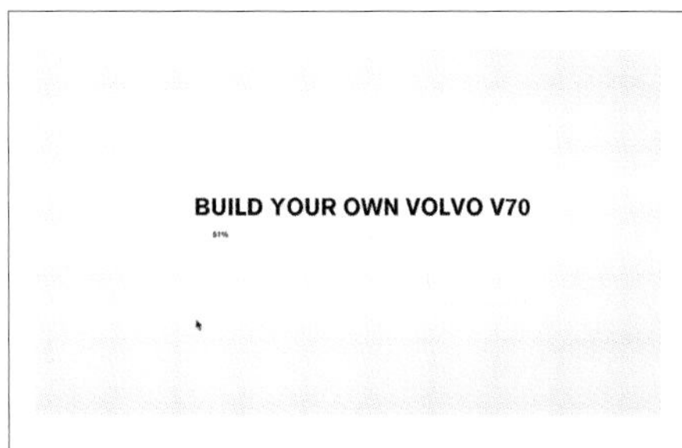

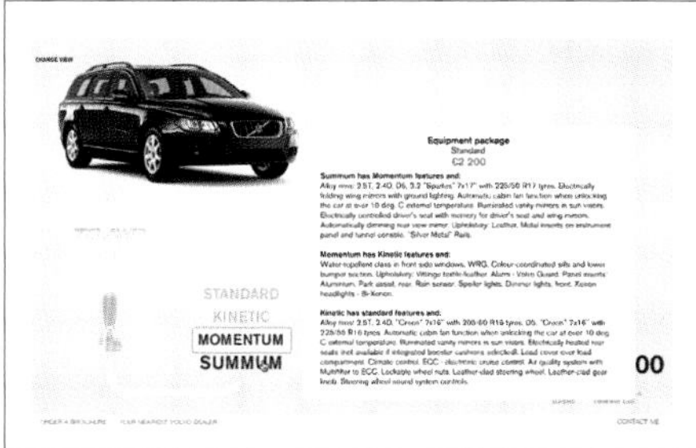

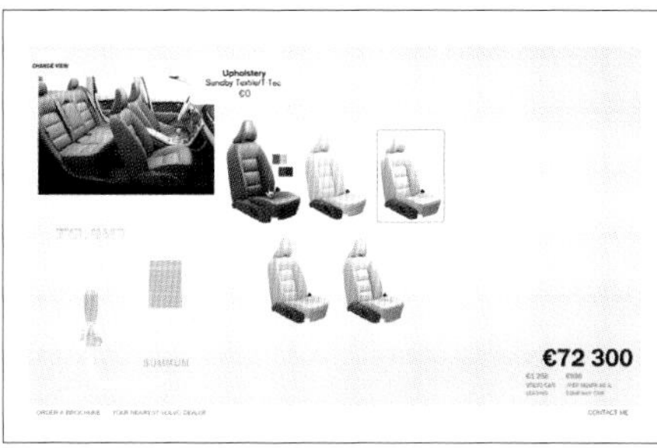

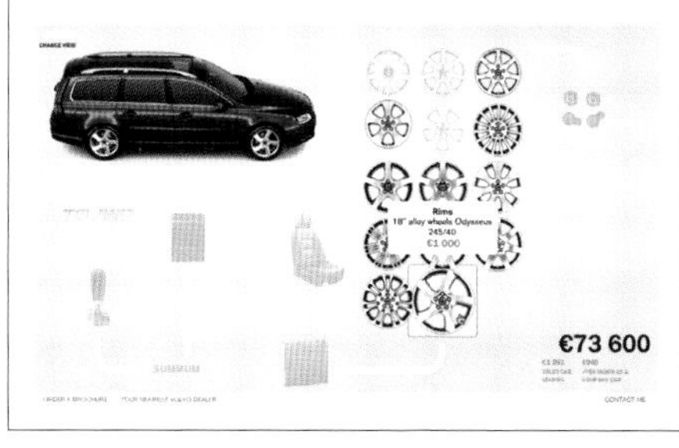

Info

DESIGN: Forsman & Bodenfors <www.fb.se>. /// **PROGRAMMING:** Kokokaka Entertainment. /// **TOOLS:** Adobe Video Production Suite, Flash, Pro Tools, Final Cut Pro, Photoshop, Illustrator, 3ds Max, After Effects.

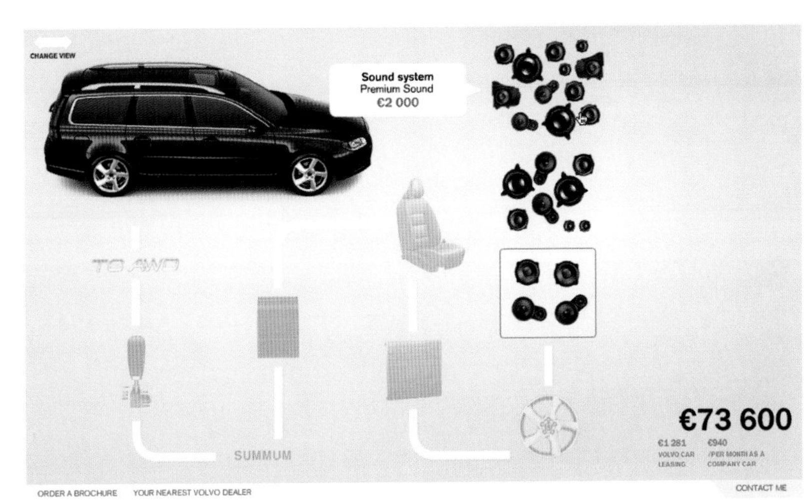
CHANGE VIEW
Sound system
Premium Sound
€2 000
SUMMUM
€73 600
€1 281
VOLVO CAR LEASING
€940
/PER MONTH AS A COMPANY CAR
ORDER A BROCHURE
YOUR NEAREST VOLVO DEALER
CONTACT ME

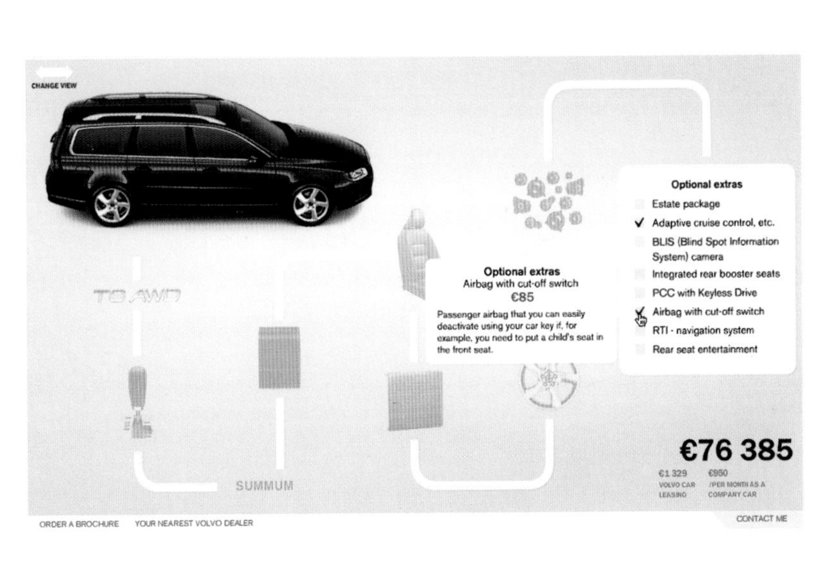
CHANGE VIEW
Optional extras
Airbag with cut-off switch
€85
Passenger airbag that you can easily deactivate using your car key if, for example, you need to put a child's seat in the front seat.
Optional extras
Estate package
Adaptive cruise control, etc.
BLIS (Blind Spot Information System) camera
Integrated rear booster seats
PCC with Keyless Drive
Airbag with cut-off switch
RTI - navigation system
Rear seat entertainment
SUMMUM
€76 385
€1 329
VOLVO CAR LEASING
€950
/PER MONTH AS A COMPANY CAR
ORDER A BROCHURE
YOUR NEAREST VOLVO DEALER
CONTACT ME

CDX

UK

http://cdx-thegame.com

2006

Concept

An interactive film containing immersive gaming elements. The storyline takes the form of a dark thriller set in the context of the TV show. The plot is key to the game and ensures dramatic purpose and historical accuracy throughout the experience. /// Ein interaktiver Film mit fesselnden Spielelementen. Die Story nimmt die Form eines düsteren Thrillers an, der in den Kontext der TV-Show gesetzt ist. Die Handlung ist der Schlüssel zum Spiel und gewährleistet dramaturgische Konsistenz und historische Genauigkeit. /// Film interactif contenant des éléments de jeu immersifs. Le scénario s'apparente à un thriller qui se déroule dans le cadre d'une émission télévisée. L'intrigue est déterminante pour le jeu et garantit tout le long tant l'aspect dramatique que la précision historique.

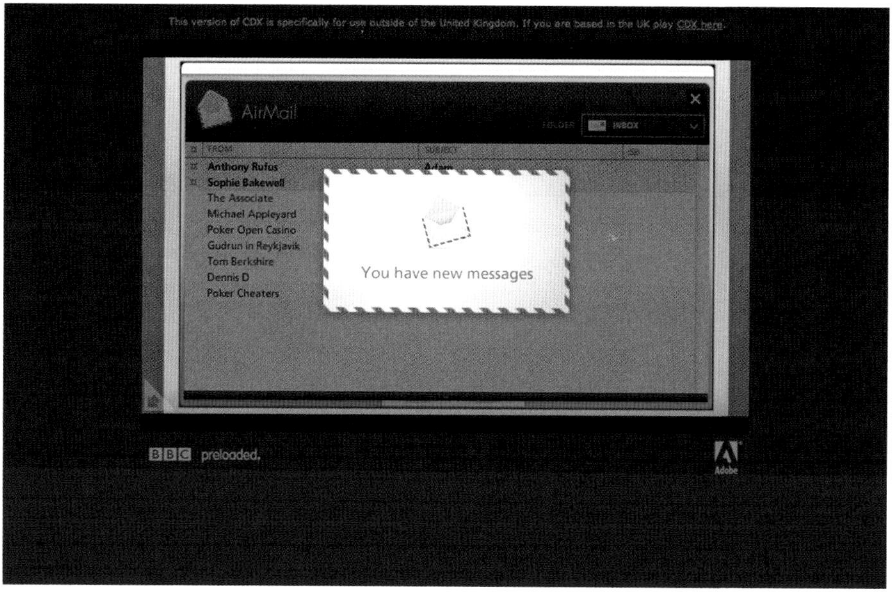

Info

Design: Preloaded <www.preloaded.com>. /// **Programming:** Preloaded. /// **Tools:** Adobe Photoshop, Flash, Maya. /// **Awards:** AOP, BAFTA, BIMA, Cannes Lions, D&AD, FlashForward, MIPCOM, Royal Television Society, SXSW, Webbies, Y Design Awards. /// **Others:** J. Wood (Writer), M. Ibeji (Historical Consultant); J. Stevenson – JS3D (3D Modelling); P. Poucher (Sound Design); B. Ledden (Producer BBC); R. Cable, M. Goodchild (Executives BBC).

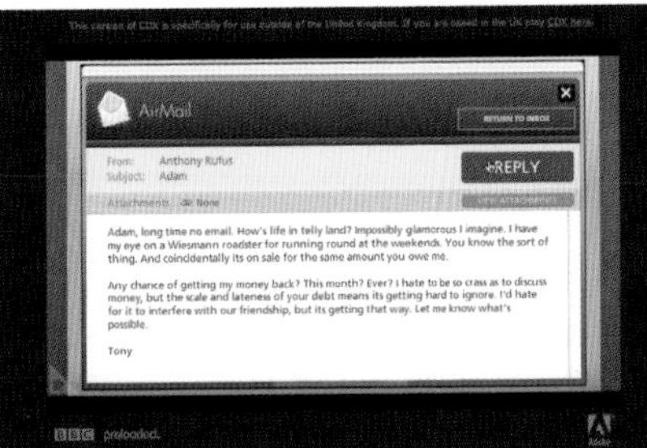
AirMail
RETURN TO INBOX
From: Anthony Rufus
Subject: Adam
REPLY
Attachments: None
Adam, long time no email. How's life in telly land? Impossibly glamorous I imagine. I have my eye on a Wiesmann roadster for running round at the weekends. You know the sort of thing. And coincidentally its on sale for the same amount you owe me.
Any chance of getting my money back? This month? Ever? I hate to be so crass as to discuss money, but the scale and lateness of your debt means its getting hard to ignore. I'd hate for it to interfere with our friendship, but its getting that way. Let me know what's possible.
Tony
BBC preloaded.

BBC preloaded.

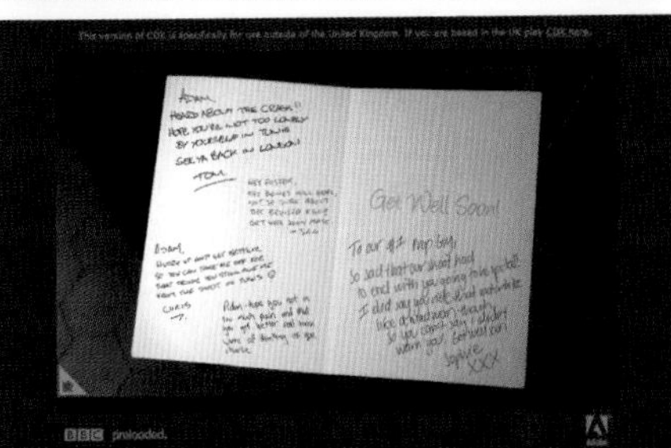
Get Well Soon!
BBC preloaded.

BBC preloaded.

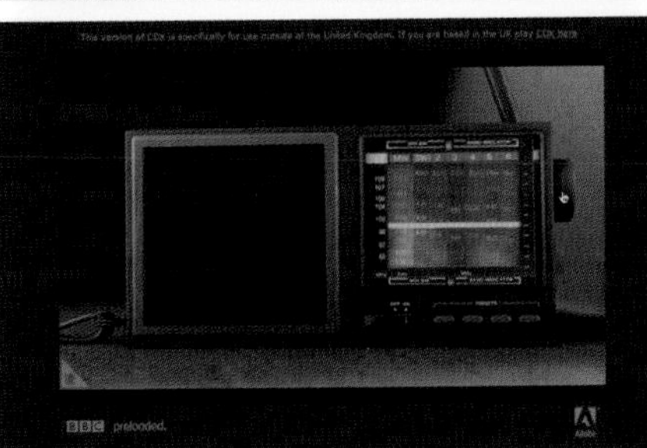
BBC preloaded.

BBC preloaded.

BBC preloaded.

BBC preloaded.

CHOOSING A MORTGAGE

USA/UK/SPAIN

www.gemoney.com/flash/Mortgage/index.html

2007

Concept

Utilising intuitive interface elements and clear summaries, this personal financial mortgage calculator is part of a suite of online tools that help bring meaningful financial information to the average person. /// Dieser Hypothekenrechner ist Teil einer ganzen Folge von Online-Tools, die intuitive Interface-Elemente und klare Zusammenfassungen einsetzen, um Normalverbrauchern Informationen und Hilfestellungen zu finanziellen Themen an die Hand zu geben. /// Grâce à des éléments d'interface intuitifs et des résumés clairs, ce calculateur personnel d'hypothèque est intégré à une suite d'outils en ligne fournissant des informations financières pertinentes à l'utilisateur moyen.

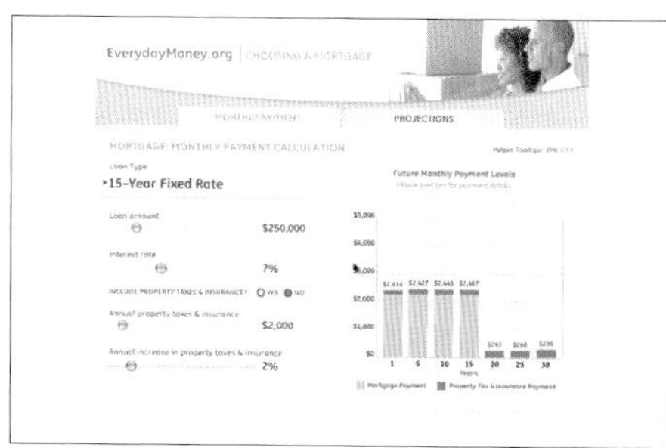

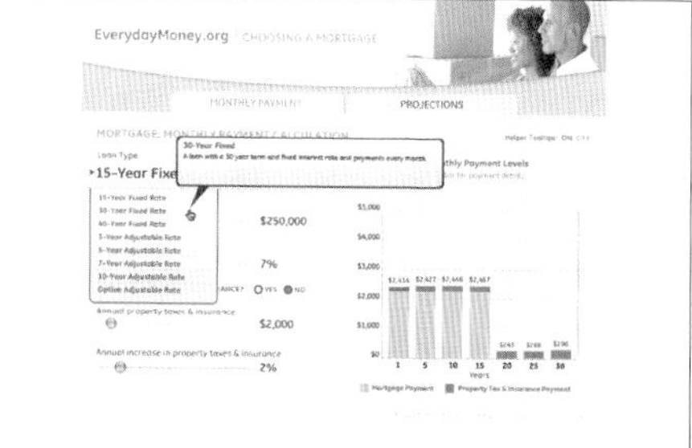

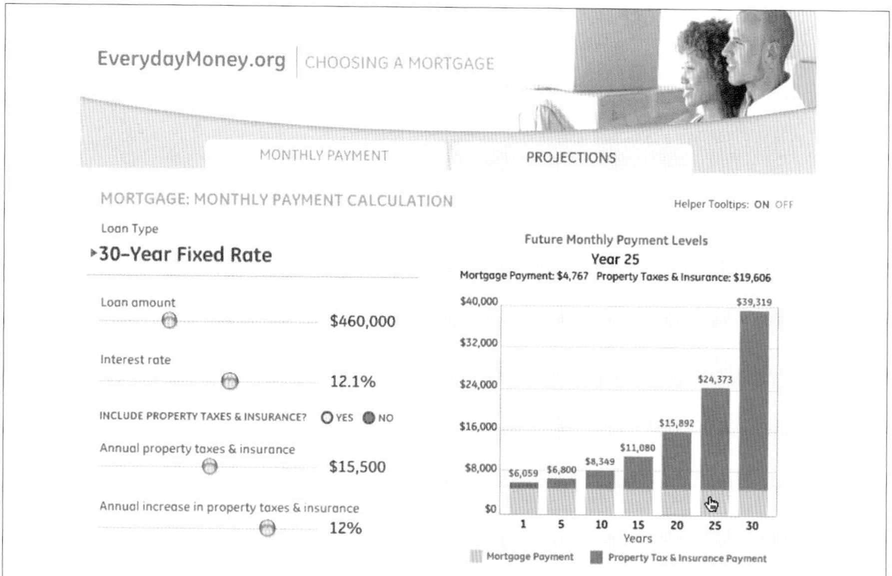

Info

Design: SiiTE Interactive <www.SiiTE.com>. /// **Programming:** SiiTE Interactive. /// **Tools:** Adobe Photoshop, Flash. /// **Awards:** Adobe (Site of the Day).

EverydayMoney.org | CHOOSING A MORTGAGE

MONTHLY PAYMENT
PROJECTIONS

PROPERTY: PROJECTIONS CALCULATION
Helper Tooltips: ON OFF
Loan Type
30-Year Fixed Rate
Current property value
How much is your home worth today? (Your loan amount is subtracted from property value to calculate the down payment).
Number of years
Current property value
$650,000
Annual change in the value of your home
2%
Projected Payments, Sale Price and Home Equity
$744,239
$600,000
$580,899
$400,000
$300,532
$200,000
$0
Total payments over 7 years (includes down payment)
Estimated sale price of home in 2015
Home equity in 2015

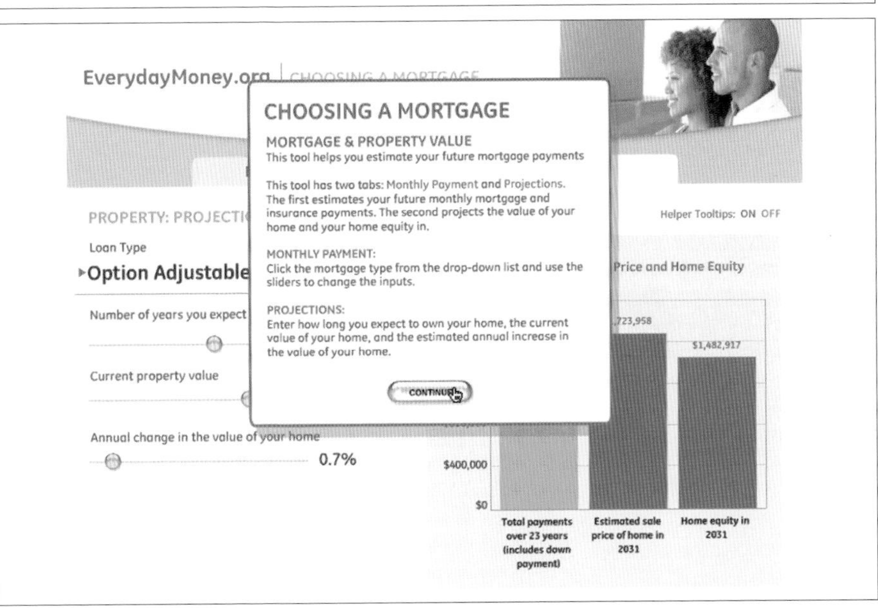

EverydayMoney.org
CHOOSING A MORTGAGE
MORTGAGE & PROPERTY VALUE
This tool helps you estimate your future mortgage payments
This tool has two tabs: Monthly Payment and Projections. The first estimates your future monthly mortgage and insurance payments. The second projects the value of your home and your home equity in.
MONTHLY PAYMENT:
Click the mortgage type from the drop-down list and use the sliders to change the inputs.
PROJECTIONS:
Enter how long you expect to own your home, the current value of your home, and the estimated annual increase in the value of your home.
CONTINUE
PROPERTY: PROJECTI
Helper Tooltips: ON OFF
Loan Type
Option Adjustable
Price and Home Equity
Number of years you expect
Current property value
Annual change in the value of your home
0.7%
$1,482,917
$400,000
$0
Total payments over 23 years (includes down payment)
Estimated sale price of home in 2031
Home equity in 2031

Results

The tools were extremely well received and have since gone on to be developed in multiple languages and for numerous countries. /// Die Tools kamen sehr gut an und sind inzwischen in zahlreiche Sprachen für viele Länder übertragen worden. /// Les outils ont reçu un accueil extrêmement positif et ont depuis été développés dans plusieurs langues et pour de nombreux pays.

CLAUS ON ICE

FRANCE/TURKEY

www.2fresh.com/2008

2007

Concept

This simple game uses basic directional keys, which allow the user to play around with a figure skating Santa Claus. /// Dieses einfache Spiel basiert auf Richtungstasten, mit denen ein eislaufender Weihnachtsmann bewegt wird. /// Dans ce jeu simple, les touches fléchées permettent à l'utilisateur de jouer avec un Père Noël sur des patins à glace.

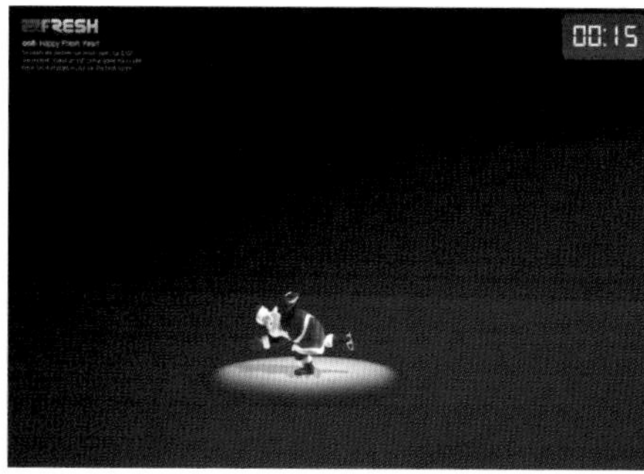

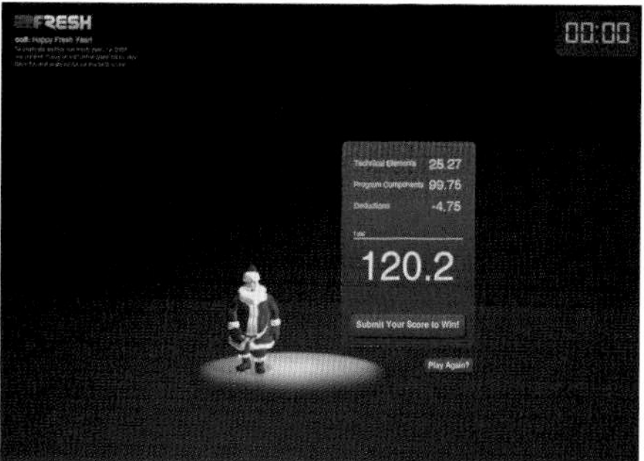

Info

Design: 2FRESH <www.2fresh.com>. /// **Programming:** 2FRESH. /// **Tools:** Adobe Photoshop, Flash, Illustrator, 3ds Max, After Effects, Dreamweaver. /// **Awards:** Interactive Media Awards. /// **Cost:** 400 hours.

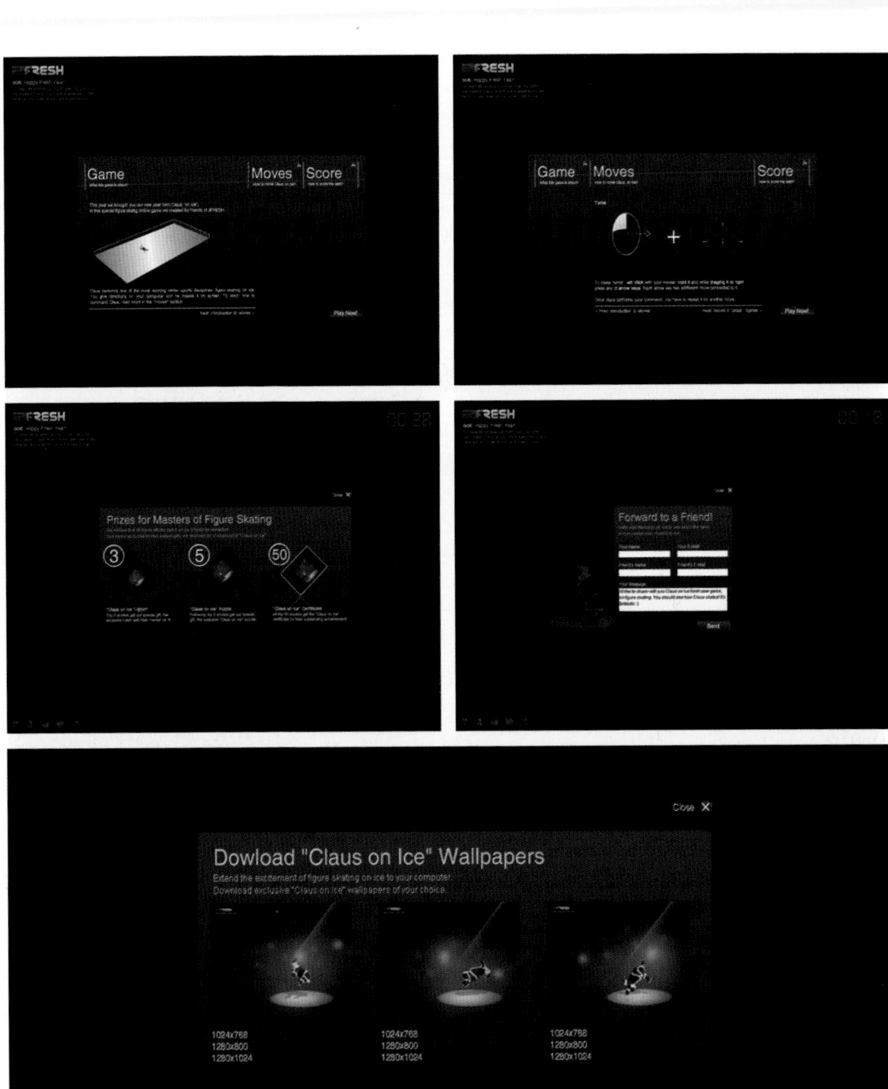
FRESH
Game
Moves
Score
Play Now!
Prizes for Masters of Figure Skating
3
5
50
Forward to a Friend!
Send
Close
Dowload "Claus on Ice" Wallpapers
Extend the excitement of figure skating on ice to your computer.
Download exclusive "Claus on Ice" wallpapers of your choice.
1024x768
1280x800
1280x1024
1024x768
1280x800
1280x1024
1024x768
1280x800
1280x1024

Concept

The Flash-based game coincided with the release of the Samsung U3 MP3 Player. The players are required to store as many tunes as possible (represented via the musical notes) into their Samsung U3. /// Das auf Flash basierende Spiel fiel zeitlich mit der Markteinführung des U3 MP3 Players von Samsung zusammen. Die Spieler müssen so viele Songs wie möglich (dargestellt durch Noten) in ihrem Samsung U3 speichern. /// Le jeu basé surFlash a coïncidé avec la sortie du lecteur Samsung U3 MP3. Les joueurs doivent stocker autant de titres que possible (symbolisés par des notes de musique) dans leur Samsung U3.

Info

DESIGN: AvantGarden <www.avantgarden.com.sg>, Vintedge. /// PROGRAMMING: Chen Yao Ming (AvantGarden). /// TOOLS: Adobe Photoshop, Flash, Dreamweaver. /// COST: 60 hours. /// OTHERS: Joint production with Vintedge.

DOCTOR IN A DASH

UK

www.bbc.co.uk/blast/games/doctorwho

2007

Concept

BBC ran a competition asking 13 to 19 year olds to come up with a fun and original game idea. They included making use of the monsters in the current series and making sure that the Doctor used his wits, rather than violence, to problem solve. /// Die BBC veranstaltete einen Wettbewerb, bei dem 13- bis 19-jährige sich eine lustige und originelle Spielidee zur TV-Serie ausdenken sollten. Die Monster der aktuellen Staffel sollten darin vorkommen, und der Doktor sollte seinen Verstand und nicht Gewalt einsetzen, um das Problem zu lösen. /// La BBC a organisé une compétition en demandant à des jeunes âgés de 13 à 19 ans de proposer une idée de jeu amusante et originale. Ils ont retenu l'idée d'intégrer des monstres dans la série et ont pris soin que le Doctor utilise son humour, et non la violence, pour résoudre des problèmes.

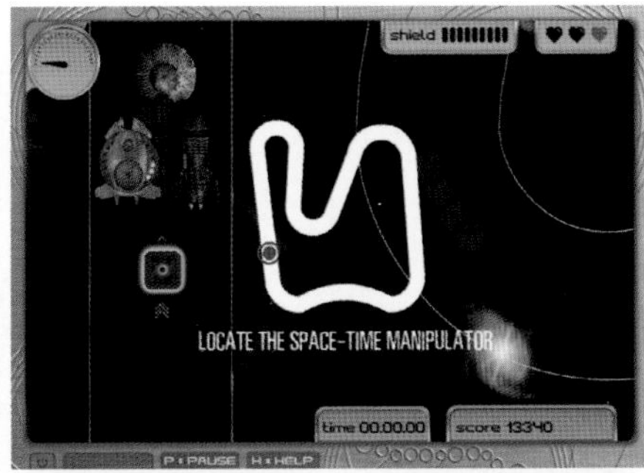

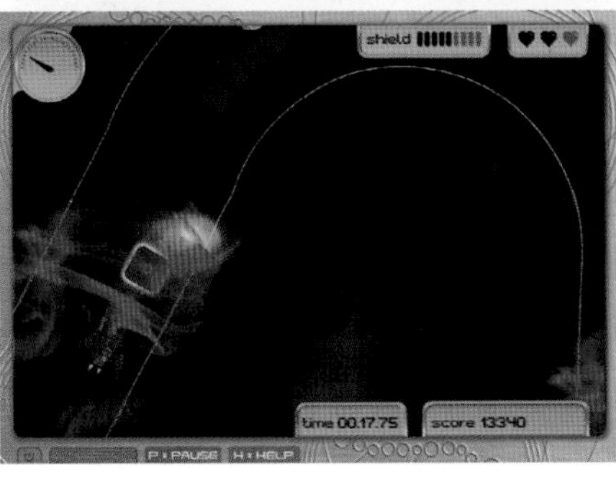

Info

Design: Sequence <www.sequence.co.uk>, Mark Johnson, Steven Goldstone, Ben Minton. /// **Programming:** Mick McNicholas, Steven Goldstone. /// **Tools:** Adobe Photoshop, Flash, Illustrator, Fireworks, Soundbooth, XML, HTML. /// **Cost:** £15,000.

DEATH IN SAKKARA

UK

http://deathinsakkara.com

2005

Concept

Death in Sakkara is an Egyptian adventure game set in a cartoon-like environment, allowing the user to follow the story and engage in various adventure sequences. Unlike many other games, this ones features a lot of dialogue with speech bubbles. /// *Death in Sakkara* ist ein ägyptisches Abenteuerspiel mit cartoonhafter Szenerie. Der Benutzer folgt der Geschichte und wird in verschiedene Abenteuer verwickelt. Im Gegensatz zu vielen anderen Spielen kommt hier viel Dialog in Sprechblasen vor. /// *Death in Sakkara* est un jeu d'aventure en Égypte dont l'environnement est semblable à un dessin animé ; l'utilisateur peut suivre l'histoire et prendre part à diverses aventures. Contrairement à beaucoup d'autres jeux, celui-ci contient de nombreux dialogues avec des bulles.

Info

DESIGN: Preloaded <www.preloaded.com>. /// **PROGRAMMING:** Preloaded. /// **TOOLS:** Adobe Photoshop, Flash. /// **AWARDS:** Winner: New Media Age, FlashForward, D&AD In-Book, Creative Review Annual In-Book. Finalist: London International Awards, BIMA, SXSW, Webbies. /// **OTHERS:** Joe Berger (Illustration); Jo Fletcher (Historical Consultant); P. Poucher (Sound Design); Ben Ledden, David Kidger, Richard Cable, Erik Upton, Iain Tatch (BBC).

INSIDE THE DOCTOR'S OFFICE
SHE HAS BEEN IN EGYPT FOR THE PAST THREE MONTHS ON AN ARCHAEOLOGICAL EXPEDITION.
I RECEIVED A TELEGRAM YESTERDAY.
FROM THE WAY IT IS WRITTEN I KNOW THAT SHE IS TRYING TO TELL ME THAT ALL IS NOT WELL.
INTERESTING. TELL ME MORE.
BBC
Terms of Use | Privacy & Cookies Policy | Close

16th March, 10am - York
Woke up feeling rotten. Must remember that drink & deadlines don't mix. A good day's work not on the cards, so crawled back into bed to wait to feel better, when the postman arrived, bringing an interesting letter from one Dr Armstrong.
Seems something I had written had fallen under the good doctor's eye. He invited me up to Hull to discuss this - "and other matters".
With nothing better to
my aching head, I decid
trip.
TURN THE PAGE HERE
NOTES
MAP
BBC
Terms of Use | Privacy & Cookies Policy | Close

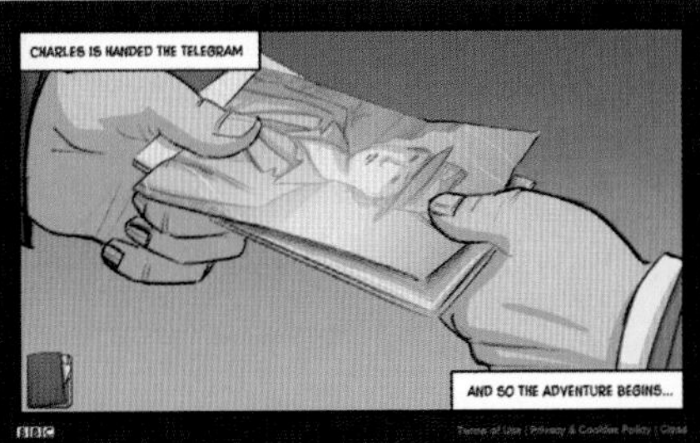
CHARLES IS HANDED THE TELEGRAM
AND SO THE ADVENTURE BEGINS...
BBC
Terms of Use | Privacy & Cookies Policy | Close

ELIZABETH'S ROOM
BBC
Terms of Use | Privacy & Cookies Policy | Close

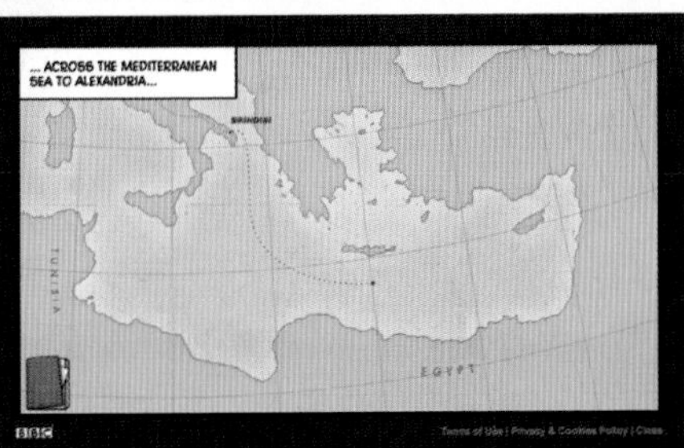
... ACROSS THE MEDITERRANEAN SEA TO ALEXANDRIA...
TUNISIA
EGYPT
BBC
Terms of Use | Privacy & Cookies Policy | Close

CAIRO, EGYPT
CHARLES ENTERS SHEPHEARD'S HOTEL...
BBC
Terms of Use | Privacy & Cookies Policy | Close

TIME FOR SOME QUICK THINKING!
GOOD AFTERNOON, I'M LOOKING FOR MISS ELIZABETH ARMSTRONG. I BELIEVE SHE IS STAYING HERE?
I'M SORRY, SIR, BUT MISS ARMSTRONG HAS NOT RETURNED TO THE HOTEL FOR A NUMBER OF DAYS NOW.
BBC
Terms of Use | Privacy & Cookies Policy | Close

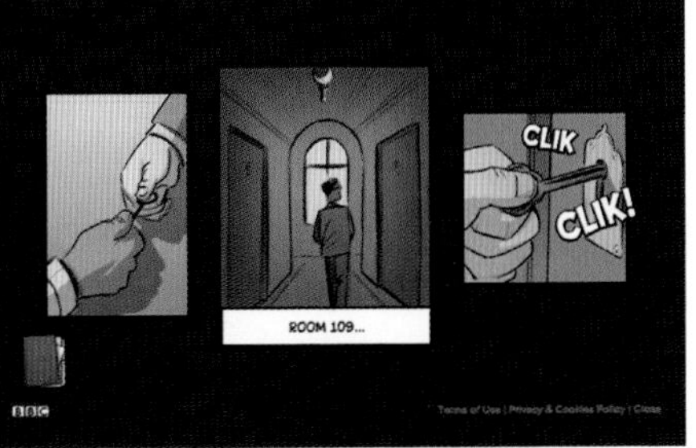
ROOM 109...
CLIK
CLIK!
BBC
Terms of Use | Privacy & Cookies Policy | Close

DELA VOLLEYBALL

NETHERLANDS

www.roadtobeijing.nl/game

2007

Concept

Play a game of volleyball with the Dutch National Ladies Volleyball Team and try to make as many combinations as possible. Prizes could be won daily by the highest score. /// Benutzer konnten mit der holländischen Damennationalmannschaft Volleyball spielen und mussten versuchen, so viele Kombinationen wie möglich zu verwenden. Der Spieler mit der höchsten Punktzahl gewann täglich einen Preis. /// Jouez un match de volley-ball avec l'équipe féminine nationale des Pays-Bas et essayez de faire le plus de combinaisons possibles. Des récompenses sont décernées chaque jour au meilleur résultat.

Info

DESIGN: THEPHARMACY <www.thepharmacymedia.com>, B. Driessen, W. van der Krieken, E. Szigetti. /// PROGRAMMING: J. Kessels. /// TOOLS: Adobe Photoshop, Flash, After Effects, PHP, MySQL. /// COST: 100 hours. /// CLIENT: DELA.

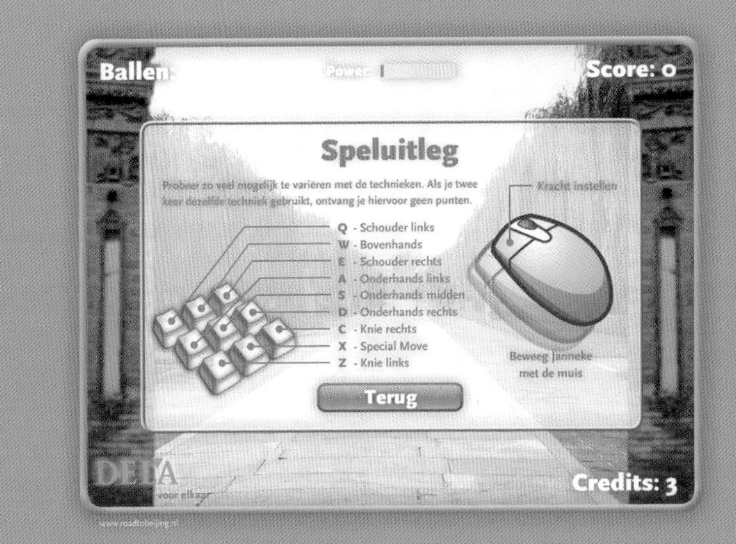
Ballen:
Power:
Score: 0
Speluitleg
Probeer zo veel mogelijk te variëren met de technieken. Als je twee keer dezelfde techniek gebruikt, ontvang je hiervoor geen punten.
Q - Schouder links
W - Bovenhands
E - Schouder rechts
A - Onderhands links
S - Onderhands midden
D - Onderhands rechts
C - Knie rechts
X - Special Move
Z - Knie links
Kracht instellen
Beweeg Janneke met de muis
Terug
DELA
voor elkaar
Credits: 3
www.roadtobeijing.nl

Ballen:
Power:
Score: 290
DELA
voor elkaar
Credits: 3
www.roadtobeijing.nl

DORITOS COLLISIONS MIXER

USA

2007

Concept

A “musical collision” with Missy Elliott’s beats and a selection of added effects and tracks. You can record your own lyrics to your phone, post it to a gallery, or send it on to your friends. /// Ein „musikalischer Zusammenstoβ“ mit Beats von Missy Elliott und einer Auswahl an Zusatztracks und –effekten. Benutzer können eigene Texte dazu aufs Handy spielen, die Tracks in eine Gallery stellen oder an Freunde versenden. /// Une « collision musicale » entre les rythmes de Missy Elliott et une sélection d’effets et de titres. Vous pouvez enregistrer vos propres paroles sur votre téléphone, les placer dans une galerie ou les envoyer à vos amis.

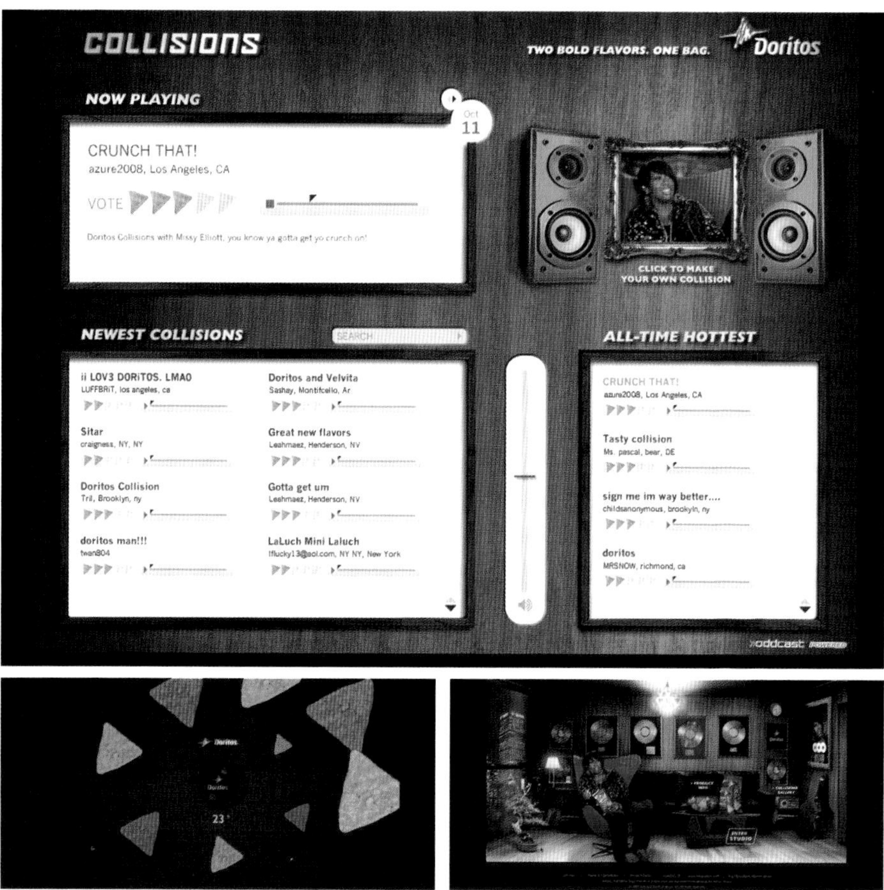

Info

DESIGN: Domani Studios <www.domanistudios.com>. /// PROGRAMMING: Domani Studios. /// TOOLS: Adobe Photoshop, Flash, After Effects, Final Cut. /// COST: 1 month. /// CLIENT: Goodby, Silverstein & Partners.

Doritos
RECORD
YOUR VOCALS
All right. Time to drop in your lyrics.
You can either use your computer's microphone
OR call our toll free number and record over the
phone.
RECORD BY MIC
RECORD BY PHONE
PREVIEW TRACK
RECORD
LYRICS
< BACK TO
WAITING ROOM
< BACK TO MIXER

NEW
DORITOS COLLISIONS™ CHIPS.
Two bold flavors. One bag.
Current available flavors:
and Blue cheese
Zesty Taco and Chipotle Ranch
< BACK
ENTER
STUDIO

DYLAN MESSAGING

USA/UK

www.dylanmessaging.com

2007

Concept

For the release of the *Dylan: His Greatest Songs* compilation, the site uses the footage from the "Subterranean Homesick Blues" video. Instead of displaying the song's lyrics, fans can upload their own message to 10 cue cards and send it to their friends. /// Anlässlich des Erscheinens von *Dylan: His Greatest Songs* verwendet die Website das Video zu „Subterranean Homesick Blues". Doch anstelle des Songtextes können Fans ihre eigenen Nachrichten auf zehn Schilder hochladen und an Freunde verschicken. /// Pour la sortie de la compilation *Dylan: His Greatest Songs*, le site se sert d'extraits de la vidéo « Subterranean Homesick Blues ». Au lieu d'afficher les paroles des chansons, les fans peuvent télécharger leur propre message dans 10 aide-mémoire et les envoyer à des amis.

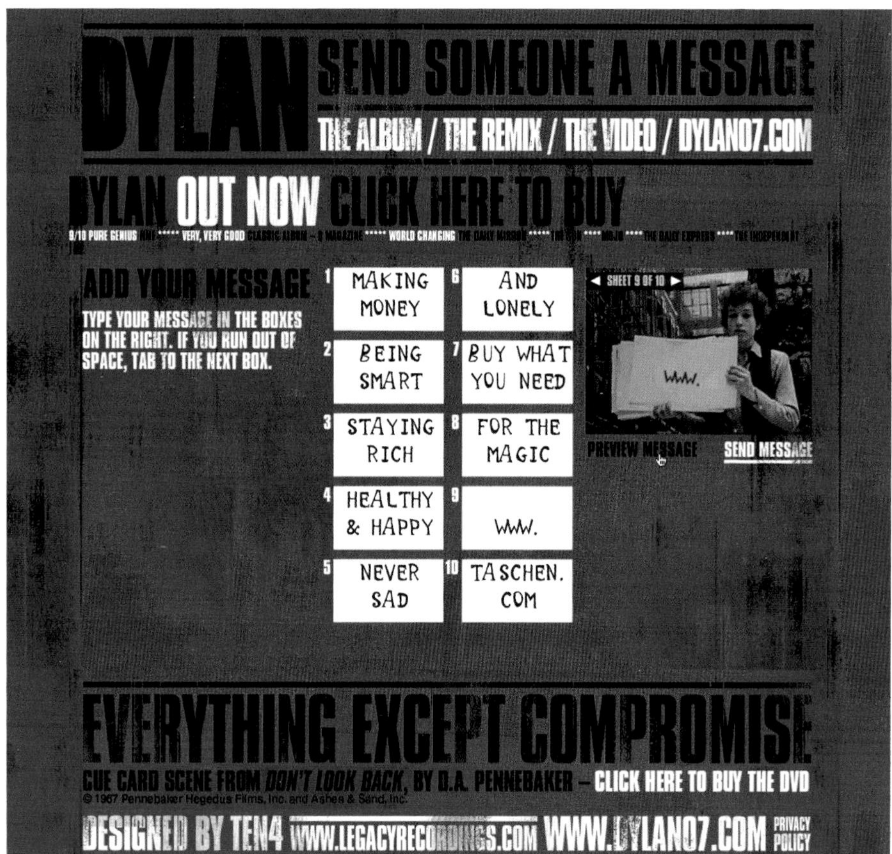

Info

DESIGN: Ten4 Design <www.ten4design.co.uk>, Owen Matthews, Adam Harte, David Adcock. /// PROGRAMMING: Oliver Lillie, David Adcock. /// TOOLS: Adobe Photoshop, Flash, HTML, PHP, MySQL. /// COST: 150 hours. /// OTHERS: Charlie Stanford (Director, Digital Marketing, Sony BMG Commercial Music Group).

DYLAN
HIS GREATEST SONGS
OUT NOW
9/10 "PURE GENIUS"
***** "VERY, VERY GOOD"
***** "WORLD CHANGING"
BUY THE ALBUM NOW
ENTER DYLANMESSAGING.COM

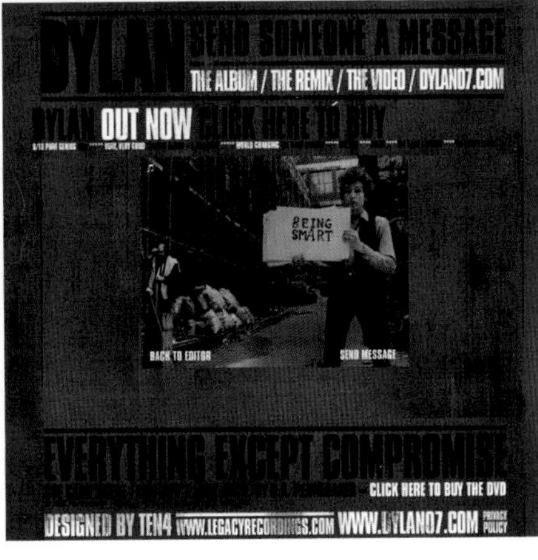

Results

With nearly 200,000 messages created, and viewings of well over 2.5 million since it's launch in September 2007, it's the most successful online campaign Sony BMG has done in terms of user uptake. 12% of users signed up to the mailing list. /// Es wurden fast 200.000 Botschaften erzeugt, und die Site konnte seit ihrem Start im September 2007 2,5 Millionen Besucher verzeichnen. Im Hinblick auf Benutzerregistrierung ist es Sony BMGs bisher erfolgreichste Kampagne: 12% der Benutzer trugen sich in die Mailinglist ein. /// Avec près de 200 000 messages générés et plus de 2,5 millions de diffusions depuis son lancement en septembre 2007, il s'agit de la campagne en ligne la plus réussie de Sony BMG en termes de captage d'utilisateurs (12 % sont inscrits à la liste d'abonnement).

EDEKA LEBENSMITTELDIPLOM

GERMANY

www.lebensmitteldiplom.de

2007

Concept

This microsite is the first interactive webspecial for the German supermarket chain Edeka. It gives the user the chance to win a special weekend break by playing different games and answering various questions about healthy food. /// Diese Microsite ist das erste interaktive Webspecial für die deutsche Supermarktkette Edeka. Der Benutzer kann durch das Spielen verschiedener Spiele und die Beantwortung von Fragen über gesunde Ernährung eine Wochenendreise gewinnen. /// Ce mini-site est la première création Web pour la chaîne allemande de supermarchés Edeka. Les utilisateurs peuvent remporter un week-end d'escapade en jouant à des jeux et en répondant à des questions sur l'alimentation saine.

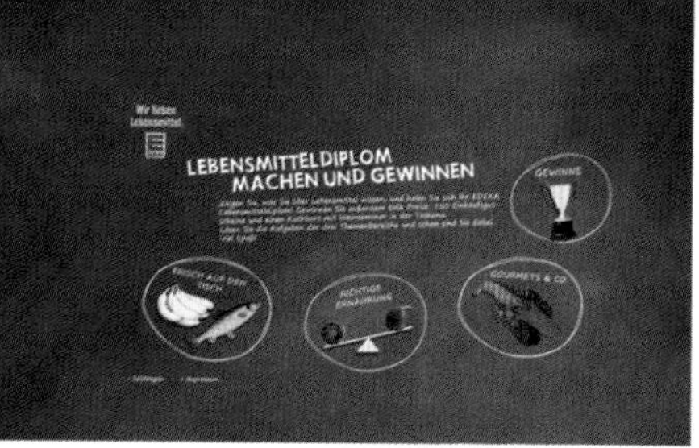

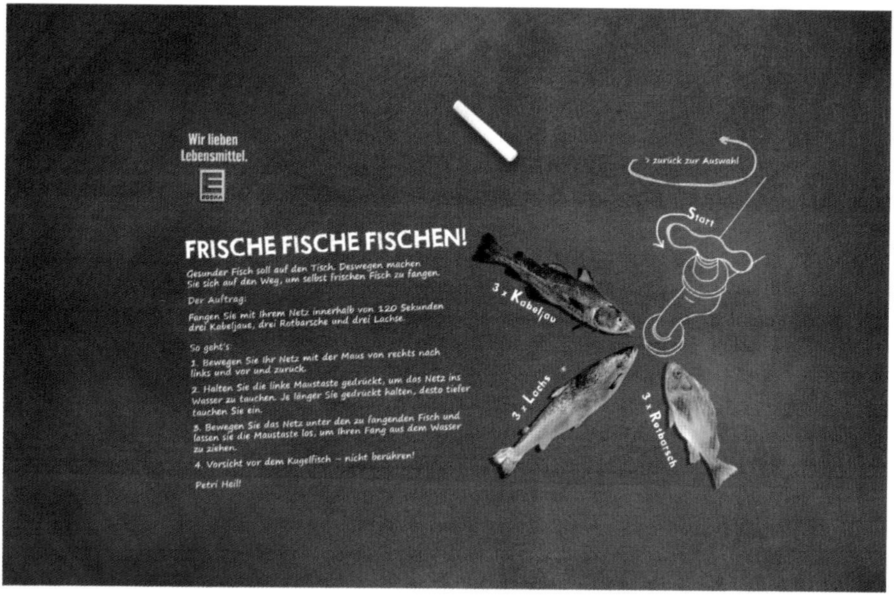

Info

Design: blackbeltmonkey <www.blackbeltmonkey.com>, Creative Director: Olver Bentz, Mike John Otto; Art Director: Kathrin Laser. /// **Programming:** Yasmine Bechmann, Marc Tricou. /// **Tools:** Adobe Photoshop, Flash, Illustrator, PHP, XML. /// **Cost:** 2 month. /// **Others:** Marcellus Gau (Project Managment).

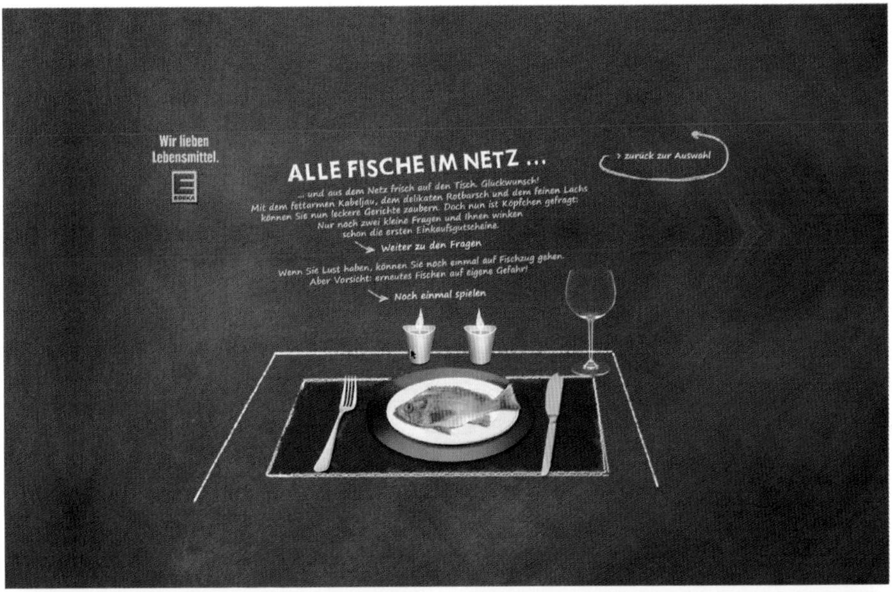

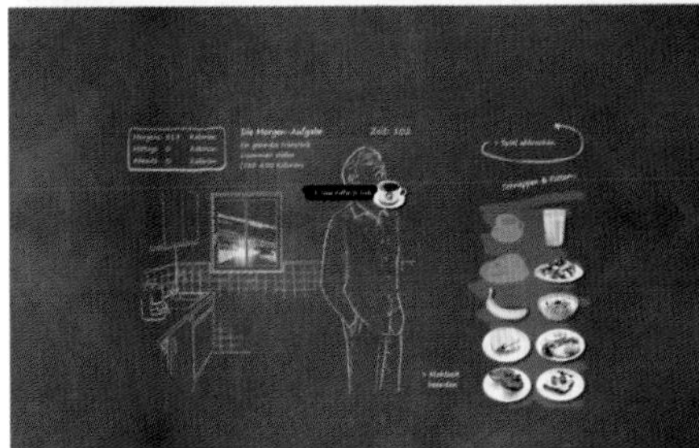

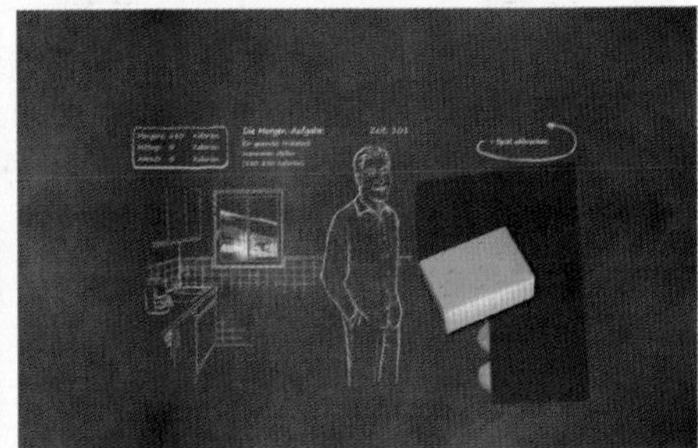

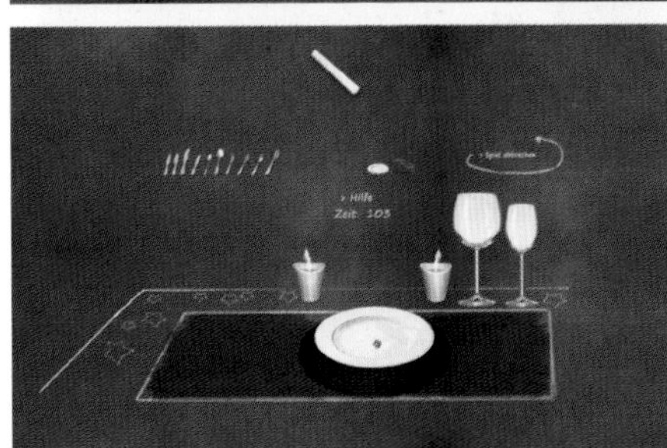

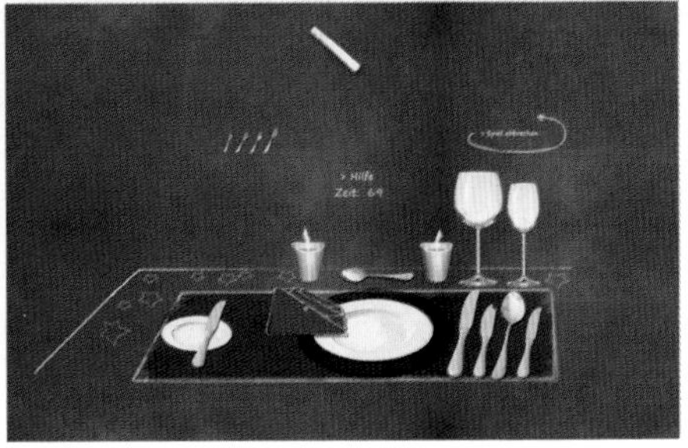

Results

The microsite generated a huge traffic push for the Edeka website and campaign, attracting many new users. /// Die Microsite hat der Website und Werbekampagne von Edeka enormen Auftrieb gegeben. /// Grâce au mini-site, le trafic pour le site Web et la campagne d'Edeka a énormément augmenté en attirant de nombreux nouveaux utilisateurs.

E-POUSSE (E-GARDEN)

FRANCE

2005

Concept

E-pousse (E-garden) is a virtual gardening experience. Whether the player connects or not, the game is playing in real time and things happen in the garden. /// E-pousse (E-garden) ist ein virtuelles Gärtnerspiel. Ob mit oder ohne Beteiligung des Benutzers: Das Spiel läuft in Echtzeit ab, und im Garten tut sich was. /// E-pousse (E-garden) offre une expérience de jardinage virtuel. Que le joueur soit connecté ou non, le jeu se joue en temps réel et il se passe des choses dans le jardin.

Info

DESIGN: LES CHINOIS <www.leschinois.com>, Ludovic Roudy. /// PROGRAMMING: Julien Bennamias. /// TOOLS: Adobe Photoshop, Flash, Illustrator. /// COST: 7 months.

Results

Over 90,000 regular players with an average of 27 player visits per month on the websit. /// Über 90.000 regelmäßige Spieler mit durchschnittlich 27 Besuchen pro Spieler pro Monat. /// Plus de 90 000 joueurs réguliers, avec une moyenne de 27 visites par mois.

EXCITING KIA

KOREA

www.kiamotors.com/Experience/exciting_kia/exciting.html 2007

Concept

The *Exciting KIA* web content intends to display how Kia Motors develops its brand concept and convey its vision as a truly global carmaker in the future. The games enables the user to build a car and choose the surrounding environment. /// Der Webcontent von *Exciting KIA* möchte zeigen, wie Kia Motors sein Markenkonzept entwickelt, und die Vision von einem wahrhaft globalen Autohersteller der Zukunft vermitteln. Anhand der Spiele können Benutzer ein Auto bauen und eine Szenerie auswählen. /// Le site Web *Exciting KIA* montre comment Kia Motors met au point son concept de marque et transmet sa vision en tant que futur constructeur automobile mondial. Le jeu permet à l'utilisateur de fabriquer un véhicule et de choisir l'environnement.

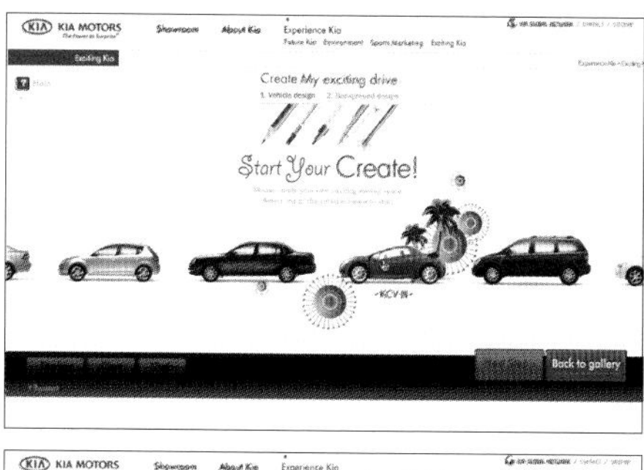

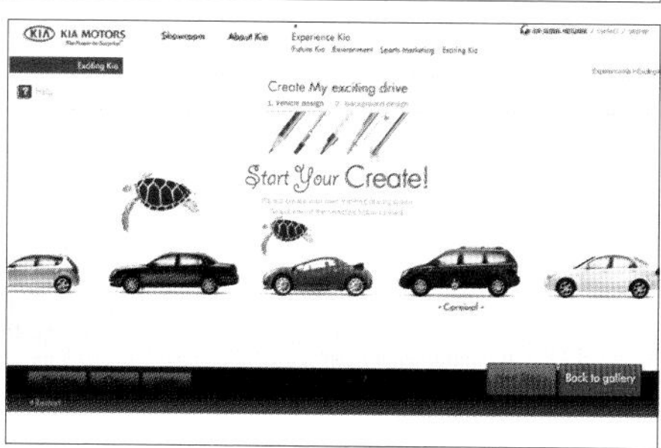

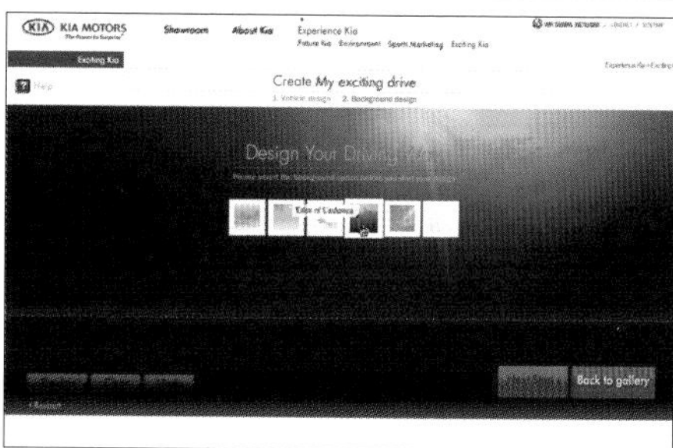

Info

DESIGN: PostVisual <www.postvisual.com>, Euna Seol, Donghoon Choi, Jieun Kim, Sinae Kim. /// **PROGRAMMING:** Seolbaek Son, Byungrak Song.

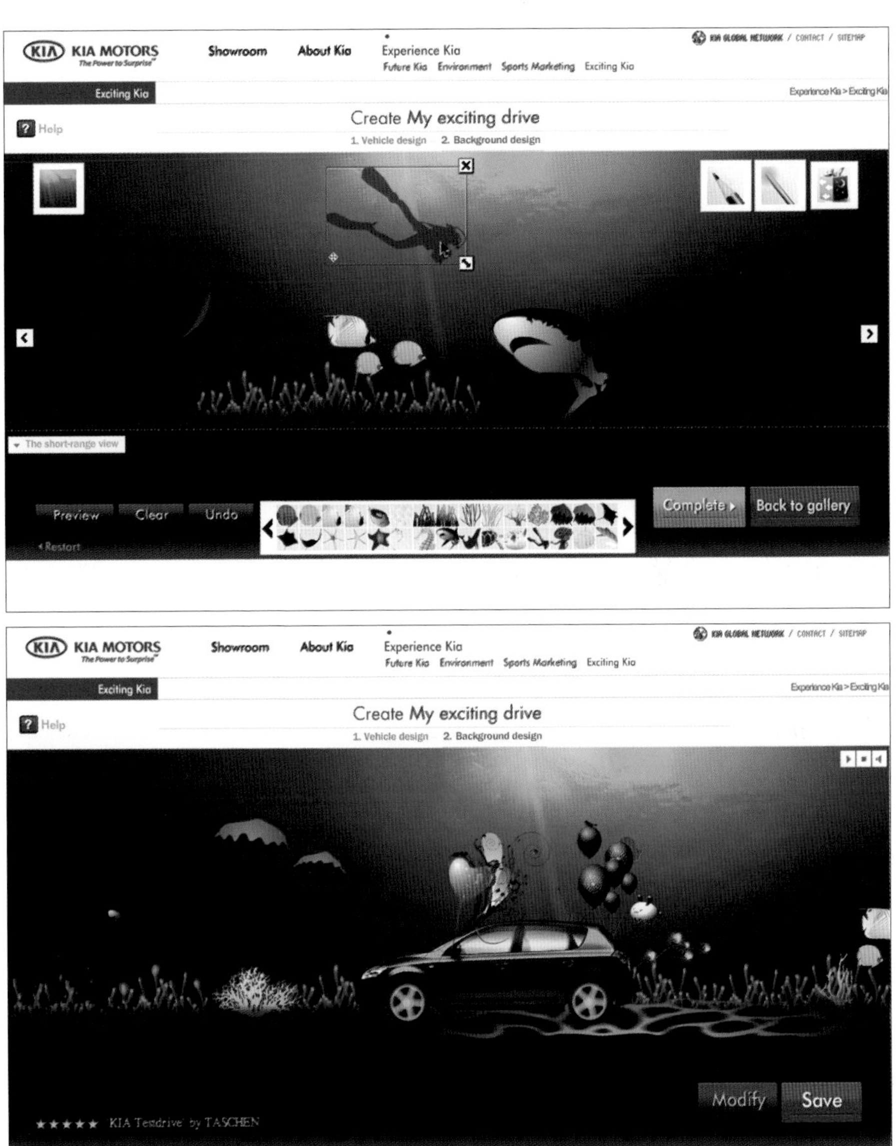
KIA MOTORS
The Power to Surprise
Showroom
About Kia
Experience Kia
Future Kia Environment Sports Marketing Exciting Kia
KIA GLOBAL NETWORK / CONTACT / SITEMAP
Exciting Kia
Experience Kia > Exciting Kia
Help
Create My exciting drive
1. Vehicle design 2. Background design
The short-range view
Preview Clear Undo
Restart
Complete
Back to gallery
KIA MOTORS
The Power to Surprise
Showroom
About Kia
Experience Kia
Future Kia Environment Sports Marketing Exciting Kia
KIA GLOBAL NETWORK / CONTACT / SITEMAP
Exciting Kia
Experience Kia > Exciting Kia
Help
Create My exciting drive
1. Vehicle design 2. Background design
Modify
Save
★★★★★ KIA Testdrive by TASCHEN

FALL OUT BOY

SOUTH AFRICA

www.falloutboy.co.za

2007

Concept

To promote the release of the new Fall Out Boy album, Prezence developed an interactive promotional site where users could listen to the new album, watch videos and play the highly addictive literal "Arms Race" game, named after the first single! /// Um das neue Album von Fall Out Boy zu bewerben, entwickelte Prezence eine interaktive Website, auf der Benutzer sich das Album anhören, Videos gucken und das süchtig machende Spiel „Arms Race“ spielen konnten, das nach der ersten Singleauskoppelung benannt wurde. /// Pour la promotion du lancement du nouvel album de Fall Out Boy, Prezence a créé un site interactif dans lequel les utilisateurs peuvent écouter des chansons, regarder des vidéos et jouer au passionnant jeu « Arms Race » intitulé comme le premier single !

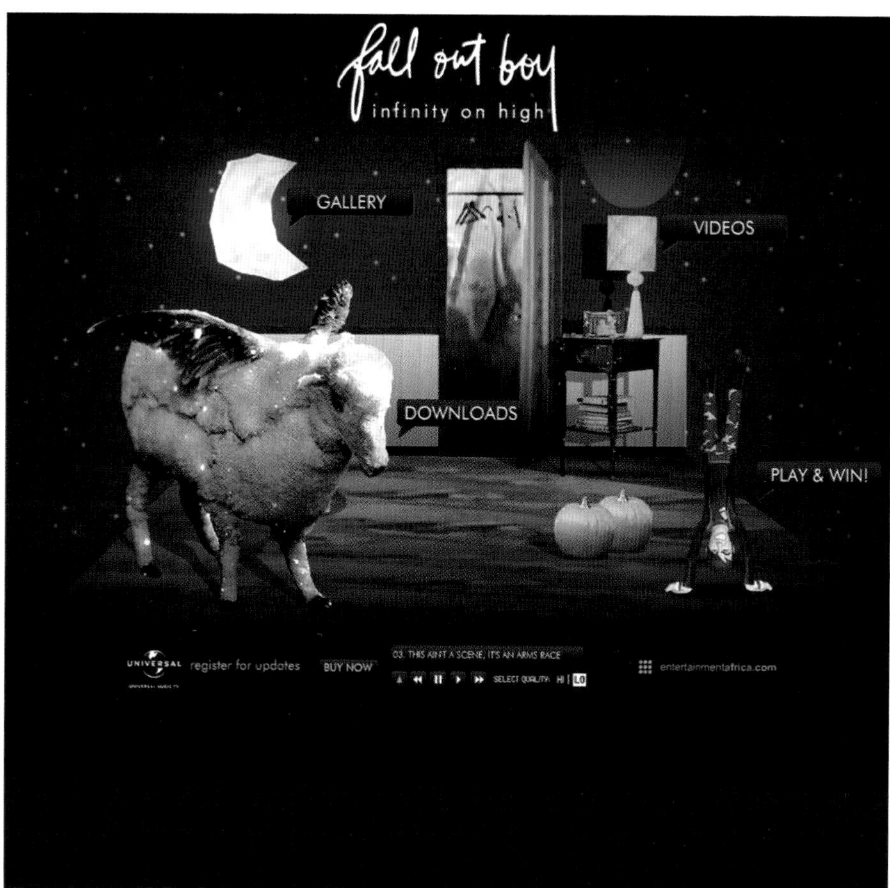

Info

Design: Prezence <www.prezence.co.za>, Andrew Potter. /// **Programming:** Andrew Potter (Action Scripting). /// **Tools:** Adobe Photoshop, Flash, XML, PHP. /// **Cost:** 50 hours.

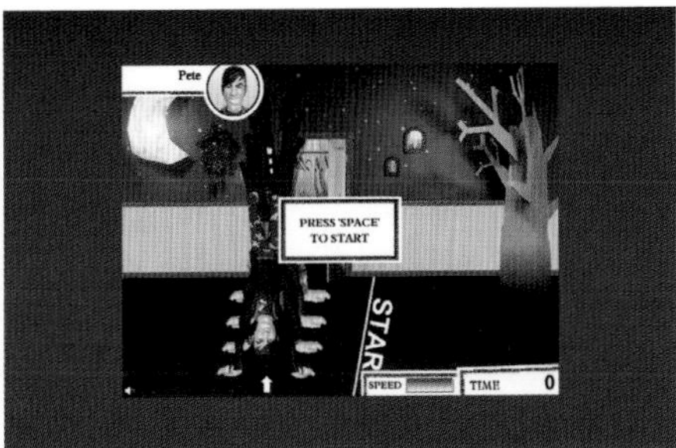

Pete
PRESS 'SPACE' TO START
START
SPEED
TIME 0

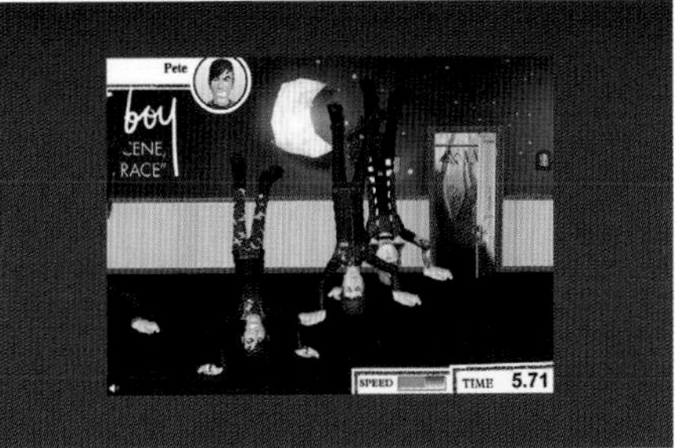

Pete
SPEED
TIME 5.71

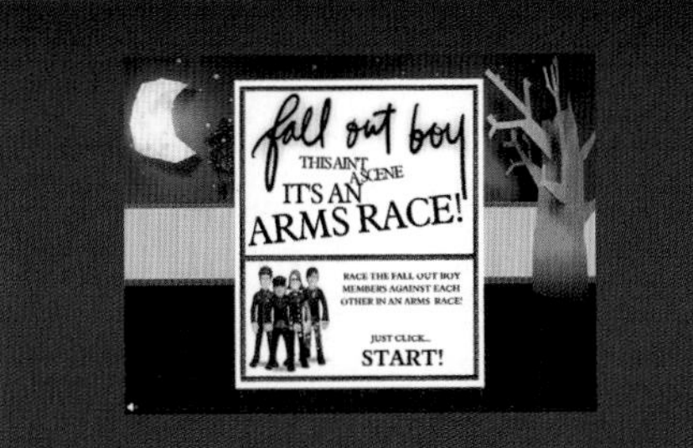

fall out boy
THIS AIN'T A SCENE
IT'S AN ARMS RACE!
RACE THE FALL OUT BOY MEMBERS AGAINST EACH OTHER IN AN ARMS RACE!
JUST CLICK...
START!

Patrick
SPEED
TIME 6.71

You are the
WINNER!
Awesome dude!
LEADER BOARD
OPTIONS
TRY AGAIN

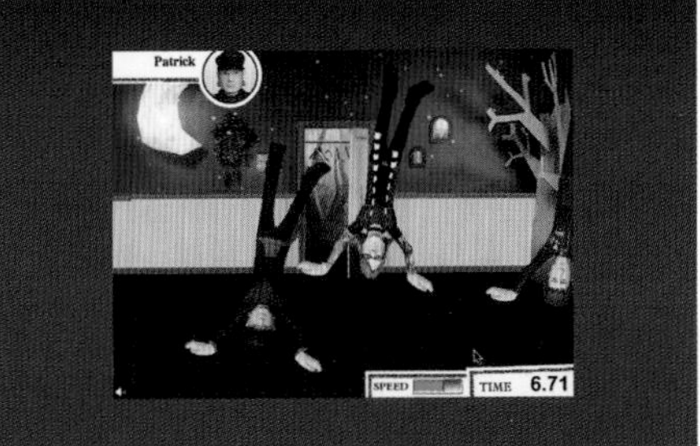

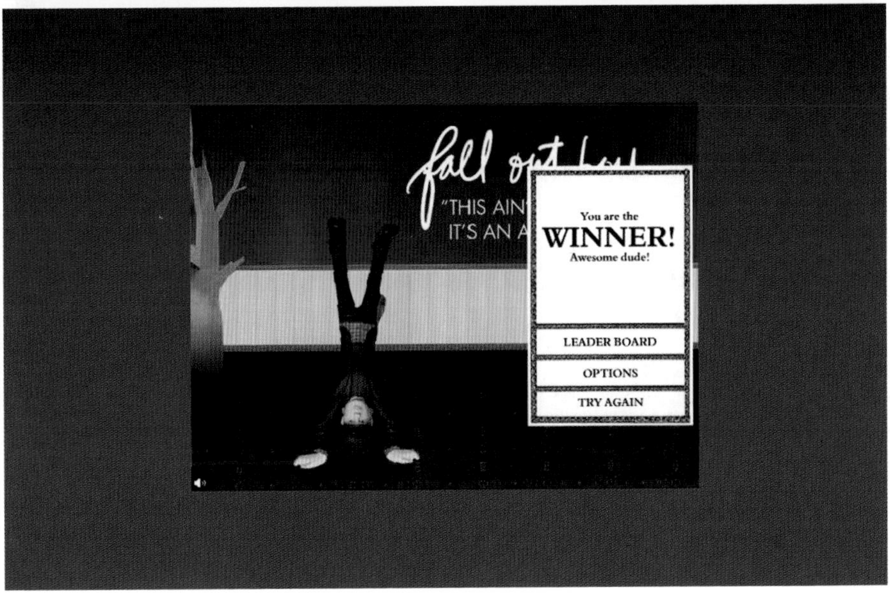

GET THE GLASS

USA

www.gettheglass.com

2007

Concept

This award winning site features a fully 3D interactive game to promote milk in the United States. /// Diese mit einem Preis ausgezeichnete Website zeigt ein interaktives 3D-Spiel, das den Milchkonsum in den USA ankurbeln soll. /// Ce site primé inclut un jeu interactif 3D pour faire la promotion du lait aux États-Unis.

Info

DESIGN: North Kingdom <www.northkingdom.com>, Jorge Calleja (Goodby Silverstein & Partners), Robert Lindström (North Kingdom). /// **PROGRAMMING:** Mikael Forsgren, Klas Kroon (North Kingdom). /// **TOOLS:** Adobe Photoshop, Flash, 3dsMax, Combustion. /// **AWARDS:** Cannes Lion (Gold), FWA (Site of the Year + People's Choice of the Year). /// **OTHERS:** Daniel Wallström, Mathias Lindgren, Lucian Trofin, North Kingdom (3D); Tomas Westermark, Johan Forslund, Annelie Jönsson (Producers); Heather Wischmann (Producers Goodby Silverstein & Partners).

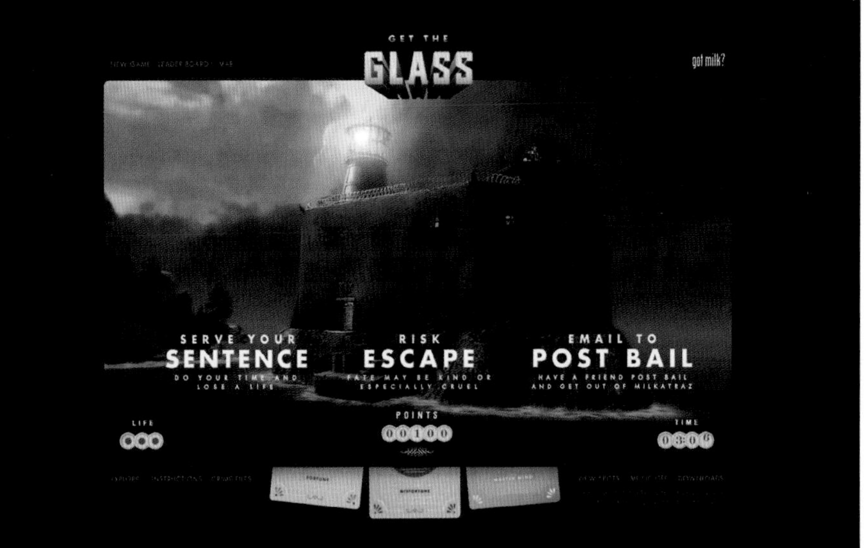

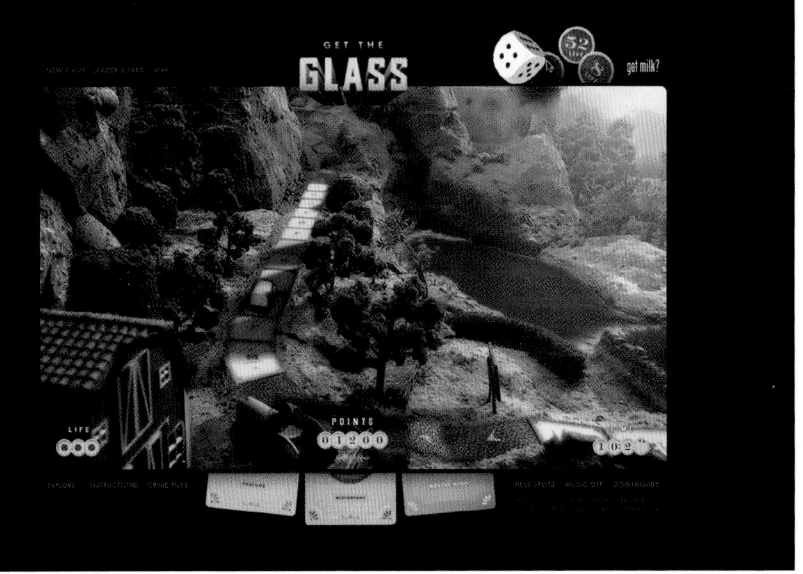

Results

10 minutes stay is average on the website. /// Die Website hat eine durchschittliche Verweildauer von 10 Minuten. /// Durée moyenne de visite de 10 minutes sur le site Web.

GET THE MESSAGE

UK

www.getthemessage.net

2007

Concept

To captivate a younger audience looking for adventurous career experiences, the website lets the user customise messages that will play as embedded content within the selected videos. /// Um ein jüngeres Publikum anzusprechen, das auf der Suche nach interessanten Berufserlebnissen ist, lässt diese Website den Benutzer eigene Botschaften verfassen, die in die ausgewählten Videos eingebaut werden. /// Pour attirer un public plus jeune en quête d'expériences audacieuses, le site Web permet à l'utilisateur de personnaliser des messages qui s'afficheront dans les vidéos sélectionnées.

Info

Design: glue London <www.gluelondon.com>, Leon Ostle, Simon Cam. /// **Programming:** Damian Mitchell, Fraser Hobbs. /// **Tools:** Adobe Photoshop, Flash, Illustrator, PHP, ffmpeg, XHTML. /// **Awards:** Cannes Lion (Bronze), Eurobest (Gold), IMA Grand Prix, Y Design Award (Best Application/Best Not-For-Profit), Campaign Digital Award. /// **Others:** Creative Team: James Leigh, Darren Giles; Mark Jenkinson (In House Director); Dominick O'Brien (Head of Technology).

ROYAL NAVY

LIFE WITHOUT LIMITS

SOUND OFF

DISCLAIMER
ACCESSIBLE VERSION

Back
Submit

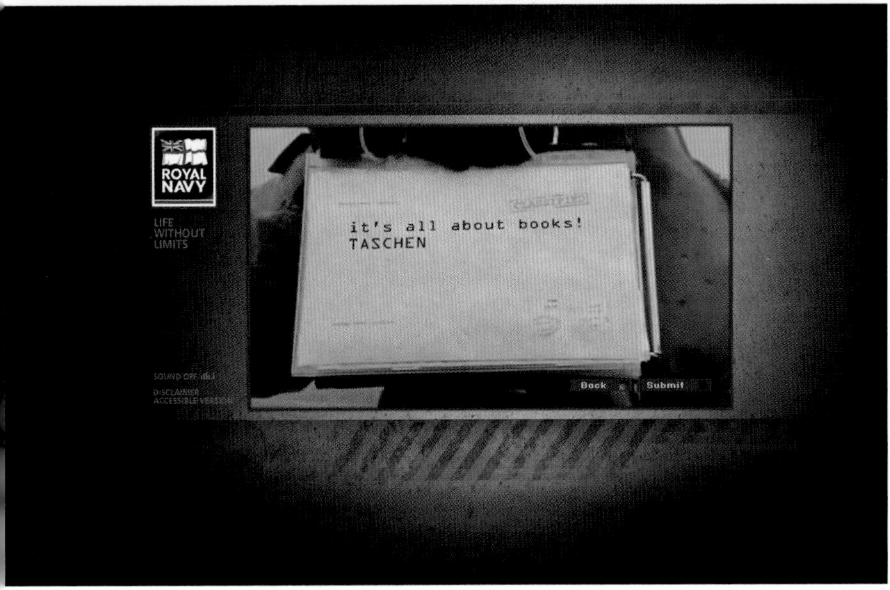

ROYAL NAVY

LIFE WITHOUT LIMITS

it's all about books!
TASCHEN

SOUND OFF

DISCLAIMER
ACCESSIBLE VERSION

Back
Submit

GUANTÁNAMO

UK

http://guantanamo.w3haus.com/home

2006

Concept

On this virtual journey to the Guantánamo Bay prison, the visitor can choose the clothes, hair style and floating tools. Users can also pick up the message about Guantánamo that they wish to leave in many language options. /// Auf dieser virtuellen Reise ins Gefangenenlager in Guantánamo Bay konnten Benutzer Kleider, Frisuren und Werkzeuge auswählen sowie eine Nachricht über Guantánamo in vielen verschiedenen Sprachen hinterlassen. /// Dans ce voyage virtuel à la prison de Guantánamo Bay, le visiteur peut choisir les vêtements, la coiffure et les outils flottants. Les utilisateurs peuvent aussi décider le message qu'ils souhaitent laisser sur Guantánamo dans plusieurs langues.

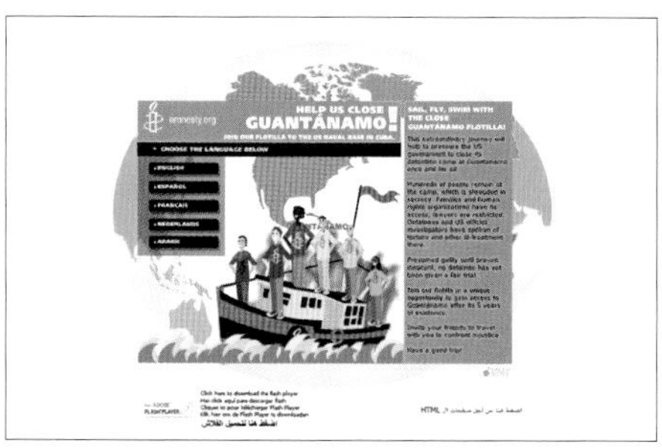

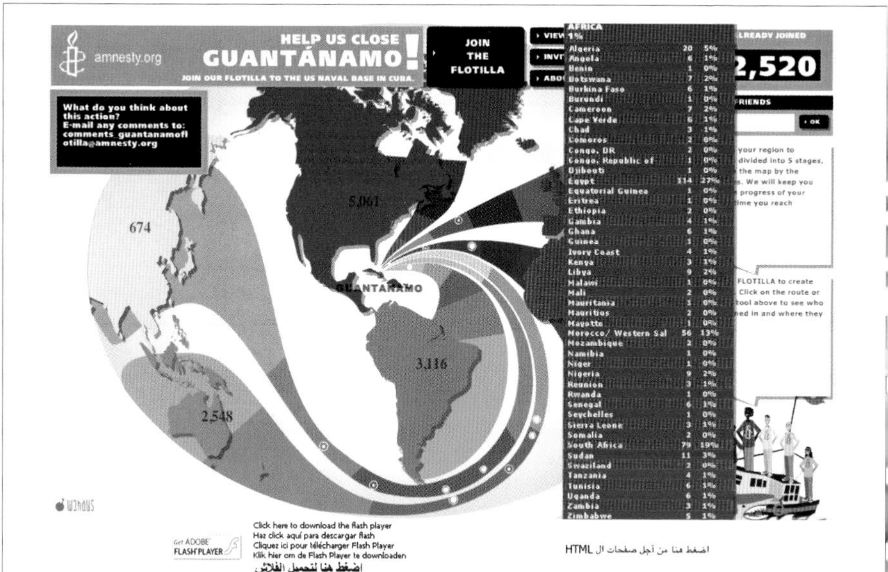

Info

Design: W3Haus <www.w3haus.com.br>, Chico Baldini. /// **Programming:** Rafael Souza, Eduardo Costa. /// **Tools:** Adobe Photoshop, Flash, PHP, HTML, XML. /// **Cost:** 800 hours. /// **Others:** Mauricio Nicolao (Account Executive).

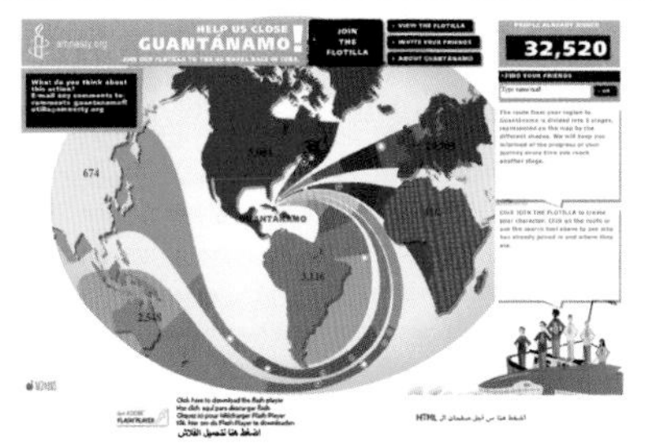

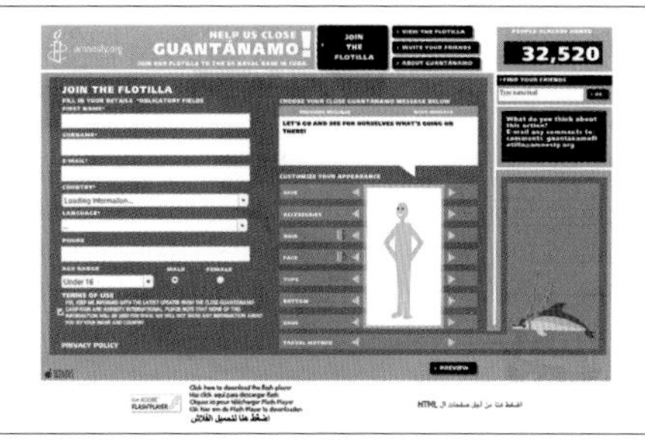

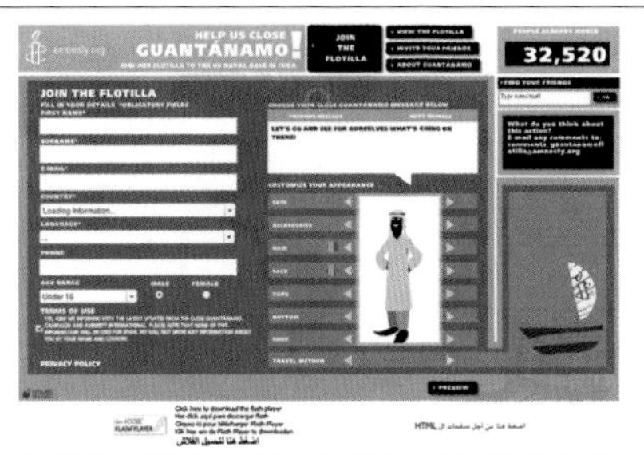

32,520 visitors from more than 90 different countries took the virtual boat to Guantànamo. The site was online until June 26th 2007 to commemorate the International Day in Support of Victims of Torture. /// 32.520 Besucher aus über 90 Ländern nahmen das virtuelle Boot nach Guantánamo. Die Website war bis zum 26. Juni 2007 online, dem Internationalen Tag zur Unterstützung von Folteropfern. /// 32 520 visiteurs de plus de 90 pays différents ont emprunté le bateau virtuel jusqu'à Guantánamo. Le site est resté en ligne jusqu'au 26 juin 2007 pour commémorer la journée internationale de soutien aux victimes de tortures.

HEALTHCARE MISSION

FRANCE

http://www.francetelecom.com/sirius/dossiers_anim/orange_esante/index_en.html

2008

Concept

A game with the objective of improving the quality of healthcare for an entire city. After choosing and learning the new technologies in the field, players can score points when using their skills properly. /// Ziel des Spiels ist es, die Gesundheitsversorgung einer ganze Stadt zu verbessern. Nachdem sie sich über die neuen Technologien in diesem Bereich informiert und diese erlernt haben, können die Spieler durch Einsatz ihrer Fähigkeiten Punkte sammeln. /// Jeu dont l'objectif est d'améliorer la qualité des services médicaux dans une ville. Après avoir choisi et appris les nouvelles technologies dans le domaine, les joueurs peuvent marquer des points en mettant correctement en pratique leurs connaissances.

Info

Design: LES CHINOIS <www.leschinois.com>, Pierre-Yves Roudy. /// **Programming:** Alexandre C. /// **Tools:** Adobe Photoshop, Flash, Illustrator. /// **Cost:** 3 months.

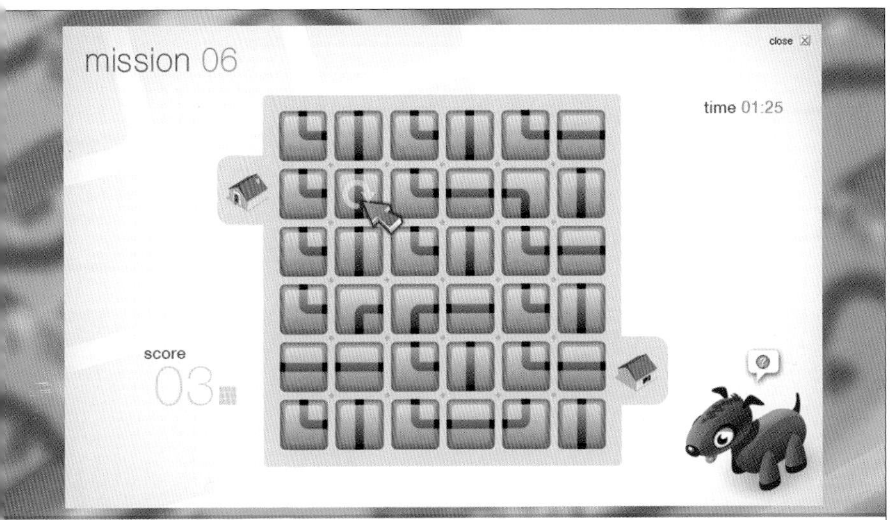
mission 06
close
time 01:25
score
03
How to play? | Tell a friend | want to know more about Orange Healthcare | legal info
design : Les Chinois

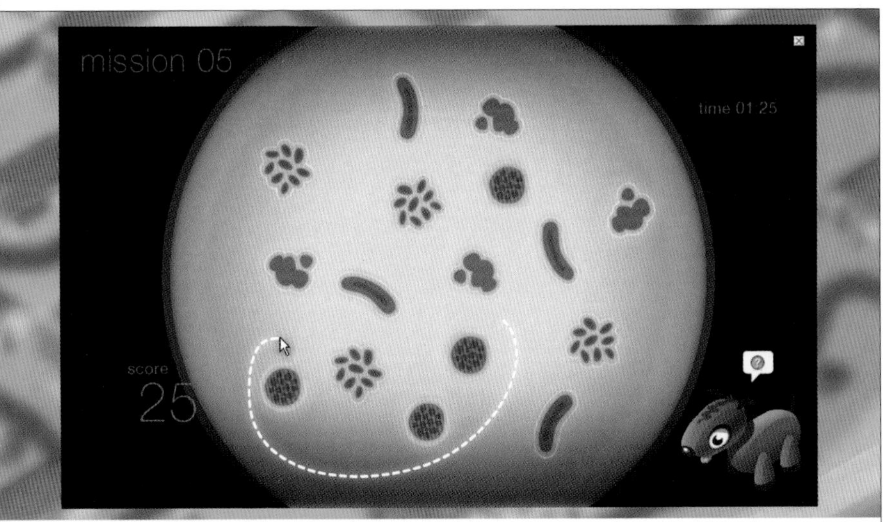
mission 05
time 01:25
score
25
How to play? | Tell a friend | want to know more about Orange Healthcare | legal info
design : Les Chinois

HET HUIS ANUBIS

NETHERLANDS

http://script03.nickelodeon.nl/anubis

2007

Concept

Kids can play and experience the mysteries of Anubis online on a daily basis. Plots and twists that are shown daily in the series can be experienced by entering the house and solving games, gradually getting closer to solving the Anubis mystery. /// Kinder können hier die Geheimnisse von Anubis spielerisch erkunden. Handlungen und Verwicklungen, die jeden Tag in der Serie gezeigt werden, vollziehen die Benutzer nach, wenn sie in ein Haus eintreten und Rätsel lösen. So offenbart sich auch Schritt für Schritt das Anubis-Rätsel. /// **Les enfants peuvent jouer et découvrir chaque jour en ligne les mystères d'Anubis. Des intrigues et des rebondissements qui ont lieu tous les jours dans la série sont à découvrir en pénétrant dans la maison et en jouant à des jeux pour résoudre peu à peu l'énigme d'Anubis.**

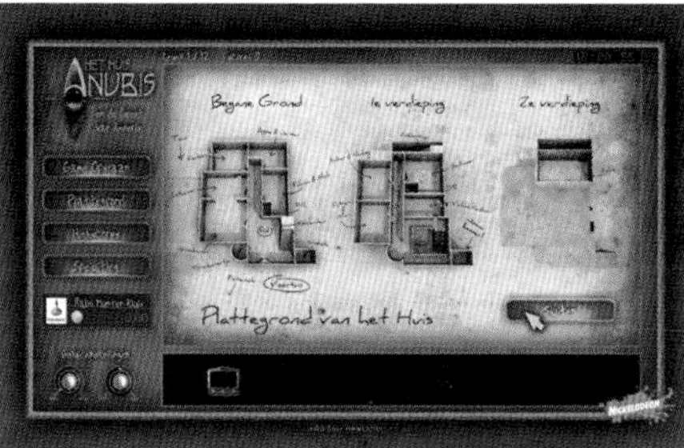

Info

DESIGN: THEPHARMACY <www.thepharmacymedia.com>, B. Driessen, W. van der Krieken, K. Elders. /// **PROGRAMMING:** J. Kessels, B. Driessen, B. van Boxtel, D. van Hout. /// **TOOLS:** Adobe Photoshop, Flash, Illustrator, 3ds Max, PHP, MySQL. /// **COST:** 3 months. /// **CLIENT:** Nickelodeon.

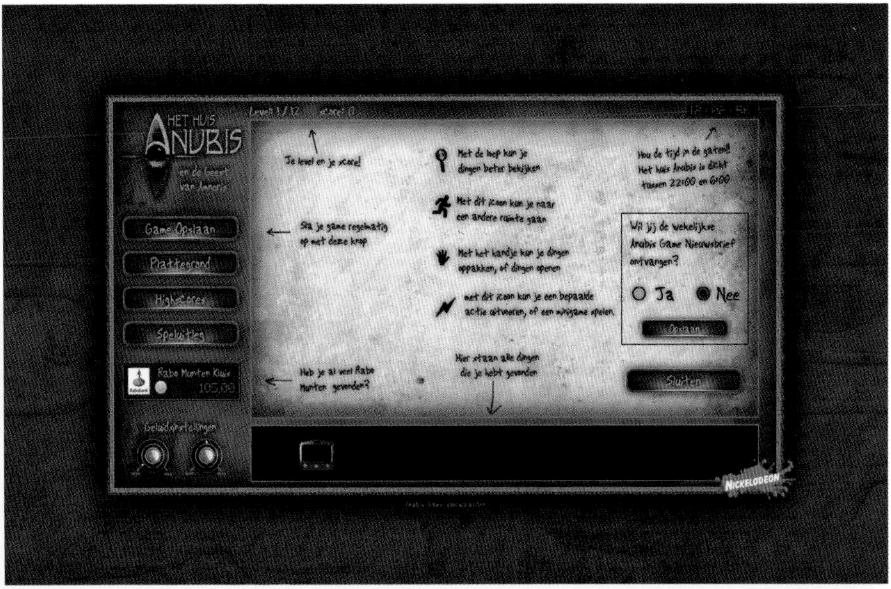

Results

15,000 unique players are experiencing the online game daily. /// 15.000 Unique User spielen das Online-Spiel täglich. /// 15 000 joueurs uniques se connectent chaque jour au jeu en ligne.

HOWL-O-SCREAM

USA

http://69.20.111.1

2007

Concept

A simple online music jukebox enables users to be the Death Jockey by mixing and recording their own scary tracks. The easy interface and zany sounds contrast with the scary aspect of the imagery. /// Durch eine einfache Online-Jukebox wird der Benutzer zum *Death Jockey* und kann seine eigenen schaurig-schönen Tracks mischen und aufnehmen. Das schlichte Interface und die lustigen Sounds kontrastieren mit dem Gruselstil der Bilder. /// Un simple juke-box en ligne permet aux utilisateurs d'être le *Death Jockey* en mixant et en enregistrant leur propres morceaux de terreur. L'interface simple et les sons loufoques contrastent avec l'aspect effrayant du graphisme.

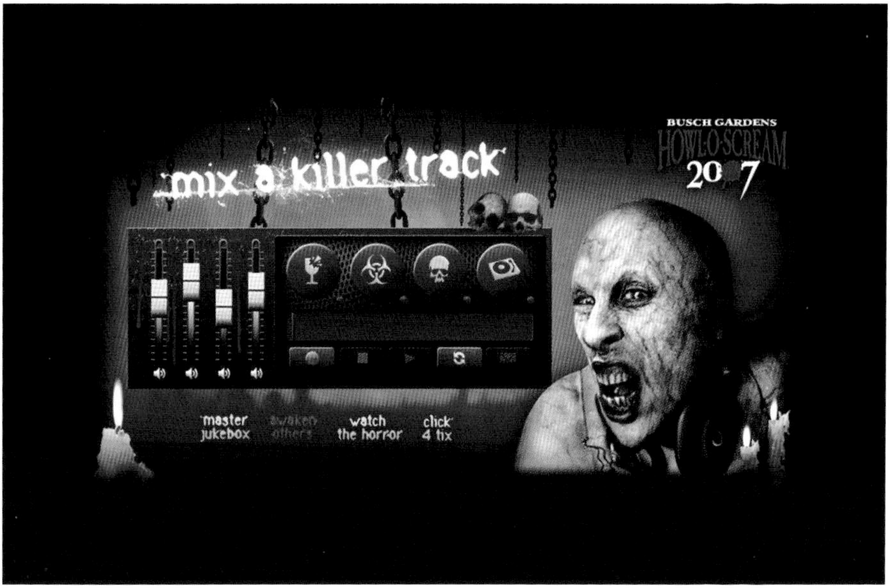

Info

Design: Domani Studios <www.domanistudios.com>. /// **Programming:** Domani Studios. /// **Tools:** Adobe Photoshop, Flash. /// **Cost:** 2 weeks. /// **Client:** DDB Chicago.

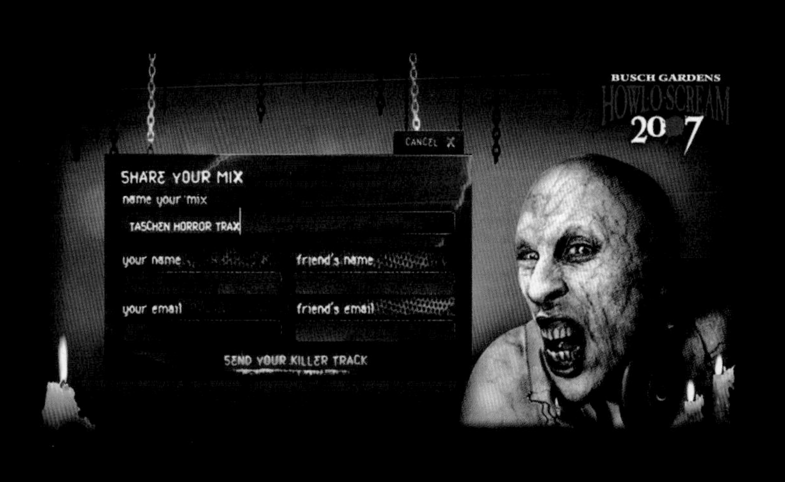
BUSCH GARDENS
HOWL-O-SCREAM
2007
CANCEL
SHARE YOUR MIX
name your mix
TASCHEN HORROR TRAX
your name
friend's name
your email
friend's email
SEND YOUR KILLER TRACK

BUSCH GARDENS
HOWL-O-SCREAM
2007
CANCEL

HUNGRY SUITCASE

www.hungrysuitcase.com

USA
2007

Concept

There is no Royal Caribbean branding on the site until the final payoff, allowing users to create their own adventure without any preconceived notions about travel and cruising. /// Die Marke Royal Caribbean taucht hier erst ganz zum Schluss auf. Dadurch können Benutzer ihre eigenen Abenteuer frei von vorgefertigten Ansichten über Reisen und Kreuzfahrten gestalten. /// La marque Royal Caribbean n'apparaît pas dans la site avant le résultat final, ce qui permet aux utilisateurs de créer leur propre aventure sans notions préconçues de voyage et de croisière.

Info

DESIGN: Big Spaceship <www.bigspaceship.com>. /// **PROGRAMMING:** Big Spaceship. /// **TOOLS:** Adobe Photoshop, Flash, After Effects, Cinema 4D, Maya, 3ds Max. /// **AWARDS:** SXSW, Flash Film Festival, FWA (Site of the Day/Site of the Month).

VACATION FUN-A-LYZER
Relaxin'
Action
Culture
TELL A FRIEND
Choose a Room
My Vacation Favorites
Show My Vacation
Fun and Games
Sign Up for Email
Plan My Vacation

VACATION FUN-A-LYZER

VACATION FUN-A-LYZER

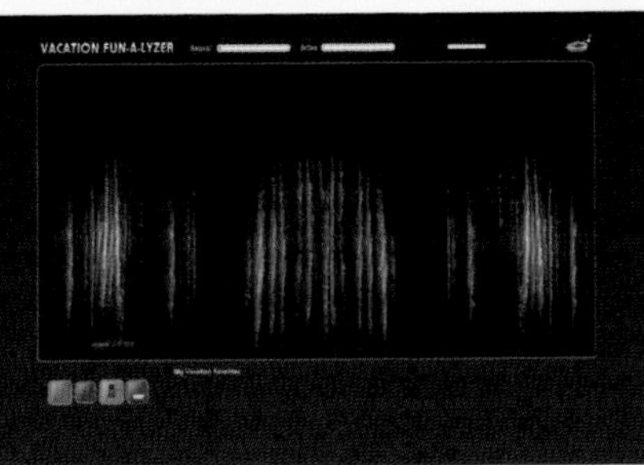
VACATION FUN-A-LYZER

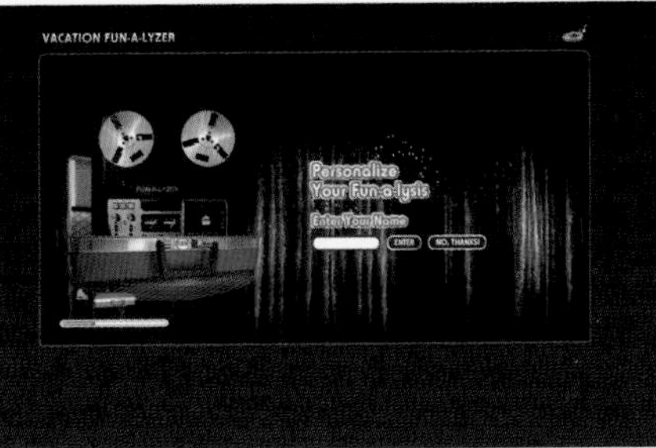
VACATION FUN-A-LYZER
Personalize
Your Fun-a-lysis
Enter Your Name
ENTER
NO, THANKS!

I'M A CYBORG, BUT THAT'S OK

KOREA

http://cyborg.d-o-e-s.com

2006

Concept "Open the Cyborg Pop-up Book, you can meet her mad fantastic world". A surprising simulation of pop-up books. /// „Öffne das Pop-up-Buch des Cyborgs und tauche ein in ihre verrückte, fantastische Welt." Eine überraschende Simulation von Pop-up-Büchern. /// *« Open the Cyborg Pop-up Book, you can meet her mad fantastic world ».* Une simulation surprenante de livres animés.

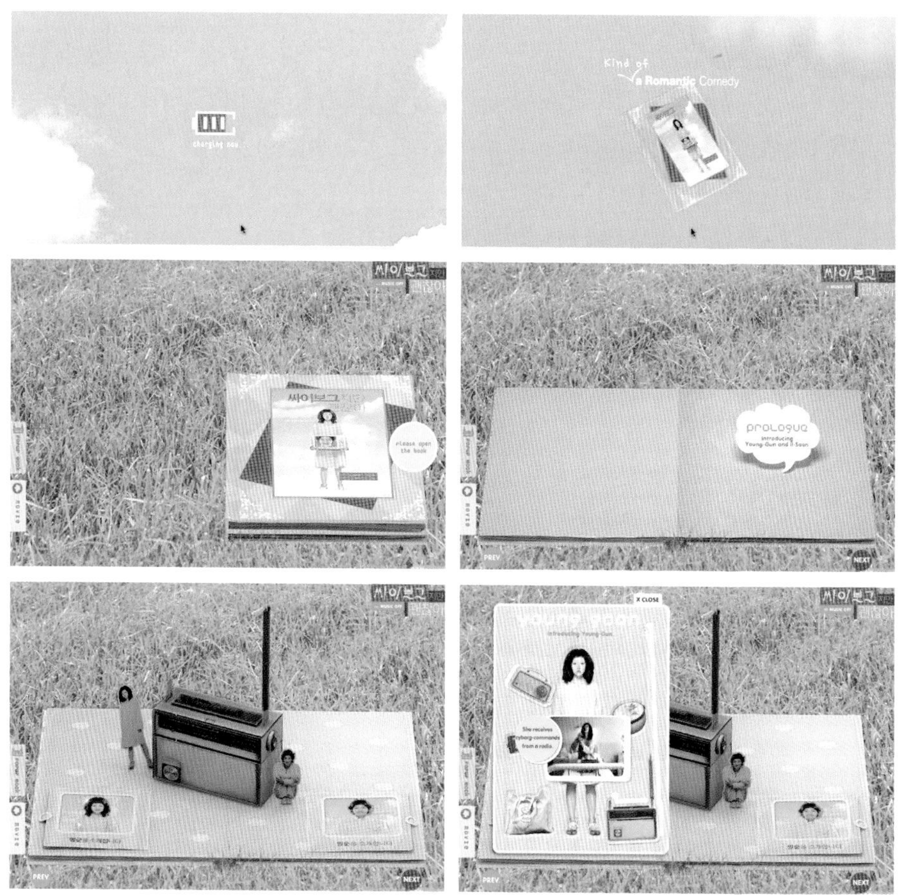

Info **DESIGN:** d.o.E.S <www.d-o-e-s.com>, Hyun Ah Yoon, Sang Jun Lee, Yong Hoon Joe. /// **PROGRAMMING:** Sin Ae Kim, Rak Kyun Kim. /// **TOOLS:** Adobe Photoshop, Flash, 3dsMax, After Effects. /// **AWARDS:** FWA (Site of the Month), Cannes Lion (Finalist), WebAward Korea (Grand Prize/People's Choice), Webby Award (Nominee). /// **COST:** 160 hours. /// **OTHERS:** 2G (3D Modeling).

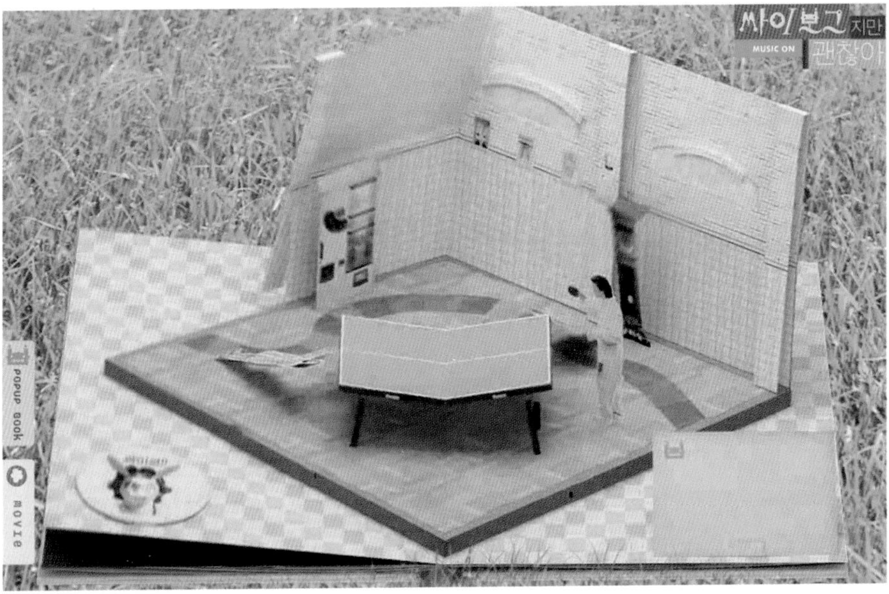

싸이보그 지만
MUSIC ON 괜찮아

POPUP BOOK
movie

싸이보그 지만
MUSIC ON 괜찮아

after talking to the phone

POPUP BOOK
movie

I'm not a **psycho** but **cyborg**

One day, in ShinSehGeh Mental Hospital, filled with bizarre thoughts and imagination, Young-Gun, who believes she's a cyborg, enters the hospital. No one understands her as she talks to vending machines and

I-MODE

www.imode.com.hk/content

HONG KONG
2007

Concept

Mobile operator 3 Hong Kong brought in *i-mode* under exclusive license in June 2007. It has revolutionised the lifestyle of mobile phone users around the world, and they can experience the interactive features of *i-mode* on this official website. /// Handybetreiber 3 Hong Kong führte *i-mode* im June 2007 als exklusive Lizenz ein. Es hat den Lebensstil von Handybenutzern weltweit verändert. Besucher können die interaktiven Elemente von *i-mode* auf dieser offiziellen Website erleben. /// En juin 2007, l'opérateur de téléphonie mobile 3 Hong Kong a lancé *i-mode* avec une licence exclusive. Il a révolutionné le mode de vie des utilisateurs de téléphones portables dans le monde entier, qui peuvent découvrir les fonctions interactives d'*i-mode* sur ce site Web officiel.

Info

DESIGN: Rice 5 <www.rice5.com>, Andrew Lee, Kevin Tsang, Tom Shum. /// **PROGRAMMING:** Eric Ho, Rex Chan, Markson Leung. /// **TOOLS:** Adobe Photoshop, Flash, Fireworks, After Effects, Maya.

Results

Pageview (game): 100,000; Game participants: 13,000; Impressions (banner ad): 8.8 million; Click rate: 16,500. /// Besucher (Spiel): 100.000+; Spieler: 13.000+; Impressions (Bannerwerbung): 8,8 Millionen+; Click rate: 16.500. /// Accès à la page (jeu) : + de 100 000 ; Joueurs : + de 13 000 ; Impressions (bannière) : + de 8,8 millions ; Taux de clics : 16 500.

IMPOSSIBLE STORY

UK

www.impossiblestory.com

2007

Concept

Inspired by the iconic hand drawn style of the "Impossible is Nothing" ad spots for TV, press and online, Impossible Story lets users create a totally personalised animation in a matter of seconds, and then send it on to their friends. /// Inspiriert durch den sehr einprägsamen handgezeichneten Zeichenstil der „Impossible is Nothing"-Werbespots in TV, Presse und Web, lässt Impossible Story die Benutzer innerhalb von Sekunden eine persönliche Animation erstellen und an Freunde versenden. /// S'inspirant du style de dessin à main levée des spots « Impossible is Nothing » pour la télévision, la presse et le Web, Impossible Story permet aux utilisateurs de créer une animation entièrement personnalisée en quelques secondes, puis de l'envoyer à des amis.

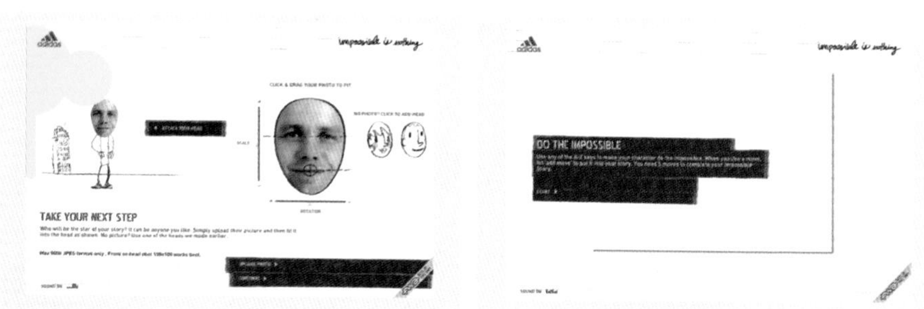

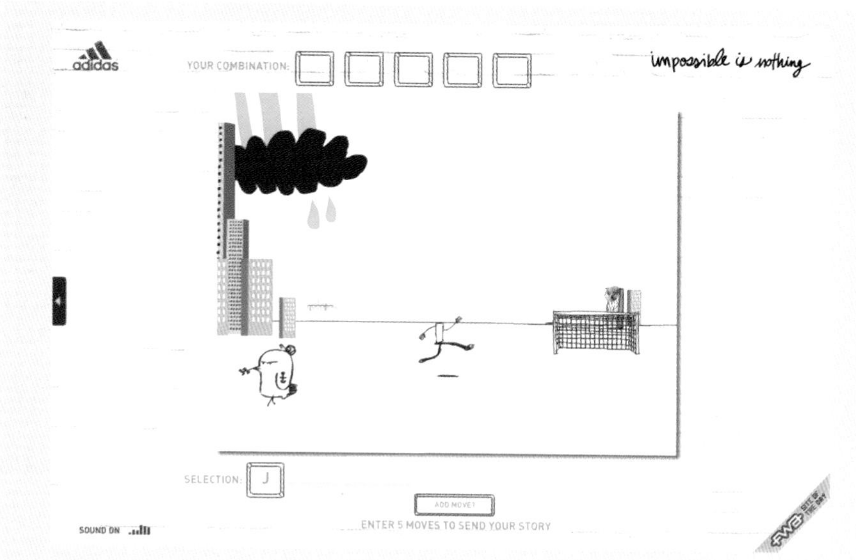

Info

Design: glue London <www.gluelondon.com>, Matt Verity, Ben Pearce, Ben Franken. /// **Programming:** Fraser Hobbs. /// **Tools:** Adobe Photoshop, Flash, Illustrator. /// **Awards:** Y Design Awards 2007 (Best Viral Campaign). /// **Others:** Adam King, Lewis Raven (Creative Team).

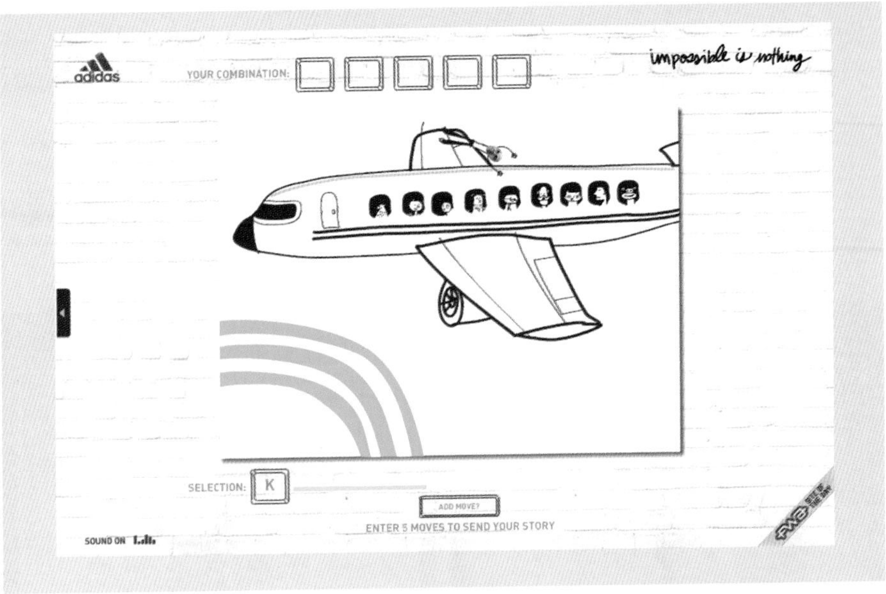

adidas
YOUR COMBINATION:
impossible is nothing
SELECTION:
K
ADD MOVE?
ENTER 5 MOVES TO SEND YOUR STORY
SOUND ON

adidas
impossible is nothing
Y

adidas
impossible is nothing
Y
K
Z

adidas
impossible is nothing
SEND THE STORY TO A FRIEND

adidas
impossible is nothing
THANKS

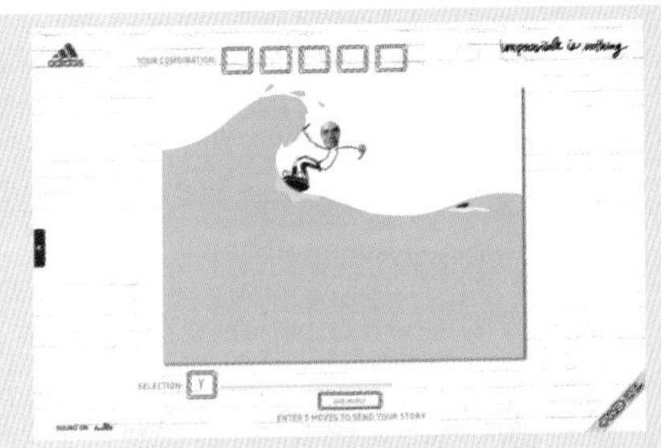

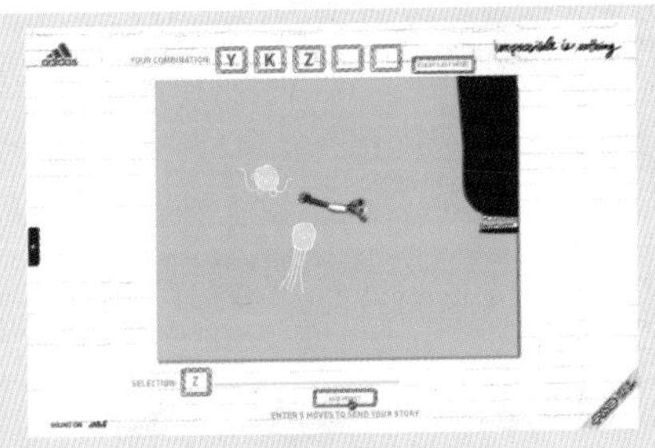

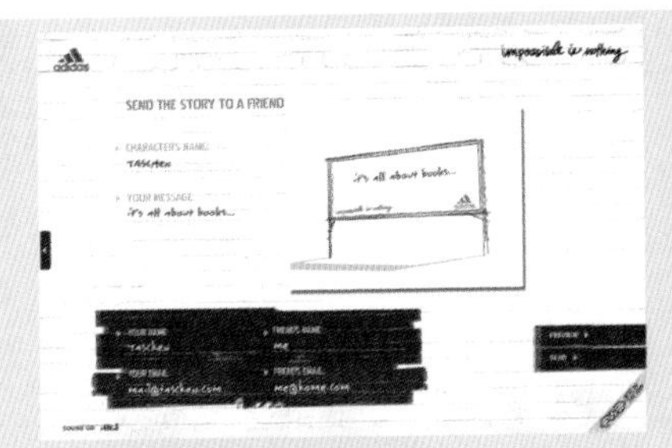

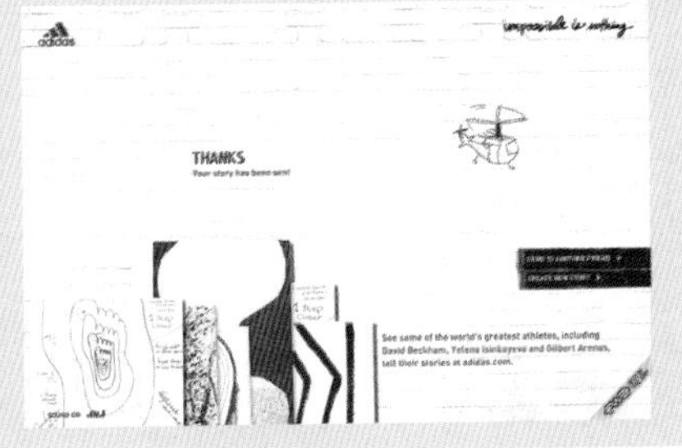

JINGLE ALONG WITH SANTA

SINGAPORE

www.avantgarden.com.sg/greetings/xmas07

2007

Concept

A novelty Christmas greeting for clients, this interactive teaser game entices them to relax and sing along with Santa by carefully observing his movements to mimic the right merry notes. /// Ein etwas anderer Weihnachtsgruß an die Kunden: In diesem interaktiven Spiel sollen sie mit dem Weihnachtsmann mitsingen, indem sie seine Bewegungen beobachten und anhand derer dann die richtigen Töne anstimmen. /// Carte de Noël fantaisie pour les clients, ce jeu interactif amusant les invite à se détendre et à chanter avec le Père Noël en prêtant attention à ses gestes pour imiter correctement les notes de la chanson.

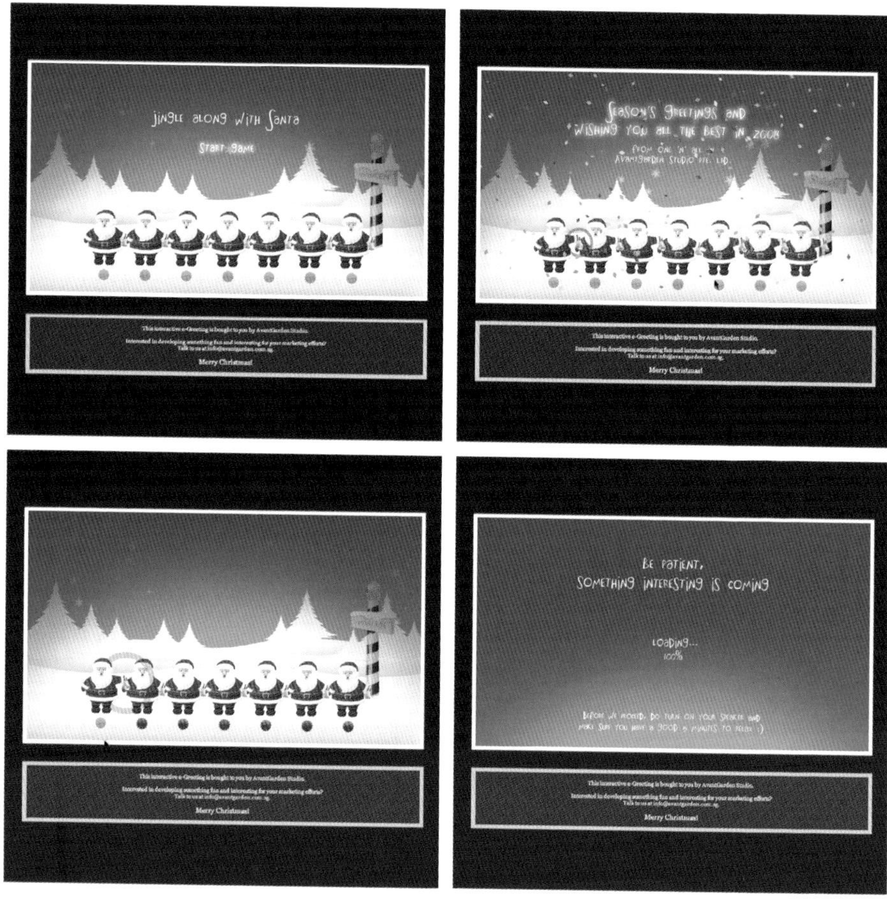

Info

DESIGN: AvantGarden <www.avantgarden.com.sg>, Chris Lim, Chen Yao Ming. /// **PROGRAMMING:** Chen Yao Ming. /// **TOOLS:** Adobe Photoshop, Flash, Dreamweaver. /// **COST:** 50 hours.

LAUNCHBALL

UK

www.sciencemuseum.org.uk/launchpad/launchball

2007

Concept

A game with the aim of making physics fun. A selection of physics phenomena blocks are available for the players to use to complete fiendish puzzles. Besides the 40 levels available to work through, players can design and share their own. /// Das Spiel möchte beweisen, dass Physik Spaß machen kann. Die Spieler müssen verschiedene physikalische Mittel einsetzen, um knifflige Puzzle zu vollenden. Über die 40 vorgegebenen Levels hinaus können Spieler auch ihre eigenen Levels entwerfen. /// Jeu dont le but est de rendre le monde de la physique amusant. Une sélection de blocs de phénomènes est disponible pour que les joueurs composent des puzzles diaboliques. En plus des 40 niveaux à découvrir, les joueurs peuvent élaborer et partager leurs propres créations.

Info

DESIGN: Preloaded <www.preloaded.com>. /// **PROGRAMMING:** Preloaded. /// **TOOLS:** Adobe Photoshop, Flash, Maya. /// **AWARDS:** Eurobest (Gold).

JUNTOS PELA NATUREZA

www.juntospelanatureza.com.br

BRAZIL

2007

Concept

An awareness campaign aimed at getting children involved in the issue of Brazil's endangered animal life, whilst promoting the new sandal from Xuxa. Kids can take care of their own virtual Golden Lion Marmoset. /// Eine Kampagne, die Kinder dazu animieren soll, sich für Brasiliens bedrohte Tierwelt zu engagieren, und dabei gleichzeitig die neueste Sandale von Xuxa bewirbt. Die Kinder können sich um ihr eigenes virtuelles Goldgelbes Löwenäffchen kümmern. /// Campagne de sensibilisation visant à impliquer les enfants dans la cause des espèces animales en danger au Brésil, tout en faisant la promotion de la nouvelle sandale de Xuxa. Les enfants peuvent s'occuper de leur propre singe lion doré virtuel.

Info

Design: W3Haus <www.w3haus.com.br>, Chico Baldini, Diego Chiarelli. /// **Programming:** Sandro Haag, Luiz Ricardo Sordi, Marcelo Arocha, Carolina Sebben. /// **Tools:** Adobe Photoshop, Flash, PHP, HTML, XML. /// **Cost:** 520 hours. /// **Others:** Kátia Rosa (Account Executive), Rodrigo Meurer (Project Manager).

Results

17,565 participations on the "Jump Golden-Lion-Marmoset" competition. /// Der „Löwenäffchen-Springwettbewerb" hatte 17.565 Teilnehmer. /// 17 565 participants à la compétition « Fais sauter le singe lion doré ».

LE PETIT OISEAU VA SORTIR

FRANCE

www.lepetitoiseauvasortir.com

2007

Concept

The main aim was to show a friendly but professional aspect of the studio. We provided a custom online pdf creation. /// Wir wollten die freundliche und gleichzeitig professionelle Atmosphäre des Studios präsentieren. Die Kunden konnten sich auf der Site individuelle PDFs erstellen lassen. /// Le but principal était d'offrir une présentation agréable mais aussi professionnelle du studio. Le site comprend une fonction de création de PDF en ligne personnalisée.

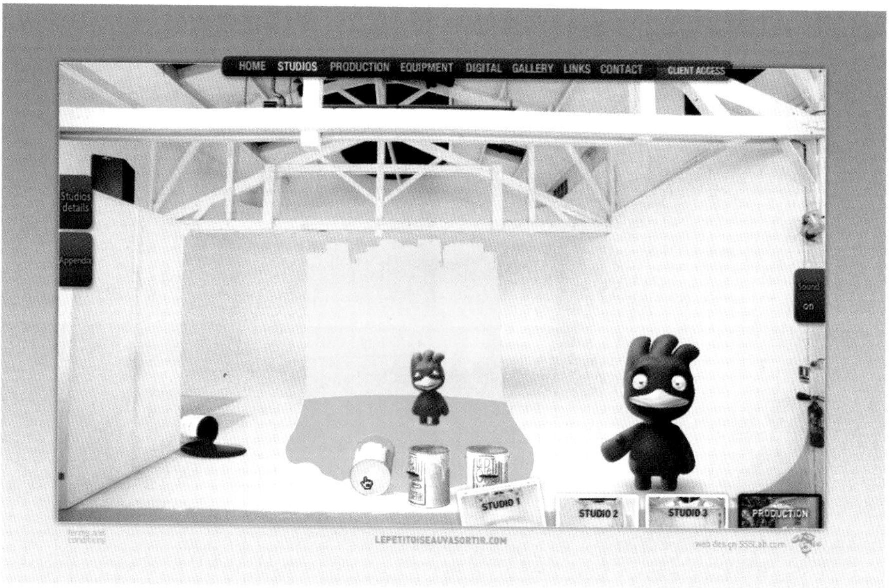

Info

DESIGN: 555Lab <www.555lab.com>, Cédric "Khan" Magne. /// PROGRAMMING: Cyrille "Pompoko" Dubois (Frontend), Tarek Ibrahim (Backend). /// TOOLS: Adobe Photoshop, Flash, Lightwave 3D, Cubase, PHP. /// COST: 960 hours. /// OTHERS: Clément "Woodini" Bachelier (Sound Design), Florent Leroy (Photo).

HOME STUDIOS PRODUCTION EQUIPMENT DIGITAL GALLERY LINKS CONTACT CLIENT ACCESS
Photo Gallery
Drag and drop the fridge magnets HERE
to reveal the photos

HOME STUDIOS PRODUCTION EQUIPMENT DIGITAL GALLERY LINKS CONTACT CLIENT ACCESS
Thierry LAYANI

HOME STUDIOS PRODUCTION EQUIPMENT DIGITAL GALLERY LINKS CONTACT CLIENT ACCESS
Thierry LAYANI

HOME STUDIOS PRODUCTION EQUIPMENT DIGITAL GALLERY LINKS CONTACT CLIENT ACCESS

HOME STUDIOS PRODUCTION EQUIPMENT DIGITAL GALLERY LINKS CONTACT CLIENT ACCESS
EQUIPMENT ONLY RENTAL
DSLR CAMERAS
DIGITAL BACKS
WORK STATIONS

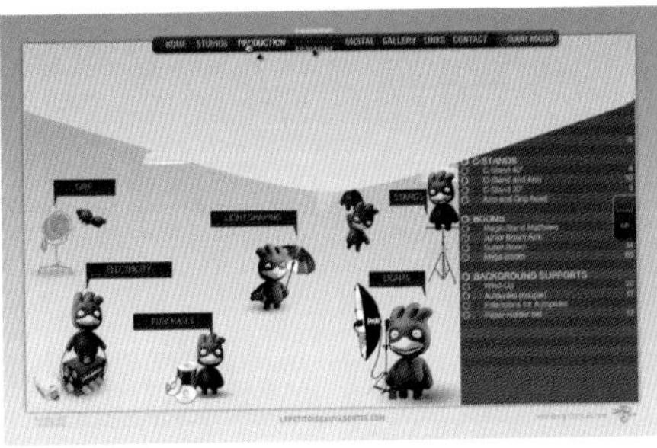
HOME STUDIOS PRODUCTION DIGITAL GALLERY LINKS CONTACT CLIENT ACCESS
STANDS
BOOMS
BACKGROUND SUPPORTS

HOME STUDIOS PRODUCTION EQUIPMENT DIGITAL GALLERY LINKS CONTACT CLIENT ACCESS
RENTAL PREMISES
WAREHOUSE
WAREHOUSE

LEVEL-UP!

http://levelup.wedonicethings.com

UK

2006

Concept

A community site for children built upon gaming metaphors right down to the site's title. The games focus on civic responsibility and social awareness, with scenarios broadly ranging from babysitting and dogwalking to shopping and litter collecting. /// Eine kommunale Website für Kinder. Die Spiele drehen sich um soziales Bewusstsein und Verantwortung, in den Spielszenen geht es zum Beispiel um Babysitting, das Ausführen von Hunden, Einkaufen oder Abfallentsorgung. /// Site communautaire pour enfants élaboré à partir de métaphores de jeu dès le titre. Le jeu prend comme thèmes la responsabilité civile et la philanthropie, avec une grande variété de scénarios allant du baby-sitting et de la promenade de chiens au shopping et au ramassage des déchets.

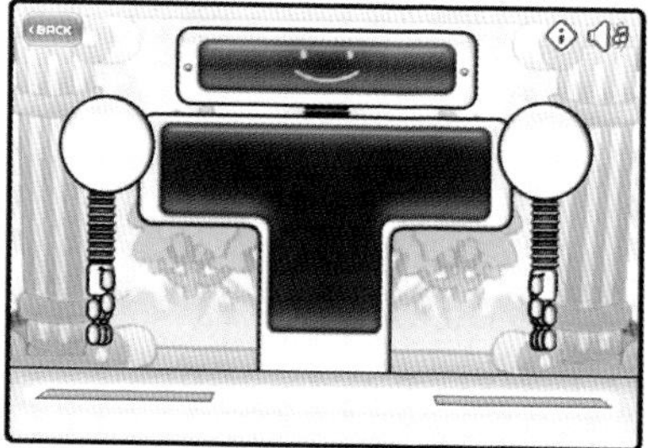

Info

DESIGN: Preloaded <www.preloaded.com>. /// PROGRAMMING: Preloaded. /// TOOLS: Adobe Photoshop, Flash. /// AWARDS: BAFTA (Winner), BIMA (Finalist).

LIGHTNING GAME

NEW ZEALAND

www.liamfinn.co.nz

2008

Concept

Keep the stars from falling into the lake by shooting and recharging them using Liam's lightning bolts. The bolt bounces off stars. The more stars you hit with a single bolt the more points you score. Be careful not to overcharge or you will be electrocuted. /// Verhindere, dass die Sterne in den See fallen, indem du sie mit Liams Blitzen triffst und dadurch wieder aufladst. Je mehr Sterne du triffst, desto mehr Punkte bekommst du. Aber hüte dich vor Überspannung, sonst erhältst du einen Stromschlag. /// **Empêcher les étoiles de tomber dans le lac en tirant dessus et en les rechargeant avec les éclairs que lance Liam. Les éclairs percutent les étoiles : plus vous touchez d'étoiles avec un seul éclair, plus vous marquez de points. Prenez garde aux surcharges, au risque de vous faire électrocuter.**

Info

DESIGN: Resn <www.resn.co.nz>. /// **PROGRAMMING:** Resn. /// **TOOLS:** Adobe Photoshop, Flash. /// **COST:** 3 weeks. /// **RESULTS:** Over 220,000 visitors in the first two months.

MENCIA MADNESS

USA

www.freedominteractivedesign.com/demos/menciamadness/main 2006

Concept

In this game for Comedy Central, Mencia Madness requires the user to try and break the balls of the same colour by putting them together in sequences of three. /// In Mencia Madness, einem Spiel für Comedy Central, muss der Spieler versuchen, gleichfarbige Bälle zu zerstören, indem er jeweils drei nebeneinanderreiht. /// Dans ce jeu pour Comedy Central, l'utilisateur doit essayer de détruire les boules en regroupant trois boules d'une même couleur.

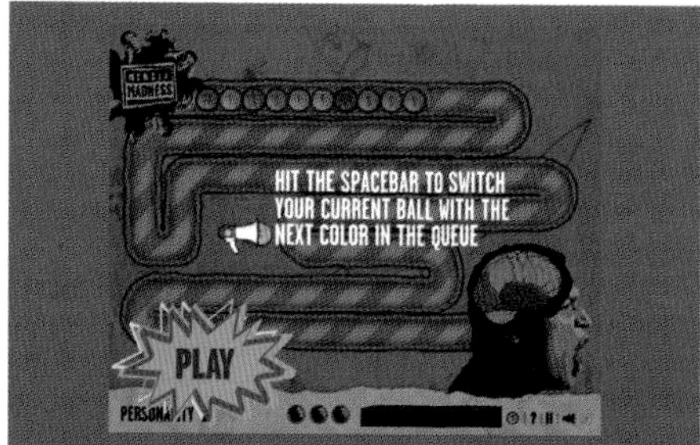

Info

DESIGN: Freedom Interactive Design <www.freedominteractivedesign.com>. /// PROGRAMMING: Freedom Interactive Design. /// TOOLS: Flash.

MENCIA MELTDOWN

USA

www.freedominteractivedesign.com/demos/menciaballs/main

2006

Concept

Mencia Meltdown proposes a game full of humour for Comedy Central. The basic idea is to try to break all the balls in the brain to avoid it from overheating. /// Mencia Meltdown ist ein lustiges Spiel für Comedy Central. Die Grundidee besteht darin, alle Bälle in einem Gehirn zu zerstören, damit dieses sich nicht überhitzt. /// **Mencia Meltdown propose un jeu plein d'humour pour Comedy Central. Le principe est de tenter de détruire toutes les boules dans le cerveau pour éviter une surchauffe.**

Info

DESIGN: Freedom Interactive Design <www.freedominteractivedesign.com>. /// **PROGRAMMING:** Freedom Interactive Design. /// **TOOLS:** Flash.

MINI SWIRLZ

USA

www.freedominteractivedesign.com/demos/kelloggsmini/main 2005

Concept

In this funny game for Kellogg's Swirlz, the player can train the tongue by lifting different objects with various weights. The user can either win or lose the game simply by swirling the cursor over the screen. /// In diesem lustigen Spiel für Kellogg's Swirlz können Spieler ihre Zungen trainieren, indem sie verschiedene Objekte mit unterschiedlichem Gewicht anheben. Dafür müssen sie nur den Cursor über den Bildschirm bewegen. /// Dans ce jeu amusant pour Kellogg's Swirlz, le joueur peut entraîner sa langue en soulevant différents objets de poids variable. Il peut gagner ou perdre le jeu en déplaçant simplement le curseur dans l'écran.

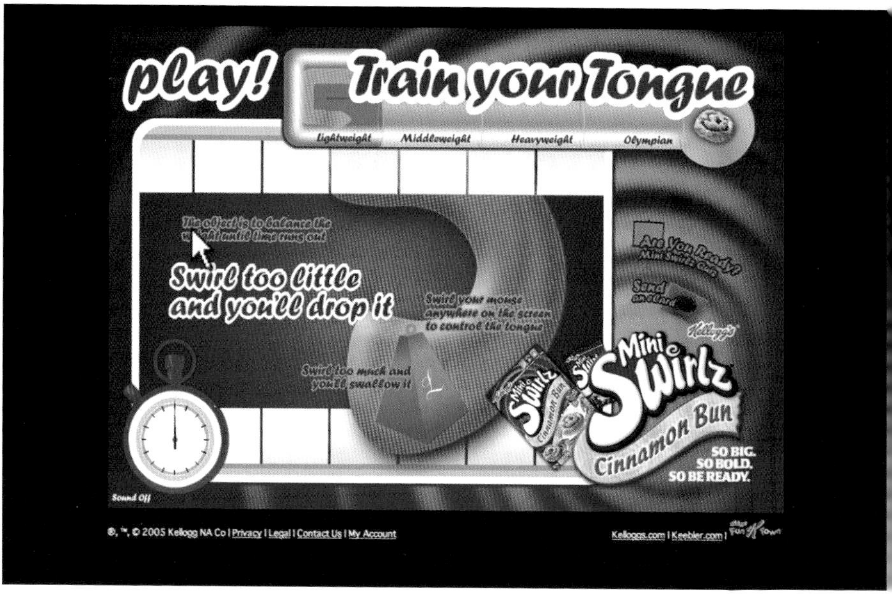

Info

Design: Freedom Interactive Design <www.freedominteractivedesign.com>. /// **Programming:** Freedom Interactive Design. /// **Tools:** Flash with a complex XML system conceived and custom-built for this exploratory game interface.

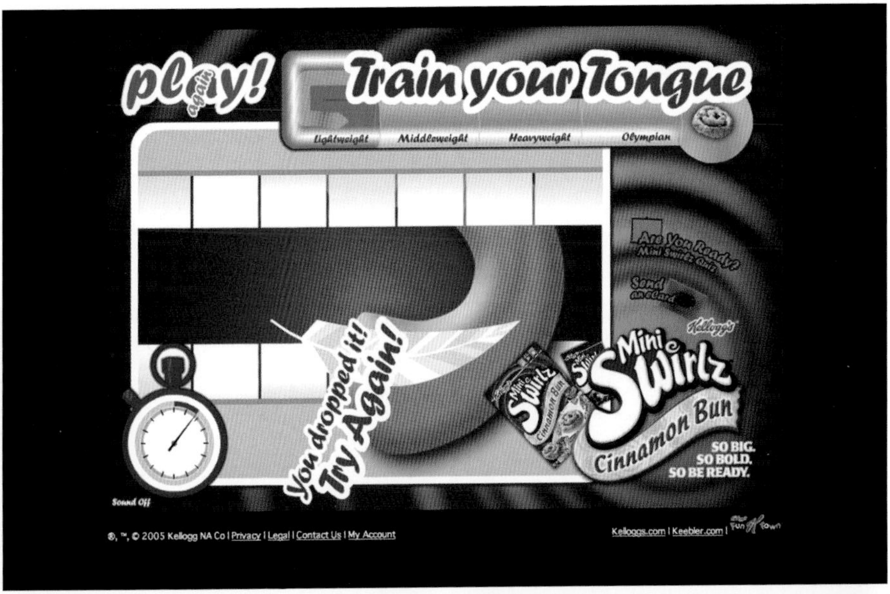

play!
again
Train your Tongue
Lightweight
Middleweight
Heavyweight
Olympian
Are You Ready?
Mini Swirlz Quiz
Send
an eCard
Kellogg's
Mini
Swirlz
Cinnamon Bun
SO BIG.
SO BOLD.
SO BE READY.
You dropped it!
Try Again!
Sound Off
®, ™, © 2005 Kellogg NA Co | Privacy | Legal | Contact Us | My Account
Kelloggs.com | Keebler.com |

play!
again
Train your Tongue
You dropped it!
Try Again!
Mini
Swirlz
Cinnamon Bun

Train your Tongue
Lightweight
Mini
Swirlz
Cinnamon Bun

Are You Ready?
Mini-Swirlz Quiz
Mini-Swirlz Contain:
A) Massive Flavorosity!
B) Chocolate-y Deliciousness
C) High Velocity Swirlz
D) All Of The Above
Submit
Mini
Swirlz
Fudge Ripple
SO BIG.
SO BOLD.
SO BE READY.

Are You Ready?
Mini-Swirlz Quiz
Correct!
Mini-Swirlz Contain
Massive Flavorosity,
Chocolate-y Deliciousness
and High Velocity Swirlz
Next
Mini
Swirlz
Fudge Ripple
SO BIG.
SO BOLD.
SO BE READY.

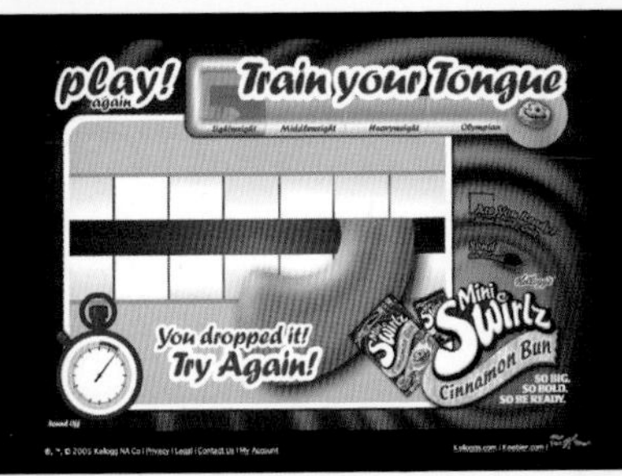

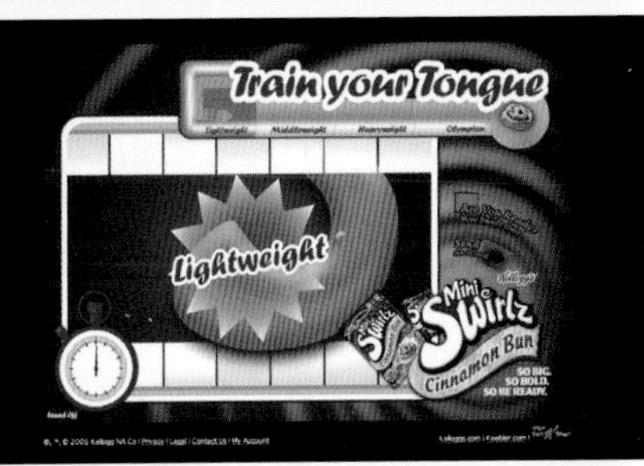

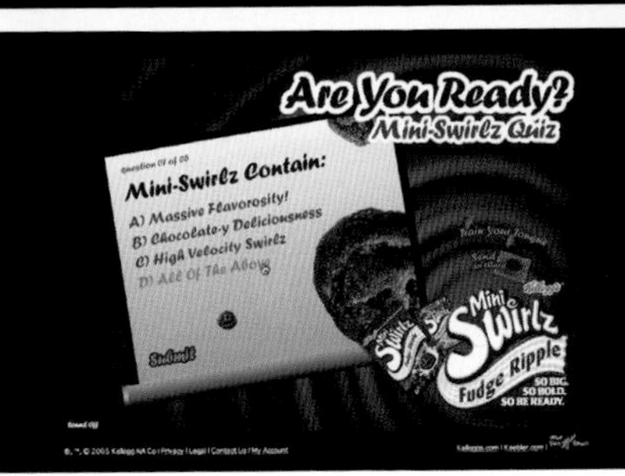

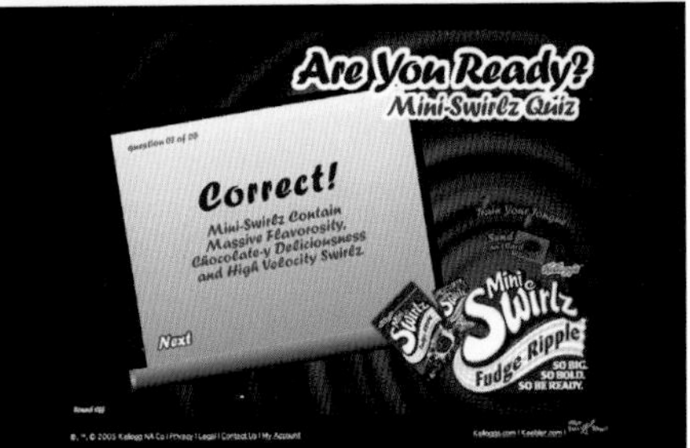

MONSTERS

BRAZIL

http://200.186.92.250/awards/2007/vw/monstro/port

2007

Concept

The hotsite launch of the new Volkswagen Crossfox was created to show the manouverability of the car, to escape beyond the cityscape and into the country. /// Diese Hotsite für den neuen Volkswagen Cross Fox sollte die Wendigkeit und Flexibilität des Autos zeigen – heraus aus der Stadt und hinein in die Landschaft. /// Le site branché de la nouvelle Volkswagen Cross Fox a été lancé pour montrer la manœuvrabilité du véhicule, pour des échappées hors des villes.

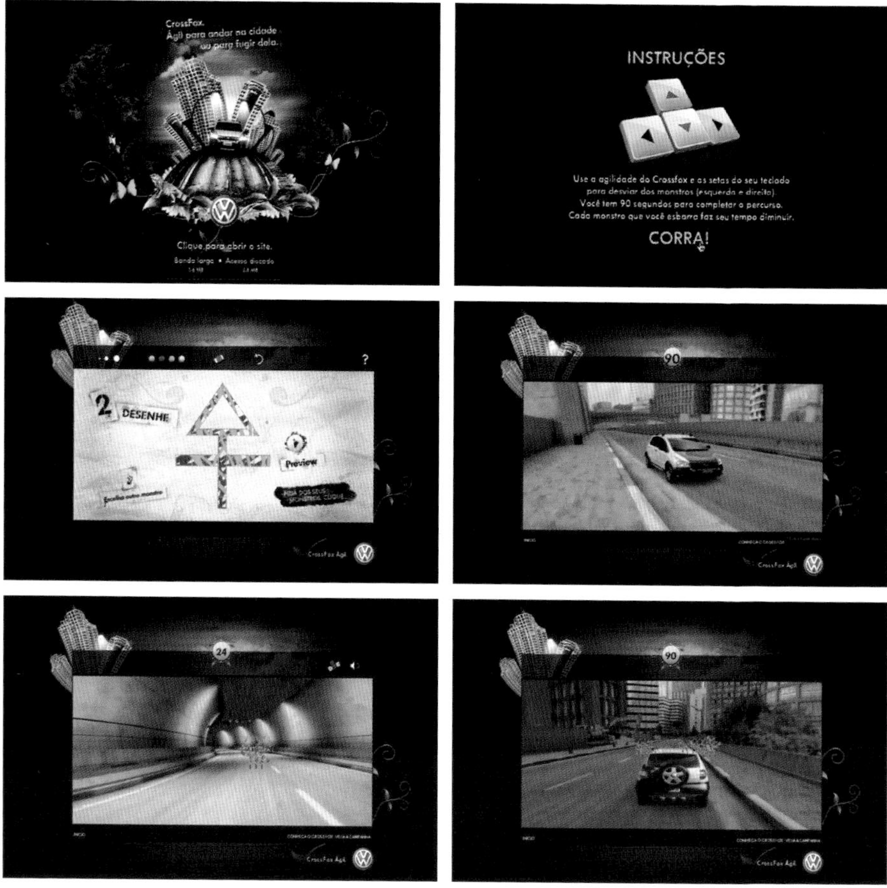

Info

Design: AlmapBBDO <www.almapbbdo.com.br>, Sergio Mugnaini (Creative Director), Marcos Paulo "Focca" (Art Director/Design), Moacyr Netto (Copywriter), TSI (3D). /// **Programming:** Fabrizio Barata (Technology Director), Raphael H. de Carvalho (Flash Developer). /// **Tools:** Adobe Photoshop, Flash, 3dsMax. /// **Awards:** MMonline/MSN (Shortlist). /// **Others:** Cromo Sonica (Sound Production).

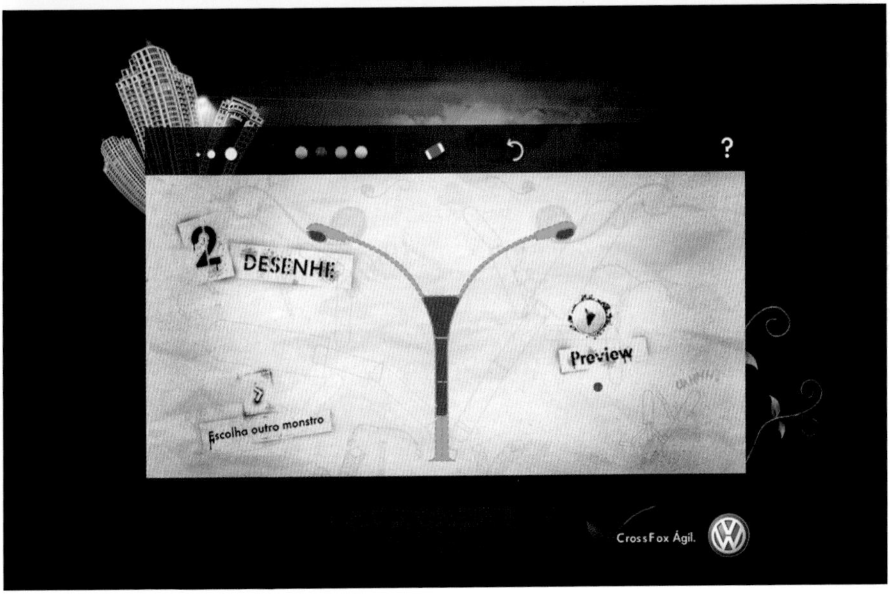

Results

Unique users: 260,000 per month. /// Unique User: 260.000 pro Monat. /// Utilisateurs uniques : 260 000 par mois.

MOTOCOLORS

INTERNATIONAL

www.motocolors.net

2007

Concept

Paint! And you will find the mobile that matches your personality. /// Male! Dann findest du das Handy, das zu dir passt. /// Peignez pour trouver le portable qui correspond à votre personnalité !

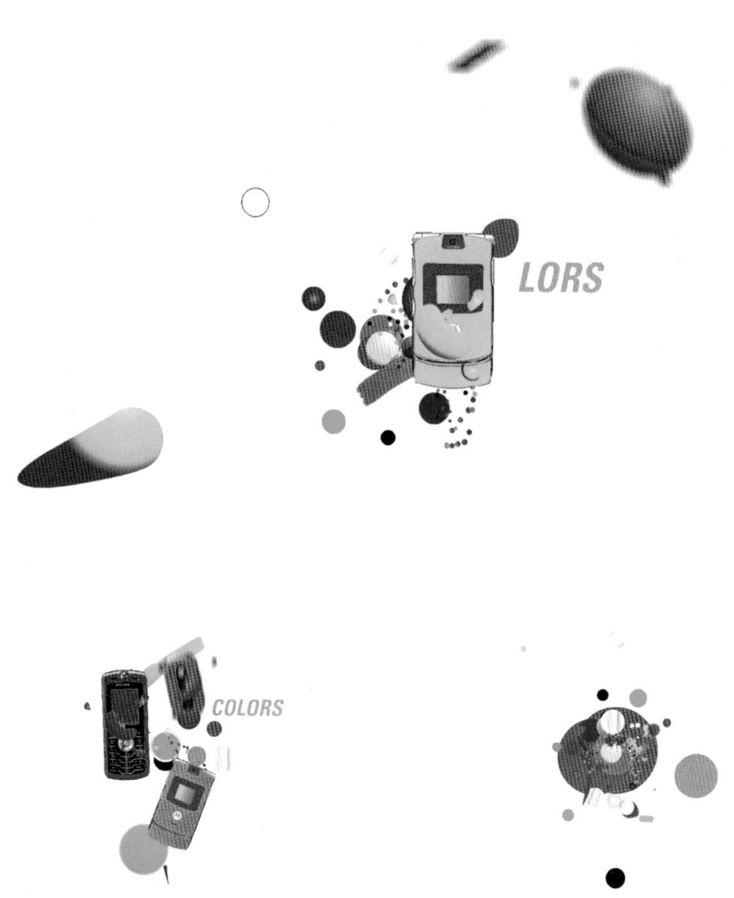

Info

Design: Theo Gennitsakis <www.theogennitsakis.com>, Theo Gennitsakis, Simon Frankart, Alexandre Pascual, Ludovic Clamens. /// **Programming:** Alexis Isaac. /// **Tools:** Adobe Photoshop, Flash, Illustrator, XML, PHP, HTML, CSS. /// **Awards:** Webby Awards, FWA (Site of the Day), New York Festivals (2x Gold, Grand Award). /// **Cost:** 190 hours. /// **Client:** Motorola.

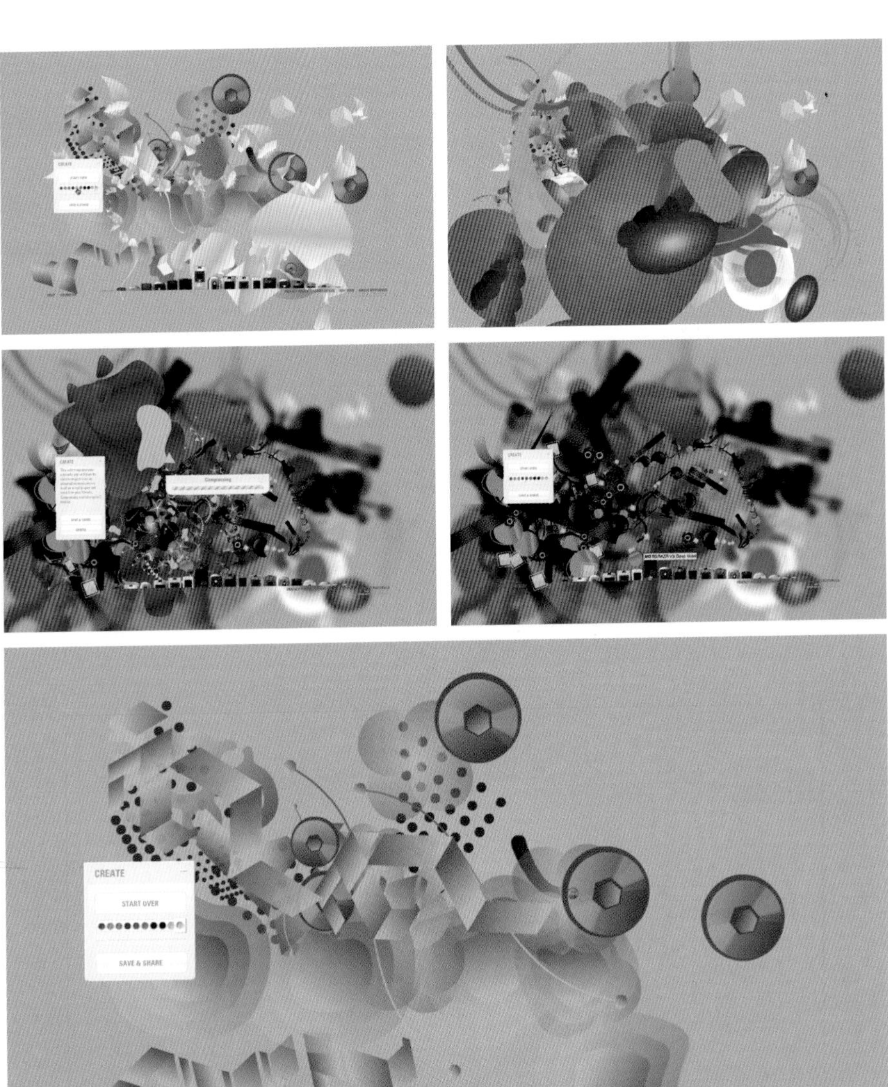
CREATE
START OVER
SAVE & SHARE
MOTO RAZR V3 Silver
HELP
SOUND OFF
PRIVACY POLICY
TERMS OF USE
BUY NOW
ABOUT MOTOROLA

MOVING DAY

USA

http://siite.com/samples/toh_game

2006

Concept

It's up to you to direct a crew of movers and prevent them from bumping into walls in this online game. /// In diesem Online-Spiel muss der Benutzer ein Team von Umzugsleuten anleiten und verhindern, dass sie gegen Wände stoßen. /// Dans ce jeu en ligne, vous devez diriger une équipe de déménageurs et les empêcher de donner des coups dans les murs.

Info

Design: SiiTE Interactive <www.SiiTE.com>. /// **Programming:** SiiTE Interactive. /// **Tools:** Adobe Photoshop, Flash, Illustrator, PHP.

NOKIA 7500 PRISM

HONG KONG

http://campaign.nokia.com.hk/7500

2007

Concept

A digital jigsaw puzzle game was created for the release of the Nokia mobile phone in Hong Kong. /// Diese digitalen Puzzle wurden zur Markteinführung des Nokia-Handys in Hongkong entworfen. /// Ce jeu de casse-tête a été créé pour le lancement du téléphone portable Nokia à Hong Kong.

Info

DESIGN: postgal workshop <www.postgal.com>, John Chan. /// **PROGRAMMING:** Samson Wong. /// **TOOLS:** Flash, Maya. /// **AWARDS:** iBLOG (Site of the Week). /// **COST:** 2 weeks. /// **OTHERS:** Edwin Chow (3D Animator). /// **RESULTS:** Information was collected for promotional purposes following an ovewhelming number of post-game email.

NA FOGUEIRA

BRAZIL

www.nafogueira.com.br/portuguese

2007

Concept

"Na Fogueira" (which means "In The Bonfire" in Portuguese) was created to allow the users to burn all the bad things that happened to them in 2007. It was a self promotional New Year project from W3Haus. /// „Na Fogueira" („Auf dem Scheiterhaufen" auf Portugiesisch) gab Benutzern die Möglichkeit, virtuell alles Schlechte zu verbrennen, was ihnen 2007 zugestoßen war. Es handelte sich um eine Neujahrs-Eigenpromotion von W3 Haus. /// « Na Fogueira » (qui signifie « dans le feu de joie » en portugais) a été créé pour permettre aux utilisateurs de brûler tout ce qui leur est arrivé de mauvais en 2007. Il s'agissait d'un projet promotionnel pour la nouvelle année réalisé par W3Haus.

Info

Design: W3Haus <www.w3haus.com.br>, Chico Baldini, Pablo de la Rocha. /// **Programming:** Matias Causa, Marcelo Arocha, Guilherme Machiavelli, Gustavo Allenbrandt. /// **Tools:** Adobe Photoshop, Flash, PHP, HTML, XML. /// **Cost:** 270 hours. /// **Others:** Leo Prestes (Creative); Fernanda Kraemer, Kátia Rosa (Production).

Results

1500 visits on the website's second day without advertising. /// 1.500 Besucher am zweiten Tag ohne Werbung. /// 1 500 visites le deuxième jour d'existence du site Web sans publicité.

NA SNIEGU

POLAND

2006

Concept

A wintertime contest in which internet users were able to ski, ride a quad and fly a kite by navigating their cursors. The aim of the project was to promote Na Sniegu — a winter event sponsored by Zywiec. /// Ein Wintersportwettbewerb, bei dem Benutzer durch Bewegen des Cursors Ski und Auto fahren oder Drachen steigen lassen konnten. Ziel war es, das von Zywiec gesponsorten Wintersportevent Na Sniegu zu bewerben. /// Concours d'hiver dans lequel les internautes pouvaient faire du ski, monter une motoquad et faire voler un cerf-volant grâce aux curseurs. L'objectif du projet était la promotion de Na Sniegu, un événement d'hiver sponsorisé par Zywiec.

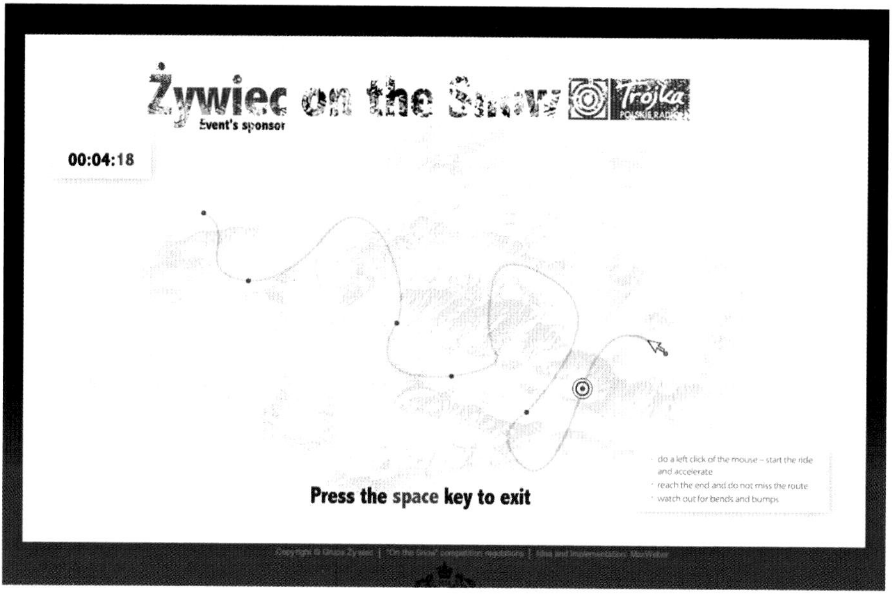

Info

DESIGN: Max Weber <www.maxweber.com>, Andrzej Kryszpiniuk, Bartek Witulski, Piotr Tracki. /// PROGRAMMING: Piotr Tracki, Marek Brun. /// TOOLS: Adobe Photoshop, Flash, Illustrator. /// COST: 3 weeks. /// OTHERS: Grzegorz Mogilewski (Creative/Art Director), Krzysztof Dykas, Marcin Talarek (Concept).

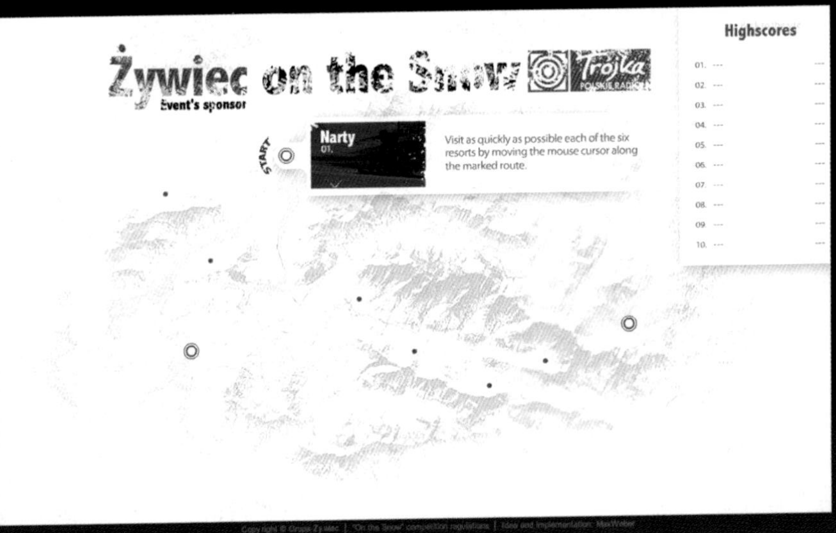
Żywiec on the Snow
Event's sponsor
Trójka
POLSKIE RADIO
Highscores
01. ---
02. ---
03. ---
04. ---
05. ---
06. ---
07. ---
08. ---
09. ---
10. ---
START
Narty
01.
Visit as quickly as possible each of the six resorts by moving the mouse cursor along the marked route.

Żywiec on the Snow
Event's sponsor
Trójka
POLSKIE RADIO
00:00:00
- start – left click of the mouse
- continue the ride – using your mouse drag the coursor along the route
- watch out – this is a ski run – ride carefully so as not to miss the route
Press the space key to exit

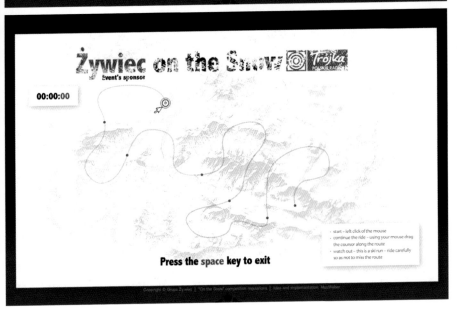

NIKE WINDRUNNER COLLECTIBLES

KOREA

www.nikewindrunner.co.kr/awards_en

2007

Concept

Creating a premium value on Nike's icon category, the Windrunner Collection. The site lets the user customise the upper and body colour of the windrunner. /// Eine neue Serie der Kultmarke: die Windrunner Collection. Auf der Website können Benutzer die Farben vom oberen und unteren Teil des Windrunners auswählen. /// Création d'une version premium pour la catégorie phare de Nike, la Collection Windrunner. Le site permet à l'utilisateur de personnaliser la couleur du haut et du reste du blouson.

Info

DESIGN: PostVisual <www.postvisual.com>, Euna Seol, Jongsoon Kim, Jieun Kim, Hyunjin Lee, Sangwook Park, Haewon Choi, Yeoni Park, Hyung Park. /// PROGRAMMING: Seolbaek Son, Byungrak Song.

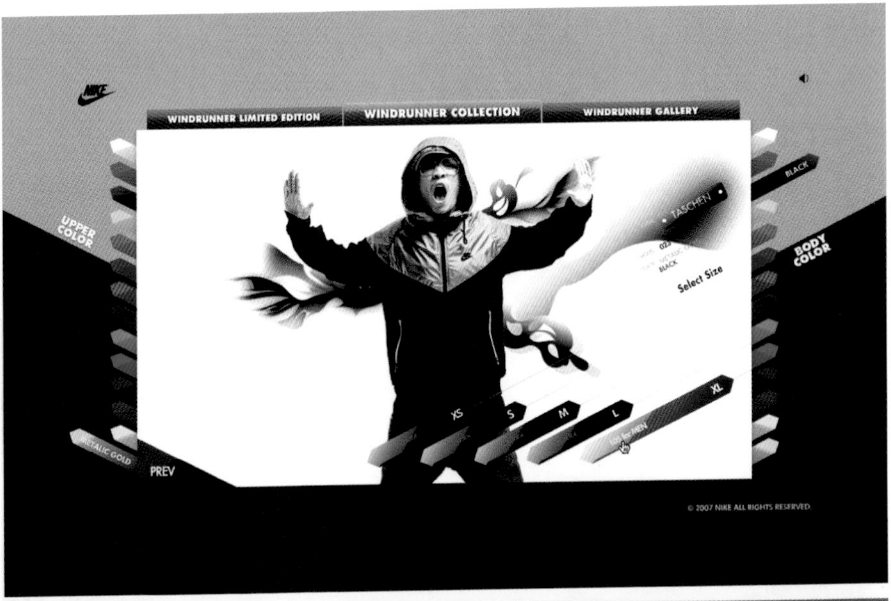

NIKE

WINDRUNNER LIMITED EDITION
WINDRUNNER COLLECTION
WINDRUNNER GALLERY

UPPER COLOR
BODY COLOR
BLACK
TASCHEN
Select Size
XS
S
M
L
XL
METALIC GOLD
PREV

NIKE

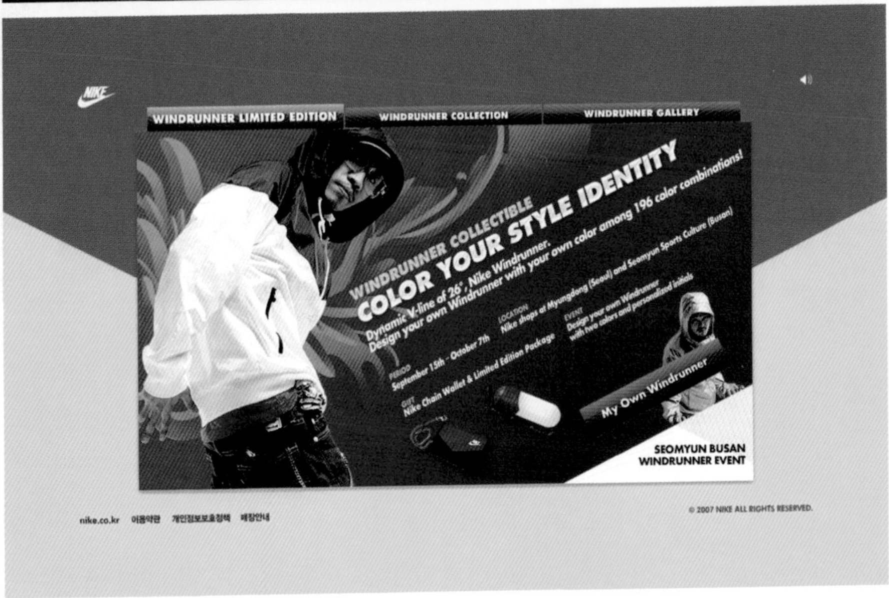

WINDRUNNER LIMITED EDITION
WINDRUNNER COLLECTION
WINDRUNNER GALLERY

WINDRUNNER COLLECTIBLE
COLOR YOUR STYLE IDENTITY
Dynamic V-line of 26", Nike Windrunner.
Design your own Windrunner with your own color among 196 color combinations!

PERIOD
September 15th - October 7th

LOCATION
Nike shops at Myungdong (Seoul) and Seomyun Sports Culture (Busan)

EVENT
Design your own Windrunner with two colors and personalized initials

GIFT
Nike Chain Wallet & Limited Edition Package

My Own Windrunner

SEOMYUN BUSAN
WINDRUNNER EVENT

nike.co.kr 이용약관 개인정보보호정책 매장안내

ONE FINE DAY IN LONDON

KOREA

www.beanpole.com/en/campaign/07ss/awards_en/shell.html

2007

Concept

The interactive music video *One fine day in LONDON* aims to provide a lively experience of British style, the heart of Beanpole designs. /// Das interaktive Musikvideo *One fine day in LONDON* möchte Benutzern den britischen Stil nahebringen, auf dem das Design von Beanpole beruht. /// Le clip vidéo interactif *One fine day in LONDON* vise à offrir une expérience vivante de style britannique, âme des créations de Beanpole.

Info

DESIGN: PostVisual <www.postvisual.com>, Euna Seol, Hyunbok Jung, Jieun Kim. /// **PROGRAMMING:** Seolbaek Son, Byungrak Song.

BEAN POLE
INTERNATIONAL
Make your own M/V
DOWNLOAD
ONE FINE DAY IN LONDON M/V
The music video to be created offers different storylines and lyrics depending on
your episode selection and presents the actual London weather of today.
With the Beatles on the crosswalk, Let it be.
SOUND OFF

PEG SOLITAIRE

BRAZIL

http://200.186.92.250/awards/2007/greenpeace/resta/eng

2007

Concept

Peg Solitaire is an entertaining and dynamic online reproduction of the ancient board game. Usually played with marbles, this one uses trees instead. /// Peg Solitaire ist eine unterhaltsame und dynamische Online-Reproduktion des antiken Brettspiels. Normalerweise wird es mit Murmeln gespielt, die hier jedoch durch Bäume ersetzt werden. /// Peg Solitaire est une reproduction en ligne amusante et dynamique de l'ancien jeu de tablier, qui se jouait normalement avec des billes. Ici, elles sont remplacées par des arbres.

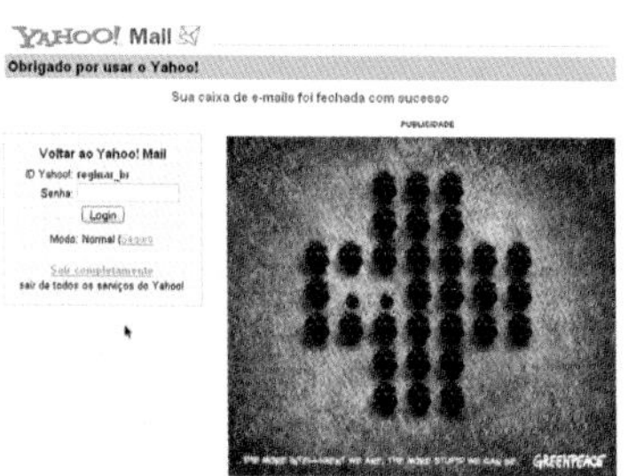

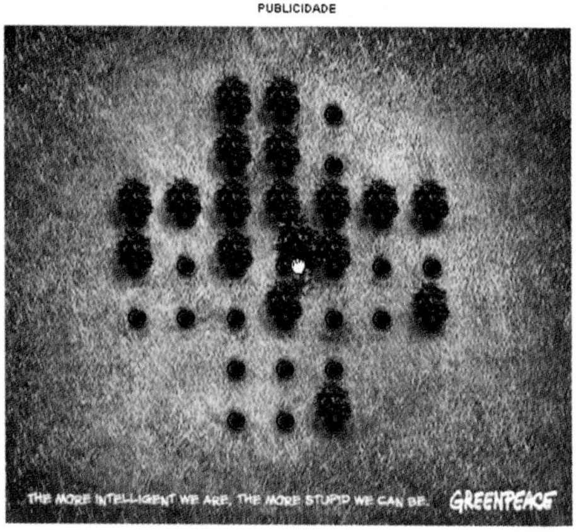

Info

Design: AlmapBBDO <www.almapbbdo.com.br>, Sergio Mugnaini, Marcello Serpa (Creative Director); Guilherme Garcia (Art Director/Design); Marcello Serpa, Moacyr Netto (Copywriter). /// **Programming:** Rodrigo França. /// **Tools:** Adobe Photoshop, Flash. /// **Awards:** One Show Interactive (Gold), D&AD (Nomination), Sinos Festivals (Bronze), MMonline/MSN (Silver), London Festivals (Shortlist), CCSP (Bronze). /// **Results:** Click rate: 7.81%.

PIGGY SCOPE

SINGAPORE 2007

www.avantgarden.com.sg/greetings/cny07

Concept

Rather than receiving a simple offline greeting, the customers had the chance to get a different message and personalised zodiac reading. /// Anstelle einer einfachen Offline-Begrüßung erhielten die Besucher unterschiedliche Botschaften und ein persönliches Horoskop. /// Au lieu de recevoir une simple salutation en ligne, les clients peuvent obtenir un message distinct et un horoscope personnalisé.

Results

Design: AvantGarden <www.avantgarden.com.sg>, Chris Lim, Chen Yao Ming. /// **Programming:** Chen Yao Ming. /// **Tools:** Adobe Photoshop, Flash, Dreamweaver. /// **Cost:** 30 hours. /// **Others:** You Quan (Illustration), Lotus On Water Feng Shui Gallery (Content Advisory).

PEPSI ROBERTO CARLOS

BRAZIL

http://200.186.92.250/awards/2007/pepsi/roberto/eng

2005

Concept

Pepsi released a campaign featuring the greatest soccer players from around the world in unusual situations. In one of the commercials of the campaign, Roberto Carlos is at the beach and has to deal with a clueless surfer. /// Pepsi startete eine Werbekampagne, die die besten Fußballspieler der Welt in ungewöhnlichen Situationen zeigte. In einem der Spots begegnet Roberto Carlos am Strand einem ahnungslosen Surfer. /// Pepsi a lancé une campagne mettant en scène les plus grands joueurs de football du monde entier dans des situations inhabituelles. Dans l'un des spots, Roberto Carlos est à la plage et face à un surfer incapable.

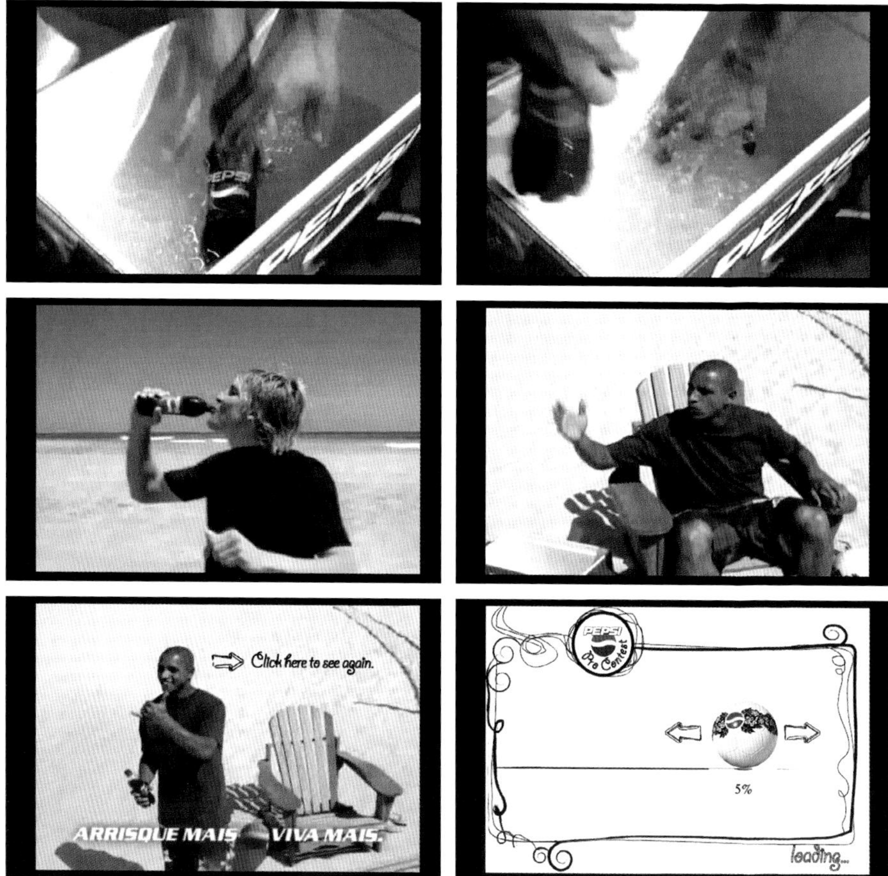

Info

Design: AlmapBBDO <www.almapbbdo.com.br>, Sergio Mugnaini (Creative Director & Art Director), Luciana Haguiara (copywritter), Dulcídio Caldeira (copywritter). /// **Programming:** Flavio Ramos. /// **Tools:** Adobe Photoshop, Flash, Illustrator. /// **Awards:** El Ojo Iberoamerica (Gold), FIAP (Gold), MMonline/MSN (Bronze). /// **Others:** Cromo Sonica (Sound Production).

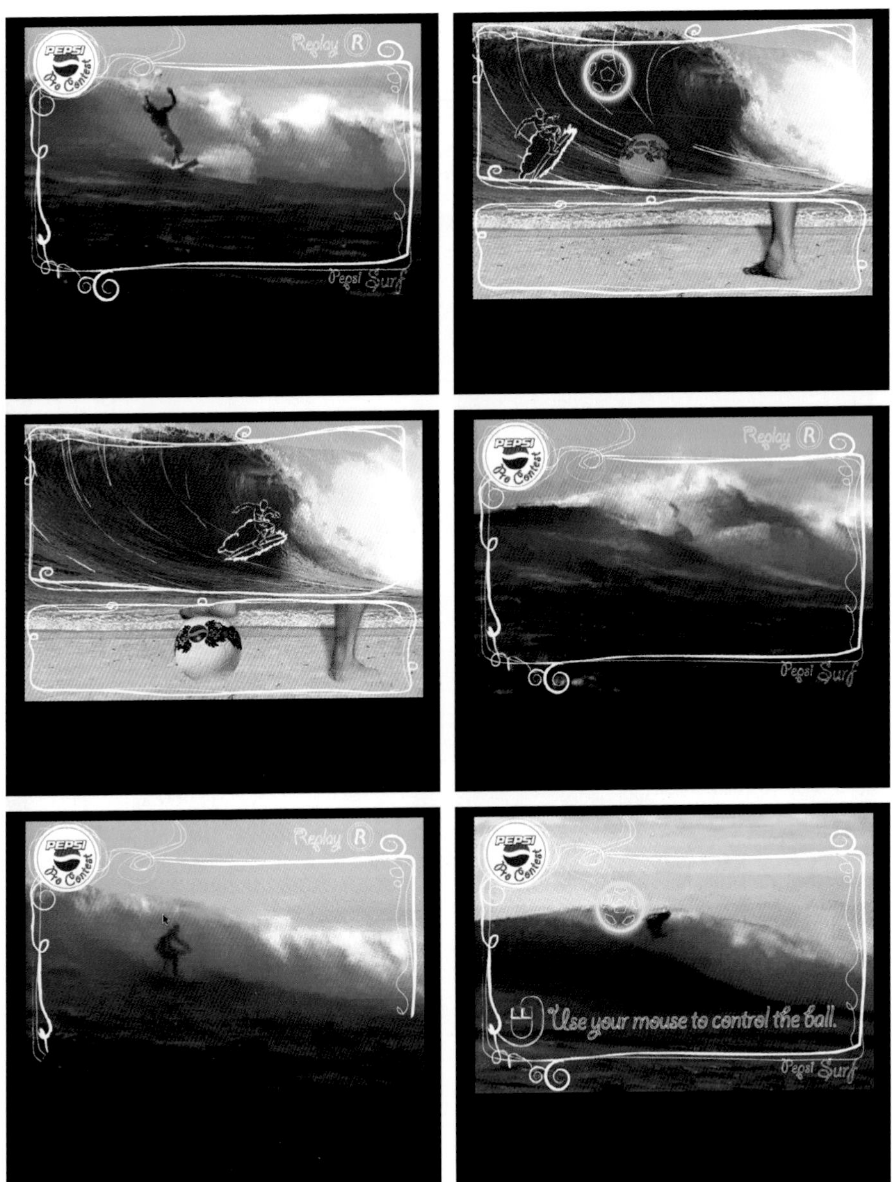

Results

Impact: 2,975,412; Click rate: 4.31%; Interaction rate: 10.29%; Exhibition time: 33". /// Besucher: 2.975.412; Click rate: 4,31%; Interaction rate: 10,29%; Anzeigezeit: 33". /// **Impact : 2 975 412 ; Taux de clics : 4,31 % ; Taux d'interaction : 10,29 % ; Durée d'exposition : 33".**

PEPSI TWISTÃO

BRAZIL

http://200.186.92.250/awards/2007/pepsi/twistao_v1/eng

2005

Concept

In Brazil, Pepsi Lime is called Pepsi Twist: Pepsi with a touch of lemon. To advertise a limited edition of the drink, a mobile game was developed: the *Twistão Operation.* /// Pepsi Lime heißt in Brasilien Pepsi Twist: Pepsi mit einem Hauch Limone. Als Werbung für eine limitierte Ausgabe des Getränks wurde ein Handyspiel entwickelt: die *Twistão Operation.* /// Au Brésil, Pepsi Lime s'appelle Pepsi Twist : du Pepsi avec une touche de citron. Pour promouvoir une édition limitée de la boisson, un jeu pour portable a été créé : le *Twistão Operation.*

Info

Design: AlmapBBDO <www.almapbbdo.com.br>, Sergio Mugnaini (Creative/Art Director), Luciana Haguiara (Copywriter). /// **Programming:** Microways. /// **Tools:** Adobe Photoshop, Javascript. /// **Awards:** El Ojo Iberoamerica (Silver), CCSP (Bronze), FIAP (Bronze). /// **Cost:** US$15,000.

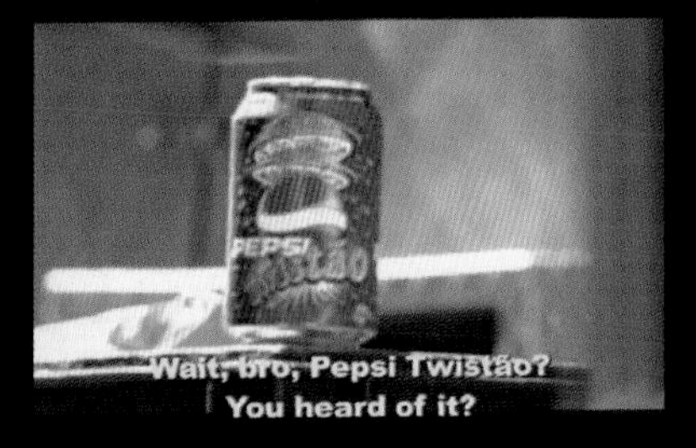

Results

50,000 people downloaded the mobile game from the website (3 months) for free. /// 50.000 Menschen luden das kostenlose Handyspiel innerhalb von 3 Monaten von der Website herunter. /// 50 000 personnes ont téléchargé gratuitement le jeu pour portable du site Web (3 mois).

PHARRELL

www.pharrell.co.za

SOUTH AFRICA

2007

Concept

To promote the release of Pharrell's new album, Prezence developed a promotional viral competition site where users could create and customise their own Pharrell character and send it on to their friends in order to win prizes. /// Um Pharrells neues Album zu bewerben, entwarf Prezence eine virale Wettbewerbs-Site, auf der Benutzer ihre eigene Pharrell-Figur gestalten und sie an Freunde verschicken konnten, um Preise zu gewinnen. /// Pour faire la promotion du lancement du nouvel album de Pharrell, Prezence a développé un site de compétition viral dans lequel les utilisateurs peuvent créer et personnaliser leur propre personnage Pharrell et l'envoyer à leurs amis pour gagner des prix.

Info

DESIGN: Prezence <www.prezence.co.za>, Wesley Reyneke. /// PROGRAMMING: Wesley Reyneke (Action Scripting). /// TOOLS: Adobe Photoshop, Flash, XML, PHP. /// COST: 40 hours.

Select a category below to customise your character. Click on "SEND IT" when you're done.

SHIRTS
PANTS
SHOES
ACCESSORIES
HAIR
SKIN / FACE

SEND IT

PHARRELL
IN MY MIND

Select a category below to customise your character. Click on "SEND IT" when you're done.

SHIRTS
PANTS
SHOES
ACCESSORIES
HAIR
SKIN / FACE

SEND IT

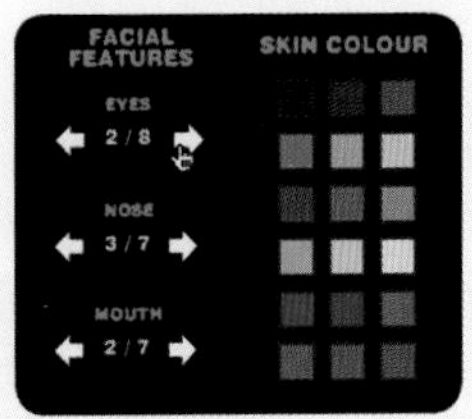

PORSCHE BLOODLINES

USA

www.porsche.com/all/bloodlines/usa

2008

Concept

On this site you can rev up the engines of the various models of Porsche and feel the sound they make. Moreover you can even download some as MP3 files or as ringtones for your mobile. /// Auf dieser Site können Benutzer die Motoren verschiedener Porschemodelle hochjagen und sich an den Geräuschen erfreuen. Einige lassen sich sogar als MP3-Dateien oder Handyklingeltöne herunterladen. /// Sur ce site, vous pouvez faire tourner le moteur de différents modèles de Porsche et en écouter le bruit. Vous pouvez même en télécharger certains comme fichiers MP3 ou sonneries pour votre portable.

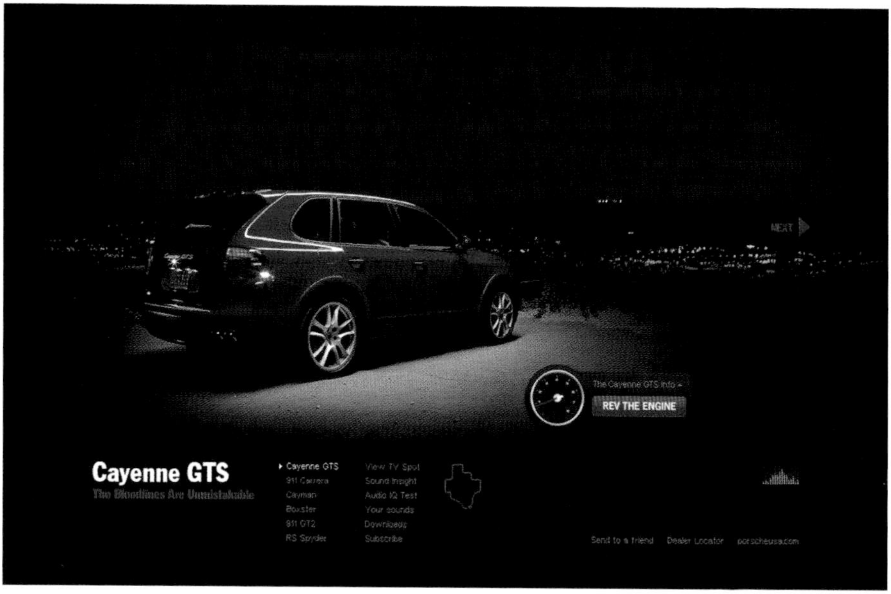

Info

Design: Fantasy Interactive <www.F--i.com>, Marcus Ivarsson (Executive Producer), Anton Repponen, Krister Karlsson. /// **Programming:** Bartek Drozdz, Simon Cave, Robert Pohl. /// **Tools:** Adobe Photoshop, Flash, After Effects, Maya. /// **Awards:** FWA (Site of the Day).

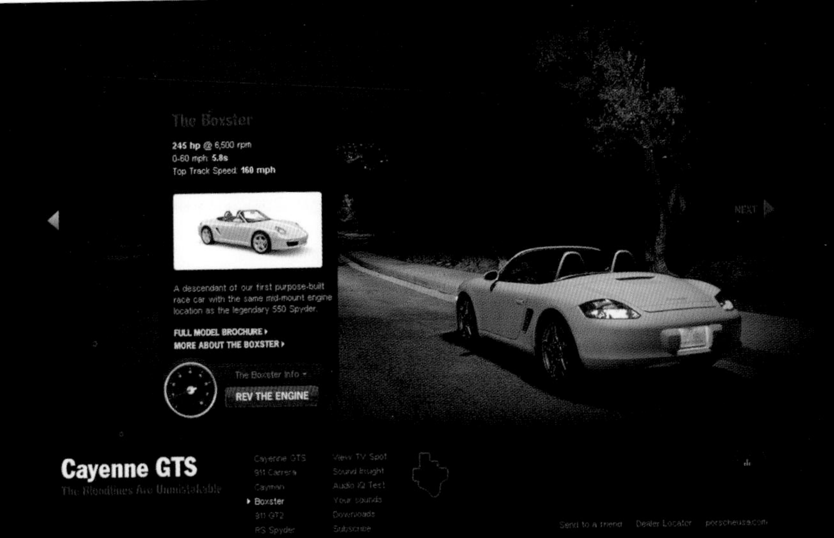

The Boxster
245 hp @ 6,500 rpm
0-60 mph 5.8s
Top Track Speed 160 mph
A descendant of our first purpose-built race car with the same mid-mount engine location as the legendary 550 Spyder.
FULL MODEL BROCHURE
MORE ABOUT THE BOXSTER
The Boxster Info
REV THE ENGINE
NEXT
Cayenne GTS
The Bloodlines Are Unmistakable
Cayenne GTS
911 Carrera
Cayman
Boxster
911 GT2
RS Spyder
View TV Spot
Sound Insight
Audio IQ Test
Your sounds
Downloads
Subscribe
Send to a friend
Dealer Locator
porscheusa.com

RS Spyder
Subscribe
911 GT2
Boxster
Downloads
Your Sounds
Audio IQ
911 Carrera
Sound Insight
TV Spot
Cayenne GTS
NEXT
Cayenne GTS
The Bloodlines Are Unmistakable
Cayenne GTS
911 Carrera
Cayman
Boxster
911 GT2
RS Spyder
View TV Spot
Sound Insight
Audio IQ Test
Your sounds
Downloads
Subscribe
Send to a friend
Dealer Locator
porscheusa.com

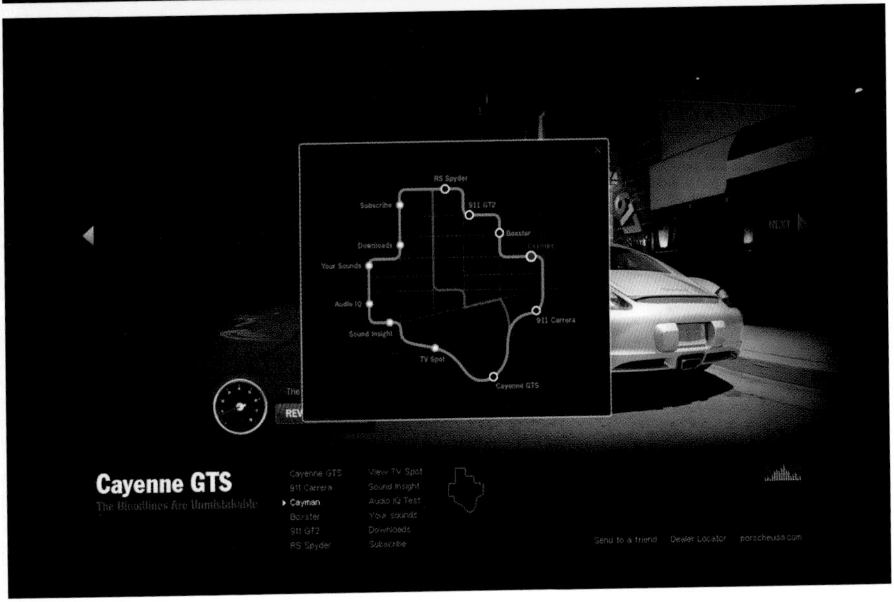

REVERZE

BELGIUM/NETHERLANDS

www.reverze.be/taschen.html

2007

Concept

Reverze is an annual dance event at the Antwerp Sportspalace. Here it is completely submerged in the mysterious concept of alien visitors that have crashed on earth. Easy to use point-and-click navigation is raised to a cinematic level. /// *Reverze* ist eine alljährlich im Antwerpener Sportpalast stattfindende Tanzveranstaltung. Hier wird sie in ein mysteriöses Konzept um Außerirdische, die auf der Erde gelandet sind, eingebettet. Die einfache Zeige-und-Klick-Navigation erreicht Kinoqualität. /// *Reverze* est un événement de danse annuel qui se tient au palais des sports d'Anvers. Le participant est totalement submergé dans le mystère d'extraterrestres qui ont atterri sur Terre. Une navigation simple d'emploi par clics est de qualité cinématographique.

Info

Design: THEPHARMACY <www.thepharmacymedia.com>, B. Driessen, W. van der Krieken, E. Szigetti. /// **Programming:** B. Driessen, J. Kessels. /// **Tools:** Adobe Photoshop, Flash, Lightwave 3D, PHP, MySQL, XML. /// **Cost:** 180 hours. /// **Client:** Bass Events.

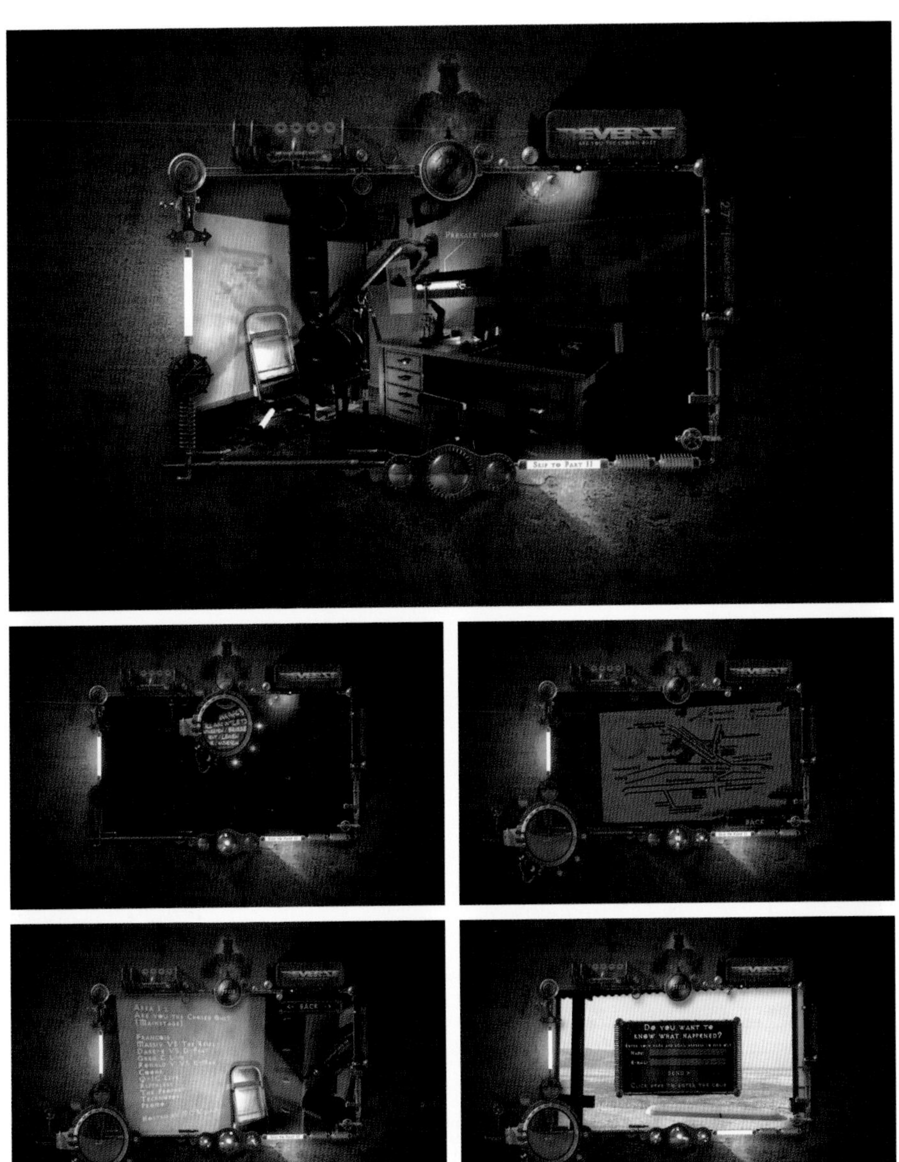

Results

The event sold out in the first week after the launch of the site. /// Die Veranstaltung war eine Woche nach Start der Website ausverkauft. /// L'événement a affiché complet la première semaine après le lancement du site.

RUBB-IT FOR HEALTHY EYES!

SINGAPORE

www.amo-eyecare-sea.com/rubbit

2008

Concept

Help our contact lens wearing froggy to catch dinner by rubbing its way to healthy eyesight. The game is an effort by Advanced Medical Optics to promote clean and comfortable lens wearing by rubbing your contacts. /// Hilf unserem Kontaktlinsen tragenden Frosch, sein Essen zu fangen, indem er sich durch Rubbeln einen klaren Blick verschafft. Mit diesem Spiel will Advanced Medical Optics für das Rubbeln der Kontaktlinsen werben, die dadurch sauber werden und gut sitzen. /// Aide notre grenouille à obtenir à manger en nettoyant correctement ses lentilles pour mieux voir. Le jeu est une initiative d'Advanced Medical Optics pour encourager le port confortable de lentilles propres grâce à un bon nettoyage.

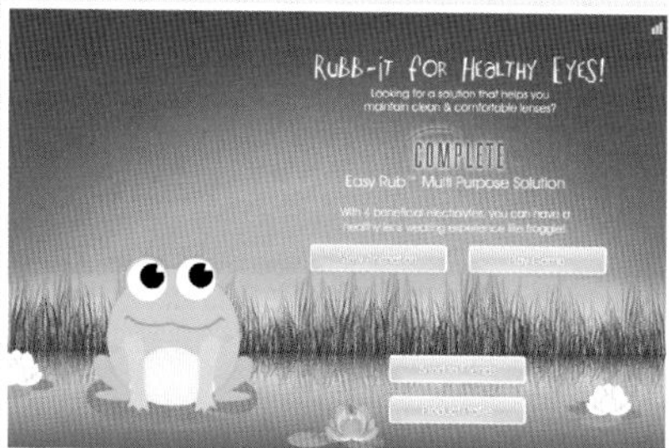

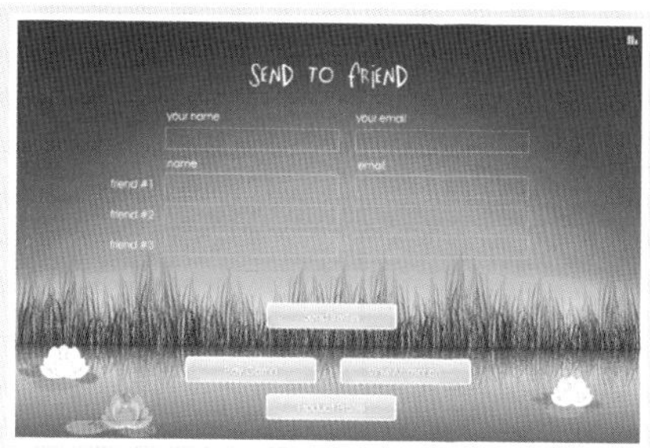

Info

Design: AvantGarden <www.avantgarden.com.sg>, Chris Lim, Chen Yao Ming. /// **Programming:** Chen Yao Ming. /// **Tools:** Adobe Photoshop, Flash, Dreamweaver. /// **Cost:** 30 hours.

STARBUCKS TIME

TURKEY
2007

Concept

Starbucks Time is a downloadable application for PC, which users set up on their computers. It activates itself when the computer is idle, shows the time on the screen and, depending on time of the day, recommends a Starbucks drink. /// Starbucks Time ist eine herunterladbare PC-Anwendung, die sich von selbst aktiviert, sobald der Computer inaktiv ist. Sie zeigt die Uhrzeit an und empfiehlt passend zur Tageszeit ein Starbucks-Getränk. /// **Starbucks Time est une application téléchargeable pour PC que les utilisateurs configurent sur leur ordinateur. Elle s'active lorsque l'ordinateur est en veille, affiche l'heure à l'écran et, selon le moment de la journée, recommande une boisson Starbucks.**

Info

Design: 2FRESH <www.2fresh.com>. /// **Programming:** 2FRESH. /// **Tools:** Adobe Photoshop, Flash. /// **Cost:** 25 hours.

SAAB PILOTS WANTED

INTERNATIONAL

www.saab.com/microsites/pilotswanted/GLOBAL/en/index2.shtml 2006

Concept

Here, the user is allowed to feel the car, engage in manouvers and see all the driving from different angles. /// Hier wird dem Benutzer ein Gefühl für das Auto vermittelt. Er kann Fahrmanöver nachvollziehen und die Fahrt aus verschiedenen Blickwinkeln erleben. /// Ici, l'utilisateur peut sentir la voiture, participer aux manœuvres et voir les déplacements depuis différents angles.

Info

Design: Perfect Fools <www.perfectfools.com>, Perfect Fools: Tony Högqvist (Creative Director); Lowe Brindfors: Niklas Wallberg (Creative Director), Tim Sheibel, Johan Tesch (Art Directors), Michael Fox (Head of Art), Alex Kerber (Assistent), Mårten Ivert (Director). /// **Programming:** Perfect Fools: Björn Kummeneje (Technical Director). /// **Tools:** Adobe Photoshop, Flash, After Effects. /// **Awards:** Cannes Cyber Lion (Bronze), NY Festivals (Silver), Eurobest (Bronze), Clio Awards (Shortlist). /// **Others:** Stefan Dufgran, Fredrik Heghammar (Producer Perfect Fools); Johanna Hibbs, Linda Karlsson, Espen Bekkebråten, Patrick O'Neill (Lowe Brindfors).

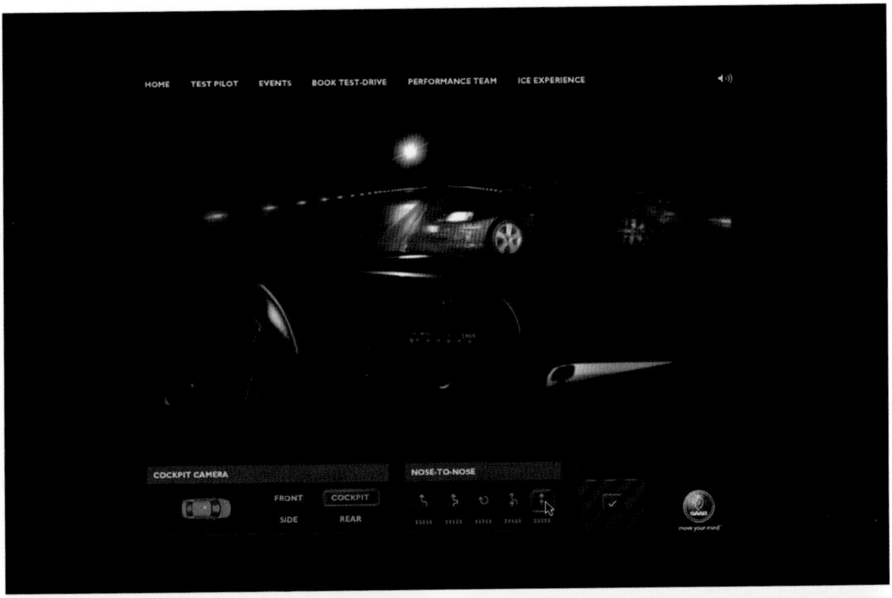

HOME
TEST PILOT
EVENTS
BOOK TEST-DRIVE
PERFORMANCE TEAM
ICE EXPERIENCE
COCKPIT CAMERA
FRONT
COCKPIT
SIDE
REAR
NOSE-TO-NOSE
SAAB
move your mind

XTX 918
Test-flight complete
DRIVE AGAIN
WATCH YOUR DRIVE

SABRINA SETLUR – ROT.FM

GERMANY

www.neue-digitale.de/projects/sabrinasetlur_2007

2007

Concept

Sabrina Setlur is a leading German hip-hop artist. For her new album *Red*, users can discover hidden song titles by sliding their cursor and exploring the online environment. /// Sabrina Setlur ist eine bekannte deutsche Hip-Hop-Künstlerin. Zu ihrem neuen Album *Red* können Benutzer versteckte Songtitel entdecken, indem sie mit dem Cursor das Online-Szenarium erkunden. /// Sabrina Setlur est une grande artiste allemande de hip hop. Pour son nouvel album *Red*, les utilisateurs peuvent découvrir des titres cachés en déplaçant le curseur et en explorant l'environnement en ligne.

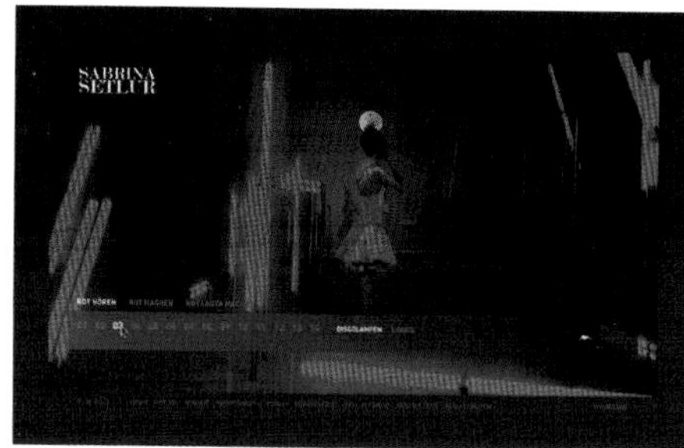

Info

Design: Neue Digitale <www.neue-digitale.de>, Olaf Czeschner, Nico Schwenke. /// **Programming:** Christoph Fischer, Heiko Schweickhardt. /// **Tools:** Adobe Photoshop, Flash, After Effects. /// **Others:** Norman Rockmann (Account Manager).

SABRINA SETLUR
HÖR DIR DIE ONLINE-VERSION VON "DAS LEBEN IN ROT" AN UND WERDE SELBST TEIL DIESES LIEDES!
SCHLIESSE EIN MIKRO UND/ODER EINE WEBCAM AN. SPRICH, RAPP ODER SINGE AUF DAS INSTRUMENTAL.
ZEIG, WIE ROT DU BIST.

SARAH JANE ADVENTURES

UK

www.thesja.com

2008

Concept

The *Sarah Jane Adventures* required an online campaign site to support the launch of DVDs and other merchandise. The game is an immersive experience that can be shared amongst the site's visitors to generate interest and awareness amongst its target audience. /// *Sarah Jane Adventures* benötigte eine Online-Werbekampagne, um DVDs und andere Merchandizing-Produkte zu unterstützen. Das Spiel bietet ein intensives Erlebnis, das die Besucher der Site miteinander teilen können. /// *Sarah Jane Adventures* a commandé un site de campagne en ligne pour le lancement de DVD et d'autres produits. Le jeu est une expérience immersive que les visiteurs du site peuvent partager pour susciter l'intérêt et sensibiliser le public cible.

Info

Design: Sequence <www.sequence.co.uk>, Mark Johnson, Steven Goldstone, Ben Minton, Jon Sully. /// **Programming:** Mick McNicholas, Steven Goldstone, Jon Sully. /// **Tools:** Adobe Photoshop, Flash, Illustrator, Fireworks, Soundbooth, XML, HTML, CSS+V89. /// **Cost:** £10,000.

Results

Take up amongst the target audience was high with the games being 'forwarded to a friend' far in excess of original expectations. /// Die Website hatte bei der Zielgruppe großen Erfolg. Das Spiel wurde viel öfter als erwartet an Freunde weitergeleitet. /// L'accroche du public cible a été importante car les jeux « envoyés à des amis » ont largement dépasséles attentes initiales.

SKATENIS BIBI

BRAZIL

www.skatenisbibi.com

2007

Concept

The website's objective is to discover what children expected from shoes for kids. To do that, the "Paint your Skatenis" competition was created, where visitors could paint the sneakers the way they liked. /// Ziel der Website war es herauszufinden, was Kinder von ihren Schuhen erwarteten. Dafür wurde der Wettbewerb „Bemale deine Skatenis" erfunden, bei dem Besucher die Turnschuhe beliebig anmalen konnten /// L'objectif du site Web est de découvrir ce que les enfants attendent des chaussures qui leur sont destinées. Pour ce faire a été organisé le concours « Peint ta Skatenis » : les visiteurs pouvaient peindre les baskets comme bon leur semblait.

Info

Design: W3Haus <www.w3haus.com.br>, Chico Baldini, Diego Chiarelli. /// **Programming:** Alessandro Cauduro. /// **Tools:** Adobe Photoshop, Flash, ASP.net, HTML, XML. /// **Cost:** 400 hours. /// **Others:** Karoline Dal Soto (Account Executive), Joseane Janner (Account Executive Assistent).

Based on the drawings that were made by the visitors Bibi, the manufacturer, created two new Skatenis models, which became two of the brand's best selling products. /// Auf der Basis der von den Kindern gemalten Bilder entwarf der Hersteller Bibi zwei neue Skatenis-Modelle, die zwei der erfolgreichsten Produkte der Marke überhaupt wurden. /// En s'inspirant des illustrations des visiteurs, le fabricant Bibi a créé deux modèles de Skatenis qui font partie des meilleures ventes de la marque.

SPOOKS

UK

www.bbc.co.uk/drama/spooks/games/index.shtml

2004

Concept

The player is invited to take part in MI5 live-op simulations, under the watchful eye of department boss, Harry Pearce. The site contains twenty games and a wealth of related content resulting in a particularly immersive experience. /// Der Spieler wird eingeladen, unter den wachsamen Augen von Abteilungschef Harry Pearce an Einsatzsimulationen des Geheimdienstes MI5 teilzunehmen. Die Website bietet mit 20 Spielen und vielen weiteren Informationen eine besonders intensive Erlebniswelt an. /// Le joueur est invité à participer à des simulations en direct du MI5, sous le regard attentif du chef de service Harry Pearce. Le site contient vingt jeux et une grande quantités d'informations relatives pour offrir une expérience particulièrement immersive.

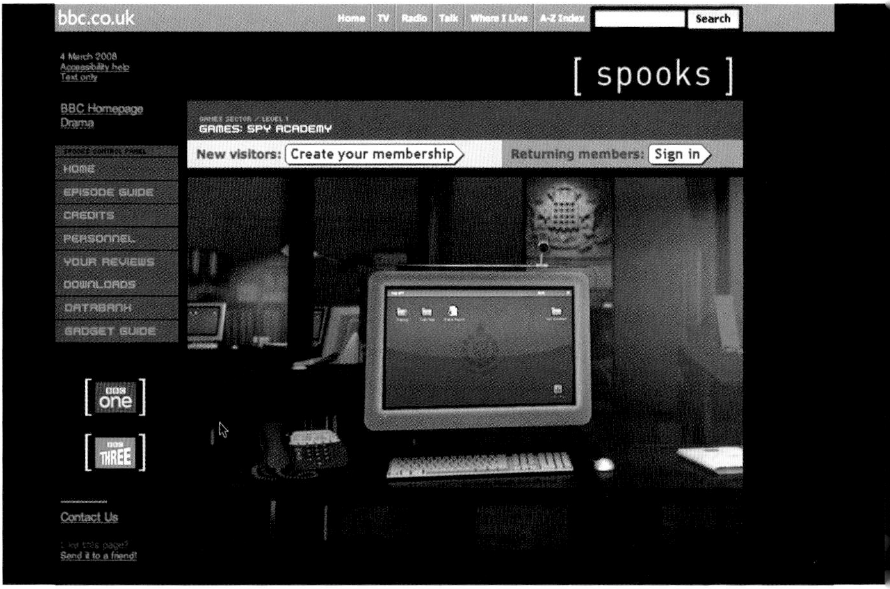

Info

Design: Preloaded <www.preloaded.com>. /// **Programming:** Preloaded. /// **Tools:** Adobe Photoshop, Flash, Maya. /// **Awards:** NMA (Entertainment, Winner), FlashForward (Games, Winnner), London International Awards (Education, Finalist), BIMA (Entertainment, Finalist), SXSW (Amusement, Finalist), D&AD In-Book.

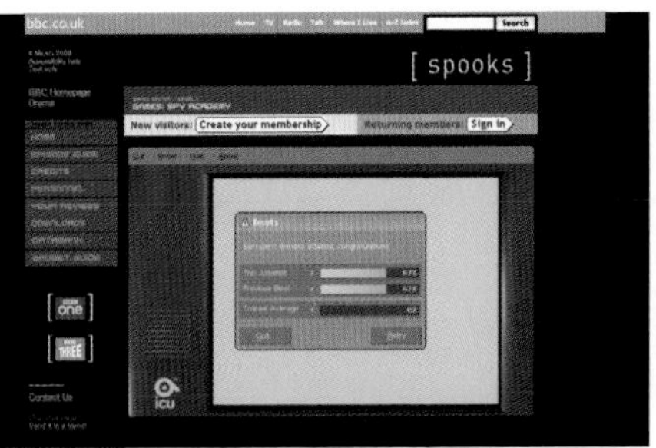

bbc.co.uk
Search
[spooks]
New visitors: Create your membership
Returning members: Sign in

bbc.co.uk
Search
[spooks]
New visitors: Create your membership
Returning members: Sign in

bbc.co.uk
Search
[spooks]
New visitors: Create your membership
Returning members: Sign in

bbc.co.uk
Search
[spooks]
New visitors: Create your membership
Returning members: Sign in
SA-emul8
Training Emulation System

bbc.co.uk
Home
TV
Radio
Talk
Where I Live
A-Z Index
Search
4 March 2008
Accessibility help
Text only
[spooks]
BBC Homepage
Drama
GAMES SECTOR / LEVEL 1
GAMES: SPY ACADEMY
New visitors: Create your membership
Returning members: Sign in
HOME
EPISODE GUIDE
CREDITS
PERSONNEL
YOUR REVIEWS
DOWNLOADS
DATABANK
GADGET GUIDE
Quit
Reset
Help
About
one
THREE
Contact Us
Like this page?
Send it to a friend!

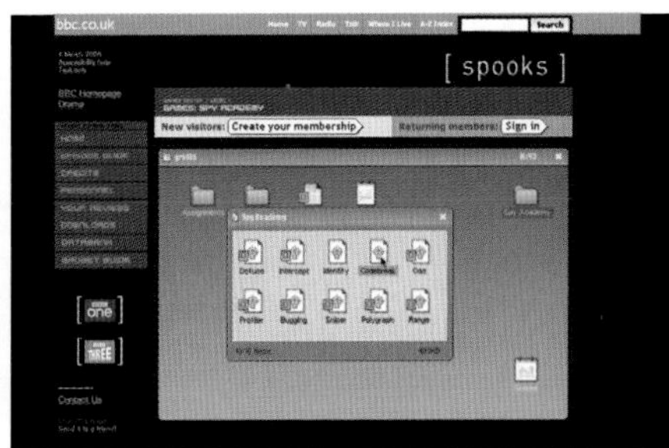

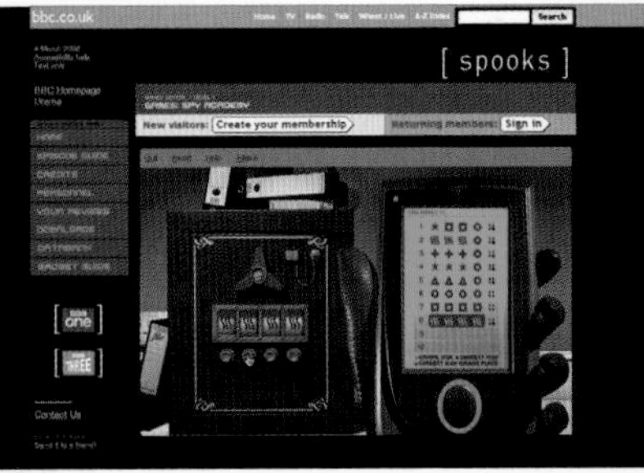

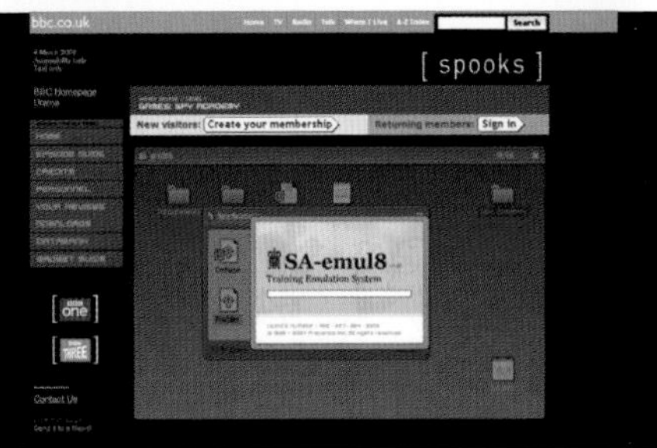

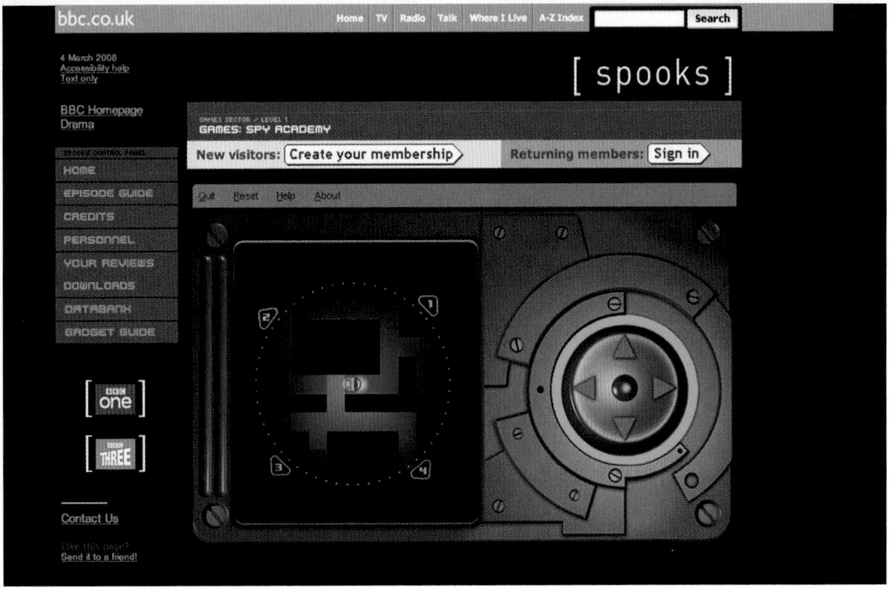

STARBUCKS PASS THE CHEER

INTERNATIONAL

http://starbucks.dev.domanistudios.com/cheerchain_rc1

2007

Concept

To celebrate Christmas, Starbucks presented its interactive online card, where users can customise the characters and "pass the cheer" to other people around the globe. /// Diese interaktive Online-Weihnachtskarte von Starbucks konnten Benutzer nach Wunsch textlich verändern und dann an ihre Lieben versenden. /// Pour fêter Noël, Starbucks a présenté sa carte interactive en ligne, dans laquelle les utilisateurs peuvent personnaliser les personnages et transmettre leur bonne humeur à d'autres personnes dans le monde.

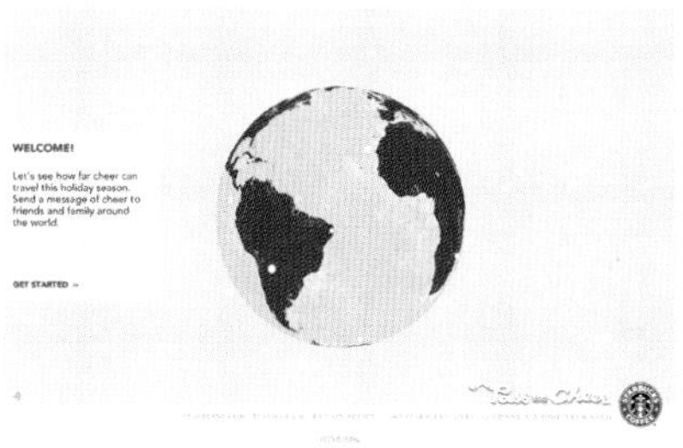

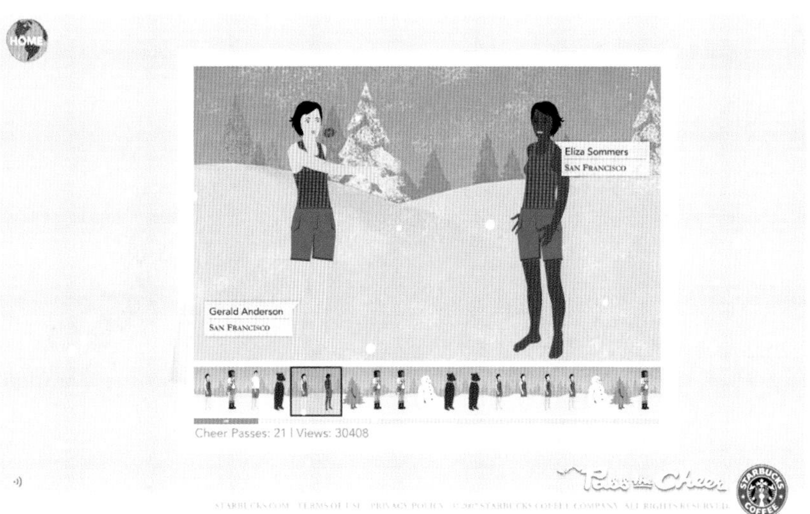

Info

DESIGN: Domani Studios <www.domanistudios.com>, Wieden + Kennedy: JD Hooge, Chean Wei-Law, Matthew Carroll, Jen Nicolazzo. /// **PROGRAMMING:** Domani Studios. /// **TOOLS:** Adobe Photoshop, Flash, Illustrator, Papervision 3D, MySQL, PHP, Dreamweaver. /// **COST:** 3 months. /// **OTHERS:** Bev Davis (Producer).

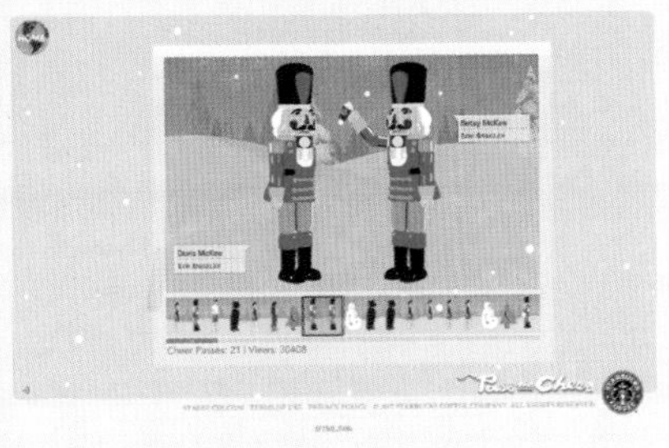

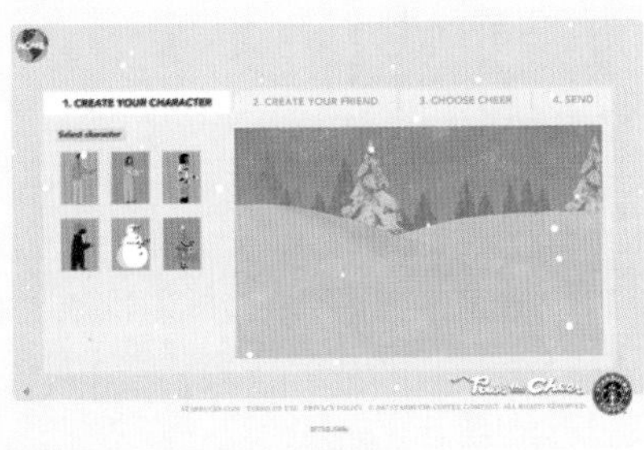

Results

Site retention rate averaged three minutes. /// Die Verweildauer auf der Site betrug durchschnittlich drei Minuten. /// **Taux moyen de rétention du site : 3 minutes.**

TDK WCA CHALLENGE

GERMAN

www.wysiwyg.de/garage/tdk_wca

200

Concept

A jump-and-run game that takes place at an airport gate. The aim is to make it to the gate in time — to qualify for a free trip to the 200 Athletic World Championships in Helsinki, sponsored by TDK. /// Ein Spring- und Rennspiel, das an einem Flughafen-Gate spielt. Ziel ist es, das Gate rechtzeitig zu erreichen. Zu gewinnen gab es eine Reise zu den Leichtathletikweltmeisterschaften 2005 in Helsinki, gesponsort von TDK /// Un jeu de course poursuite qui se déroule dans un aéroport. L'objectif est d'arriver à temps à la porte d'embarquement pour gagner u voyage au championnat du monde d'athlétisme 2005 à Helsinki, sponsorisé par TDK.

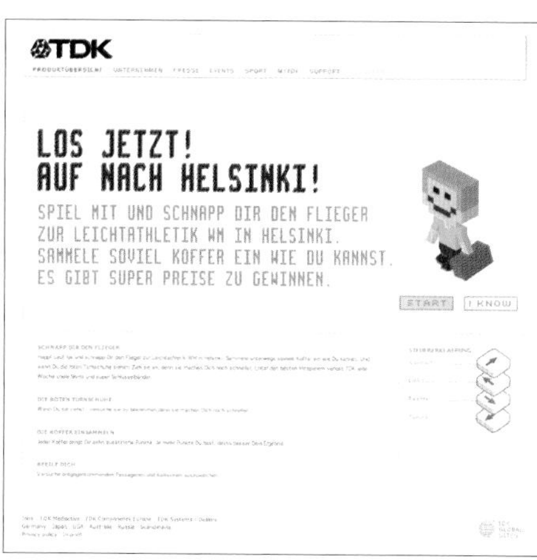

Info

DESIGN: wysiwyg* software design <www.wysiwyg.de>, Alexander Koch, Oliver Heib. /// **PROGRAMMING:** Oliver Michels. /// **TOOLS:** Flash, Illustrator. /// **OTHERS:** Lars Loik <www.lollekundbollek.de> (Illustration).

TDK
66
04

TDK
COME TO HELSINKI
37
08

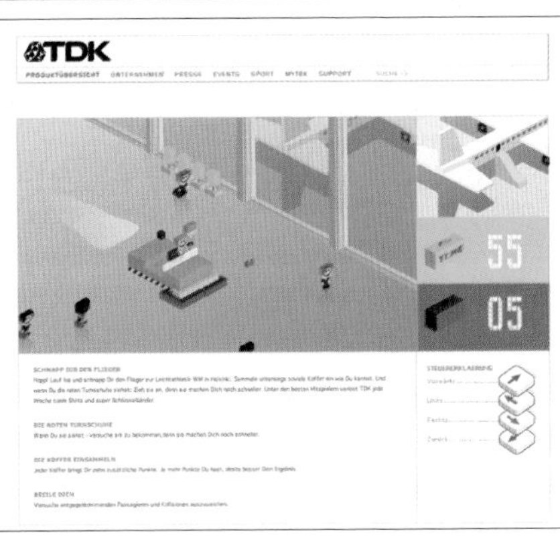
TDK
55
05

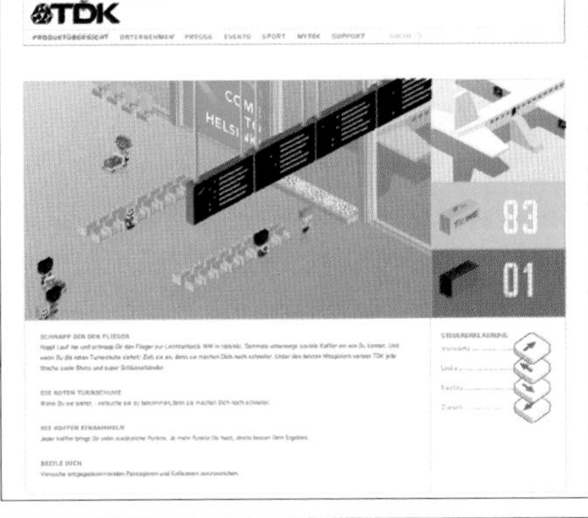
TDK
83
01

TDK
FLIGHT TO HELSINKI
wysiwyg*
****
30500
REGISTER
SEND SCORE

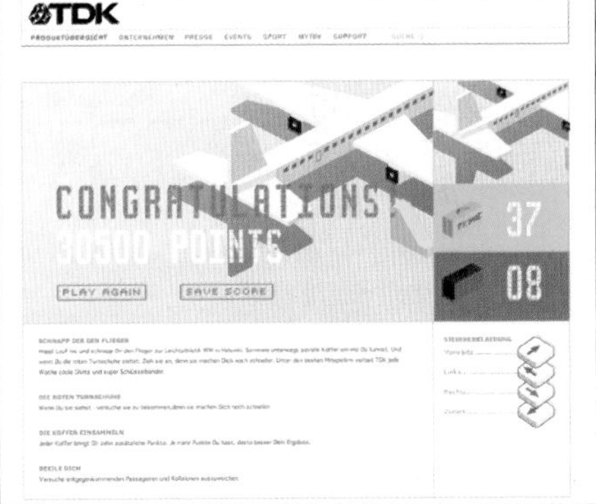
TDK
CONGRATULATIONS!
30500 POINTS
PLAY AGAIN
SAVE SCORE
37
08

THE COKE ZERO GAME

GERMANY

www.cokezerogame.de

2008

Concept

The website features a densely produced game for the beverage, packed with video and graphics. With a high degree of customisation, this car racing game features Hollywood-like special effects in all its stages. /// Dieses aufwendig produzierte Spiel ist vollgepackt mit Videos und Grafiken. Das Autorennen lässt viele individuelle Anpassungen zu und bietet durchgängig Special Effects à la Hollywood. /// Le site Web contient un jeu sophistiqué pour la boisson, avec des vidéos et des graphiques. D'un degré élevé de personnalisation, cette course de voitures présente des effets spéciaux dignes d'Hollywood à tous les niveaux.

Info

Design: North Kingdom <www.northkingdom.com>, Robert Lindström, Kenny Lindström. /// **Programming:** Klas Kroon, Mikael Forsgren. /// **Tools:** Adobe Photoshop, Flash, Illustrator, 3ds Max, Maya. /// **Others:** Jessica Nordlund, Roger Stighäll, Daniel Wallström, Lucian Trofin, Mathias Lindgren, Tomas Westermark, Johan Forslund, Patrik Berglund, Anton Eriksson, Ted Kjellson, David Eriksson.

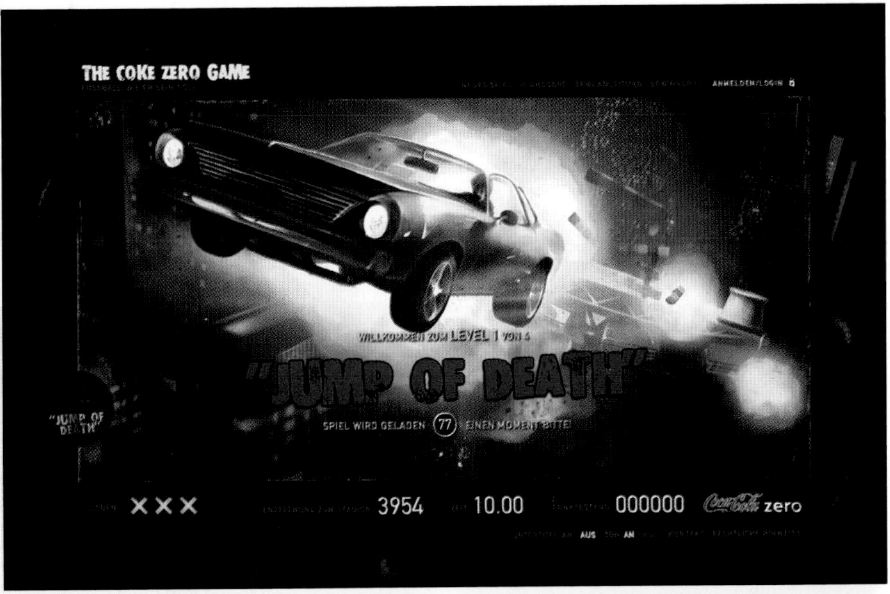

THE COKE ZERO GAME

ANMELDEN/LOGIN

WILLKOMMEN ZUM LEVEL 1 VON 4

"JUMP OF DEATH"

SPIEL WIRD GELADEN 77 EINEN MOMENT BITTE!

"JUMP OF DEATH"

XXX 3954 10.00 000000 Coca-Cola zero

AUS AN

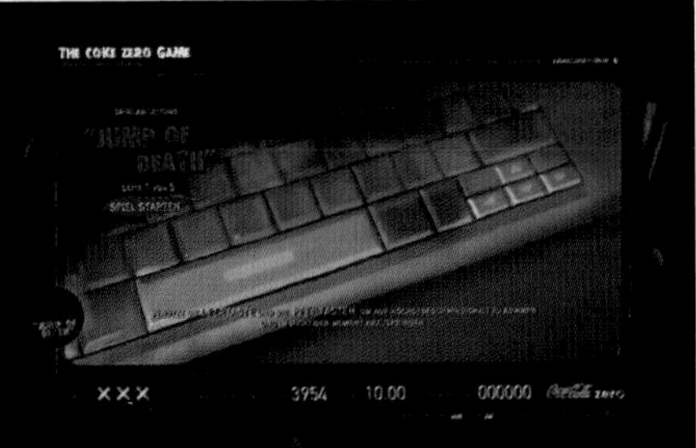

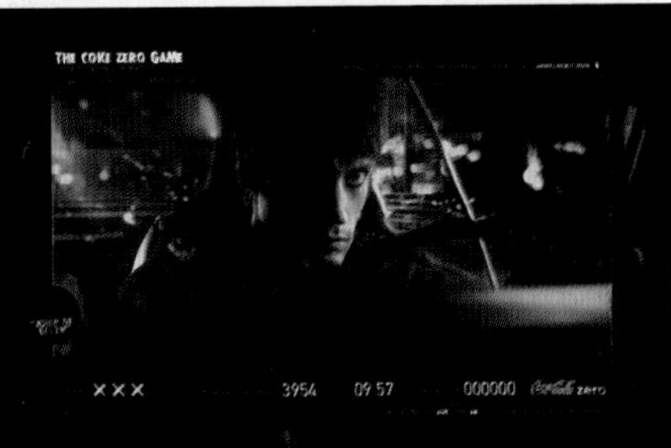

THE GRUDGE 2

NETHERLANDS

www.thegrudge2.nl

2007

Concept

Promotional site and game for the DVD movie release of *The Grudge 2*. If you escape from "the grudge" by running through the remodelled 3D scenes of the hospital in the movie, you receive a real life call on your phone! /// Promotion-Website mit Spiel zum Erscheinen der DVD von *The Grudge 2*. Spielern, denen es gelang, durch die 3D-Krankenhausszenerie des Films zu rennen und dabei dem „Grudge" zu entkommen, erhielten einen echten Telefonanruf! /// Site promotionnel et jeu pour la sortie du film *The Grudge 2* en DVD. Si vous vous échappez en courant dans les scènes 3D remodelées de l'hôpital dans le film, vous recevez un véritable appel sur votre téléphone !

Info

Design: THEPHARMACY <www.thepharmacymedia.com>, E. Szigetti, JW. Reuling, F. Litjens. /// **Programming:** JW. Reuling, J. Kessels, V. Hornikx. /// **Tools:** Adobe Photoshop, Flash, Lightwave 3D, PHP, MySQL, XML. /// **Cost:** 160 hours. /// **Client:** Dutch FilmWorks.

GAME
THE GRUDGE 2
NU OVERAL TE KOOP

GAME
THE GRUDGE 2
NU OVERAL TE KOOP

THE PIRATES' LAIR

FRANCE

www.lerepairedespirates.com

2008

Concept

An online cartoon-like game on a pirate land with various levels and multiplayer options. /// Ein Piraten-Online-Spiel im Cartoonstil mit verschiedenen Levels und Multiplayer-Optionen. /// Jeu en ligne de type dessin animé sur un territoire pirate, avec différents niveaux et des options pour plusieurs joueurs.

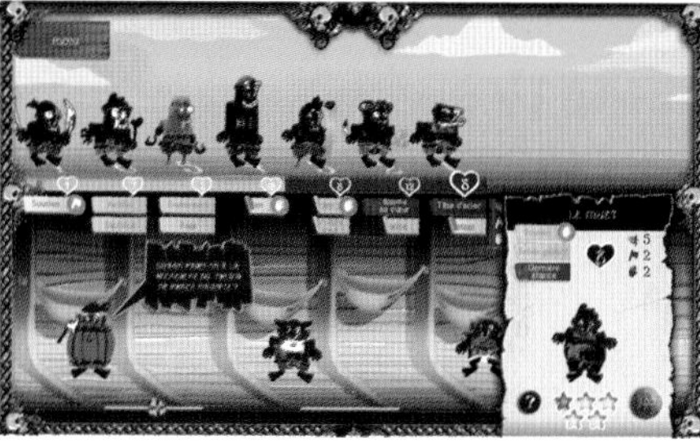

Info

Design: LES CHINOIS <www.leschinois.com>, Ludovic Roudy. /// **Programming:** Julien Bennamias. /// **Tools:** Adobe Photoshop, Flash, Illustrator.

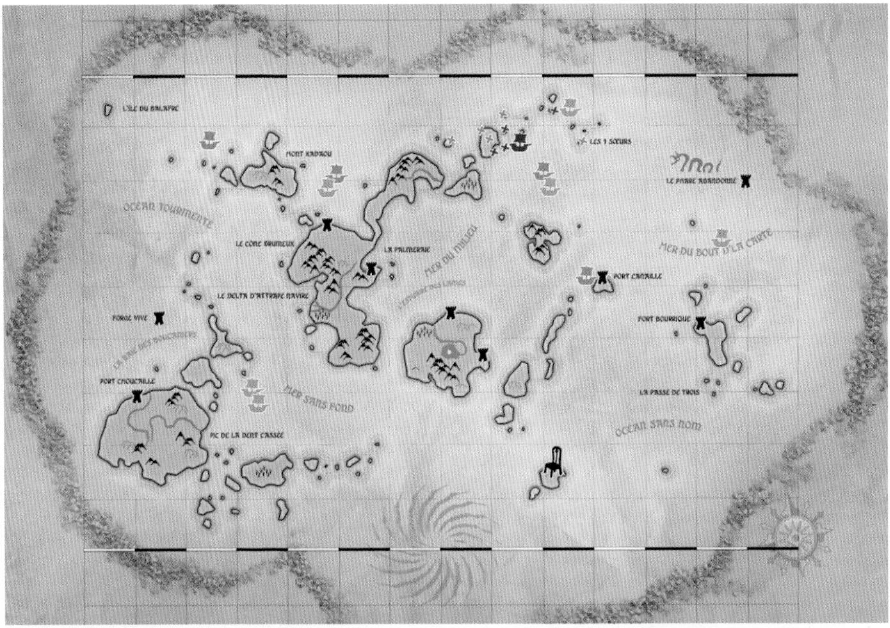
L'ILE DU BALAFRE
MONT KADAOU
OCEAN TOURMENTE
LE CONE BRUMEUX
LA PALMERAIE
MER DU MILIEU
LE DELTA D'ATTRAPE NAVIRE
FORGE VIVE
PORT CHOUCAILLE
MER SANS FOND
PIC DE LA DENT CASSÉE
LE PHARE ABANDONNE
MER DU BOUT D'LA CARTE
PORT CANAILLE
PORT BOURRIQUE
LA PASSE DE TROIS
OCEAN SANS NOM

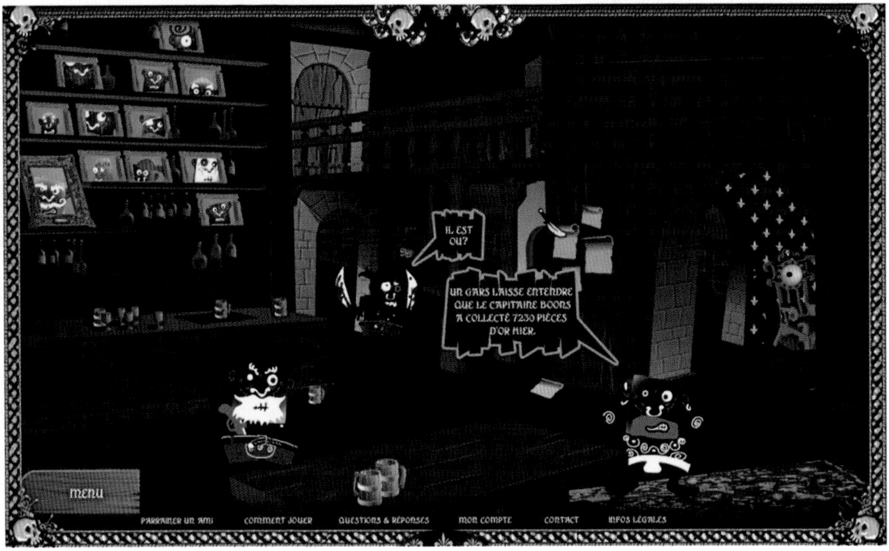
IL EST OU?
UN GARS LAISSE ENTENDRE QUE LE CAPITAINE BOONS A COLLECTÉ 7230 PIÈCES D'OR HIER.
MENU
PARRAINER UN AMI
COMMENT JOUER
QUESTIONS & RÉPONSES
MON COMPTE
CONTACT
INFOS LÉGALES

THYSSEN GLEISTECHNIK

GERMANY

2008

Concept

An online game for multiple users. The aim is to lay as many railroad tracks to a small planet as the terrain and opponents let you. Picking up material and goodies prolongs time and adds points. This was a special terminal setup for Ideenpark 2008. /// Ein Online-Spiel für mehrere Spieler. Ziel ist es, so viele Zuggleise auf einem kleinen Planeten zu verlegen, wie Gelände und Gegner es erlauben. Material und Zusätze einzusammeln kostet Zeit, gibt aber Punkte. Das Spiel wurde auf dem Ideenpark 2008 an speziellen Terminals installiert. /// Jeu en ligne pour plusieurs joueurs. L'objectif est d'installer autant de lignes de chemin de fer sur une petite planète que le terrain et les opposants le permettent. En sélectionnant le matériel et des goodies, le joueur fait durer le jeu et gagne des points. Il s'agissait d'une création spéciale pour Ideenpark 2008.

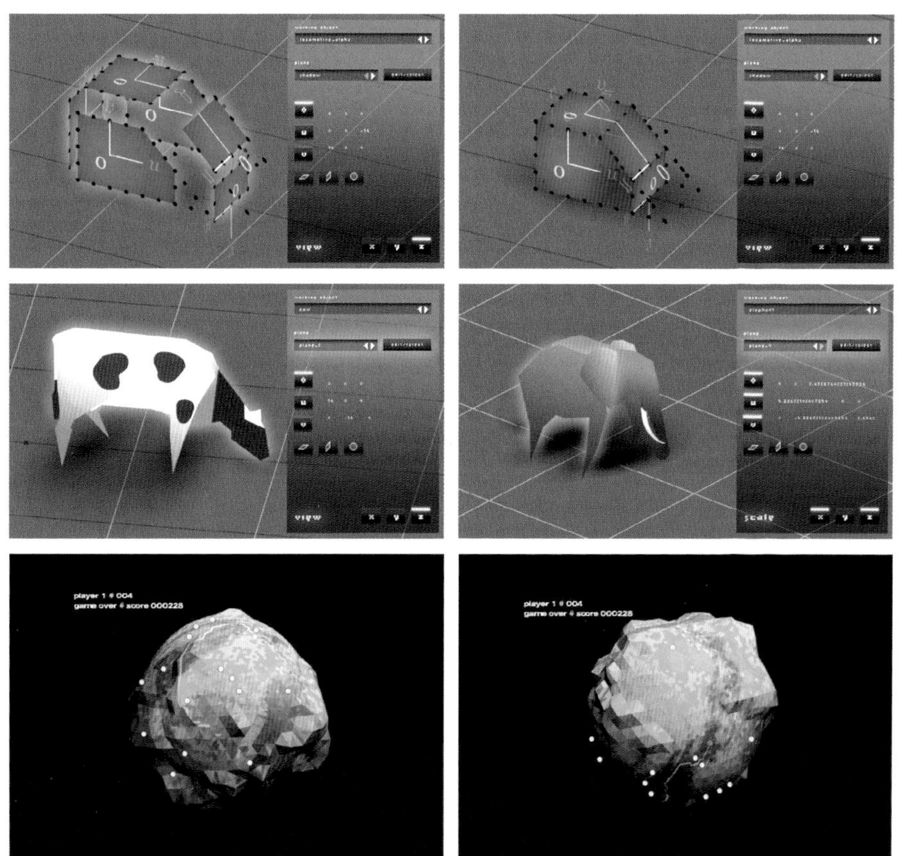

Info

Design: wysiwyg* software design <www.wysiwyg.de>, Pattrick Kreutzer, Florian Breiter. /// **Programming:** Pattrick Kreutzer. /// **Tools:** Flash, Java.

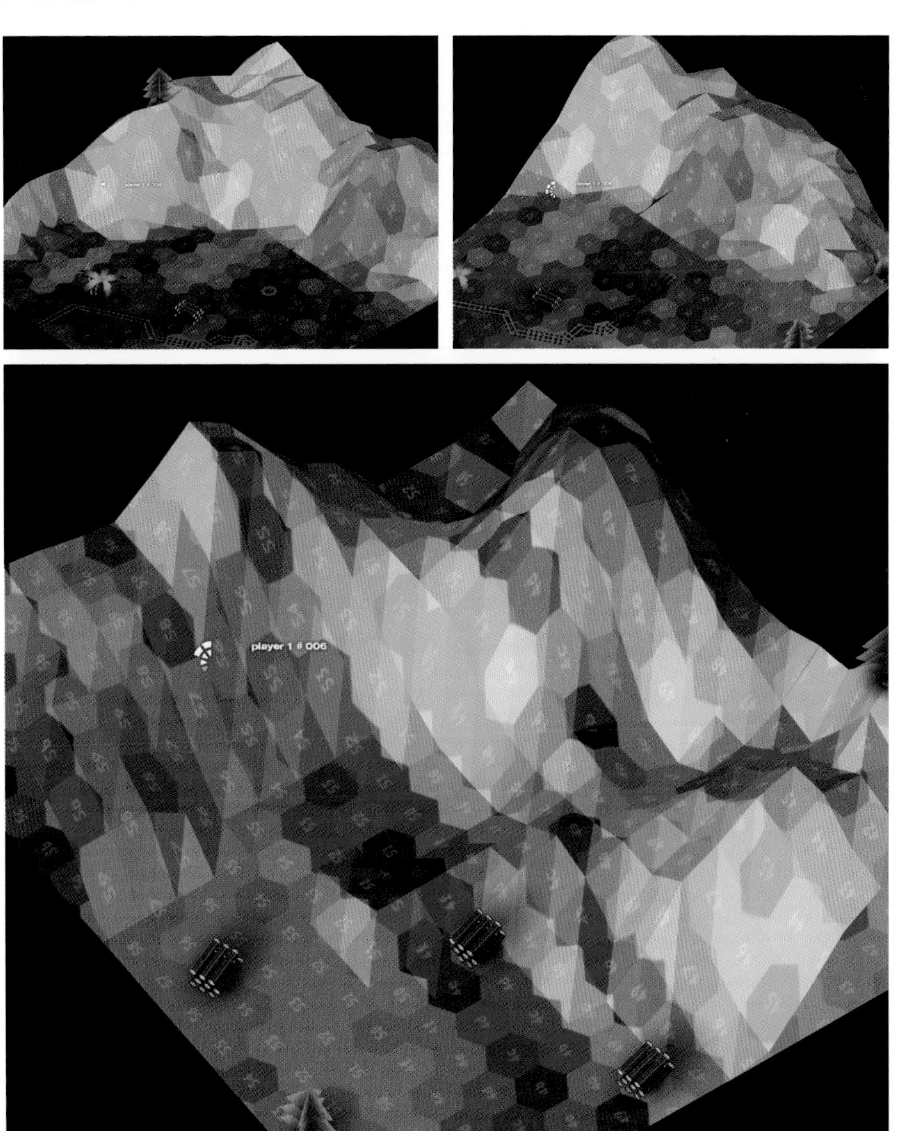
player 1 # 006

TORONTO TOURISM

CANADA

http://velocitystudio.com/tourism_toronto/toronto_tourism_flash.html

2007

Concept

Velocity was chosen to execute on the design and branding provided by Arc Worldwide, developing all interactive areas of the microsite, including a custom built and dynamic parallax navigation and intuitive shopping map. /// Velocity sollte, basierend auf Marke und Design von Arc Worldwide, alle interaktiven Bereiche der Microsite entwickeln, inklusive einer maßgeschneiderten dynamischen Parallaxen-Navigation und eines intuitiven Shoppingplans. /// Le studio Velocity a été choisi pour le design et la marque créés par Arc Worldwide, à l'origine de tous les aspects interactifs du mini-site, dont une navigation différentielle dynamique et personnalisée et une structure d'achats intuitive.

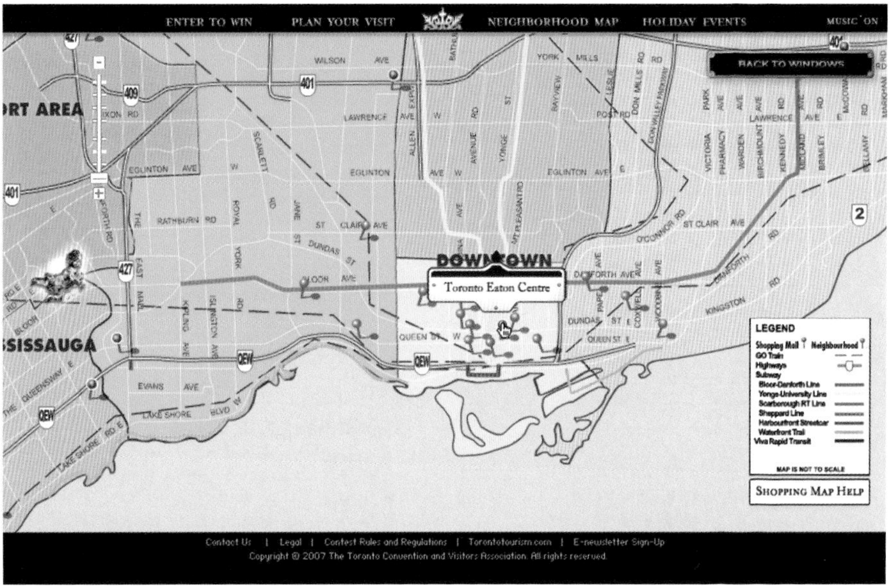

Info

Design: Velocity Studio & Associates <www.velocitystudio.com>, Ian Kay (Creative Group Head Arc Worldwide). /// **Programming:** Jonathan Coe, Alexander Davis. /// **Tools:** Flash.

ENTER TO WIN
PLAN YOUR VISIT
NEIGHBORHOOD MAP
HOLIDAY EVENTS
MUSIC ON
BACK TO WINDOWS

ENTER TO WIN
PLAN YOUR VISIT
NEIGHBORHOOD MAP
HOLIDAY EVENTS
MUSIC ON
WIN A HOLIDAY SHOPPING SPREE
gabba
BACK TO WINDOWS

ENTER TO WIN
PLAN YOUR VISIT
NEIGHBORHOOD MAP
HOLIDAY EVENTS
MUSIC ON

ENTER TO WIN
PLAN YOUR VISIT
NEIGHBORHOOD MAP
HOLIDAY EVENTS
MUSIC ON
LG

ENTER TO WIN
PLAN YOUR VISIT
NEIGHBORHOOD MAP
HOLIDAY EVENTS
MUSIC ON
WIN A HOLIDAY SHOPPING SPREE
LG
BACK TO WINDOWS

ENTER TO WIN
PLAN YOUR VISIT
NEIGHBORHOOD MAP
HOLIDAY EVENTS
MUSIC ON
PLAN YOUR VISIT
close X
Holiday Packages
Get great savings on your visit with Toronto Holiday Packages! Save big with Shop'n'Stay, Rest & Relax and fabulous Family Packages.
Click here for more
FPO
Hotel Breakfast'n'Bed
Hotel Breakfast'n'Bed packages starting at $89 / night! Stay at one of our regional hotels and receive a $25 Petro-Canada Gift Card.
Click here for more
AIR CANADA
Air Canada
Get easy booking, travel rewards and a full range of competitive fare options with Air Canada.
Click here for more
VIA Comfort, VIA Savings
Save 40% on Comfort class tickets straight to downtown Toronto aboard eco-friendly Via Rail.
Click here for more
Call us at 1-800-499-2514 to plan your visit to Toronto! Our Call Centre is ready to help with your travel plans from 10 am to 6 pm, EST, Monday to Friday.
Travel After Christmas
Can't make it during the holidays? Unwind in Toronto afterwards instead. Use up all your gift certificates while taking advantage of great Boxing Week sales!

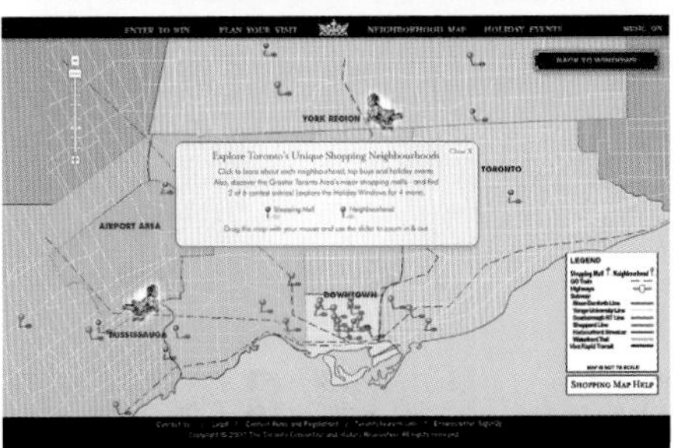
ENTER TO WIN
PLAN YOUR VISIT
NEIGHBORHOOD MAP
HOLIDAY EVENTS
MUSIC ON
BACK TO WINDOWS
YORK REGION
Explore Toronto's Unique Shopping Neighbourhoods
Close X
TORONTO
AIRPORT AREA
DOWNTOWN
MISSISSAUGA
LEGEND
SHOPPING MAP HELP

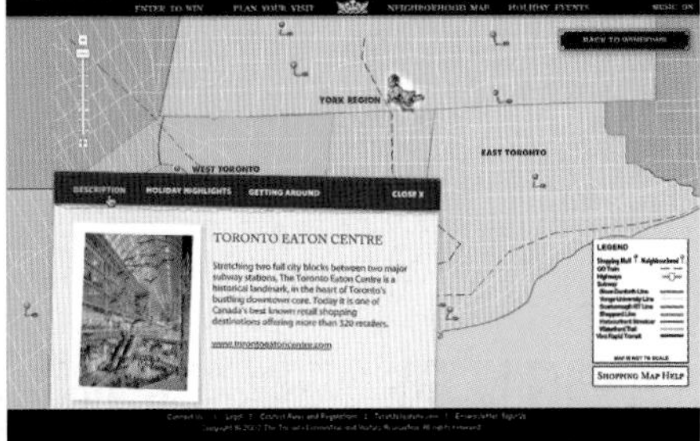
ENTER TO WIN
PLAN YOUR VISIT
NEIGHBORHOOD MAP
HOLIDAY EVENTS
MUSIC ON
BACK TO WINDOWS
YORK REGION
WEST TORONTO
EAST TORONTO
DESCRIPTION
HOLIDAY HIGHLIGHTS
GETTING AROUND
CLOSE X
TORONTO EATON CENTRE
Stretching two full city blocks between two major subway stations, The Toronto Eaton Centre is a historical landmark, in the heart of Toronto's bustling downtown core. Today it is one of Canada's best known retail shopping destinations offering more than 320 retailers.
www.torontoeatoncentre.com
LEGEND
SHOPPING MAP HELP

TRAVEL FINDER

SWEDEN

http://demo.fb.se/e/ving/travelfinder

2007

Concept

The Travel Finder helps you find your perfect trip to almost anywhere. Once you have found your destination, book it online immediately. /// Mit dem Travel Finder finden Sie die perfekte Reiseroute nach fast überall. Sobald Sie sich für ein Ziel entschieden haben, können Sie online direkt buchen. /// Le Travel Finder vous permet d'organiser le voyage parfait presque n'importe où. Une fois la destination choisie, faites immédiatement une réservation en ligne.

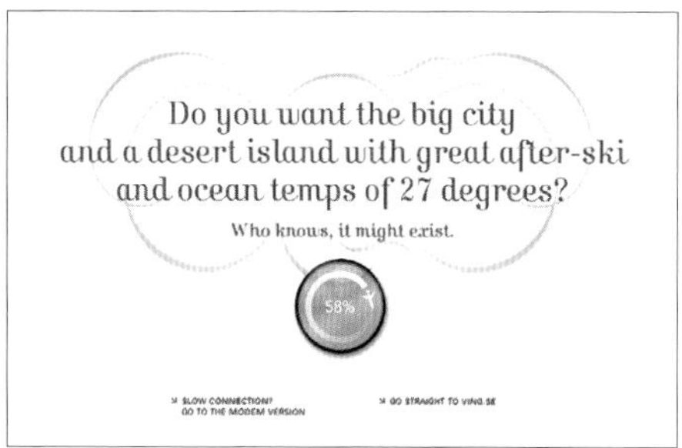

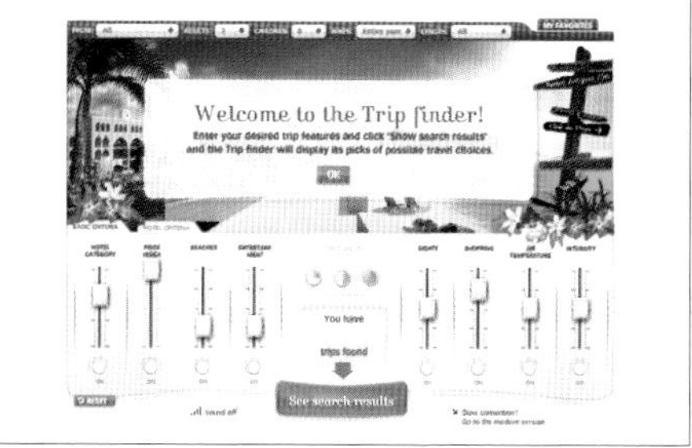

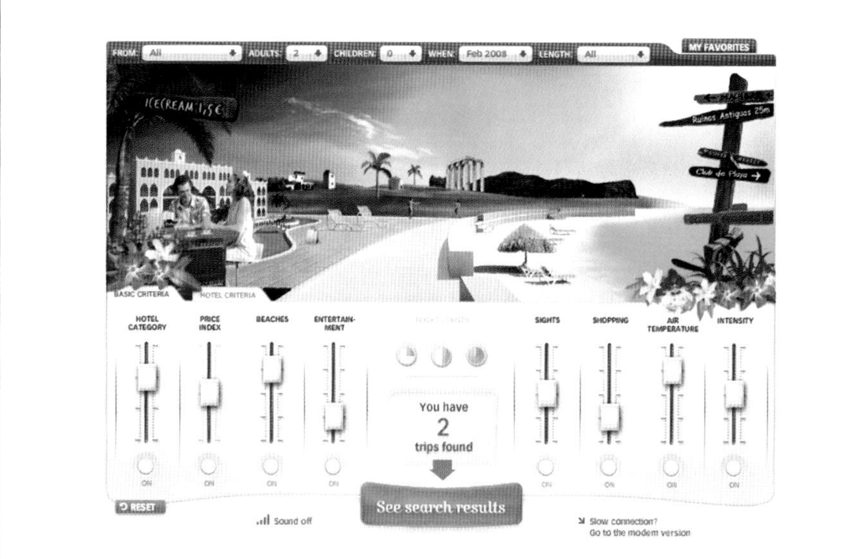

Info

Design: Forsman & Bodenfors <www.fb.se>. /// **Programming:** B-Reel. /// **Tools:** Adobe Photoshop, Flash, Illustrator, 3ds Max, After Effects. /// **Awards:** Eurobest (Finalist), LIA Awards (Finalist).

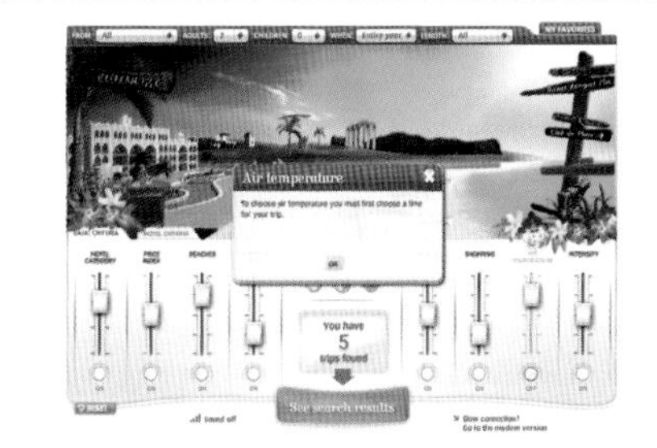

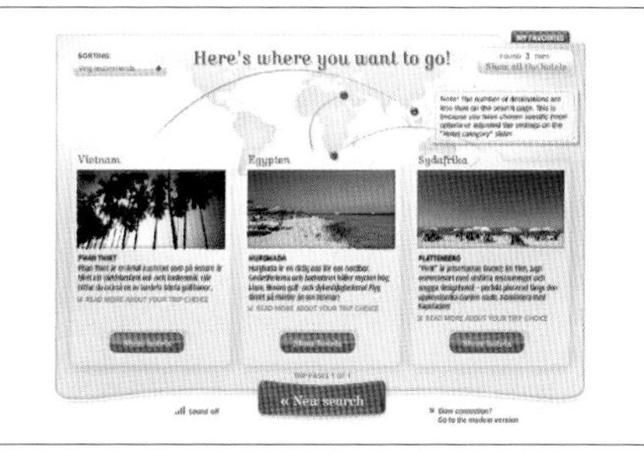
Here's where you want to go!
Vietnam
Egypten
Sydafrika
« New search

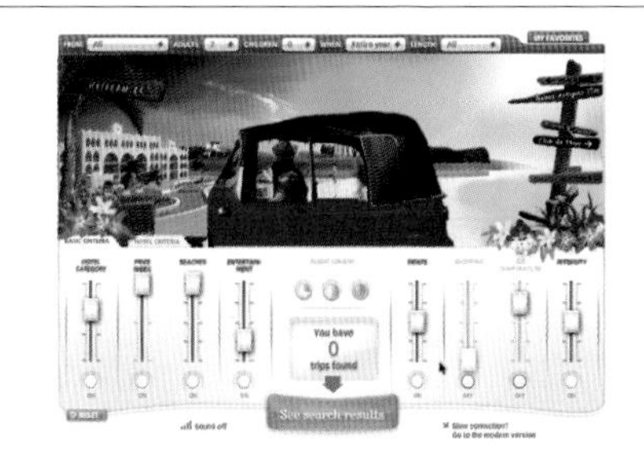

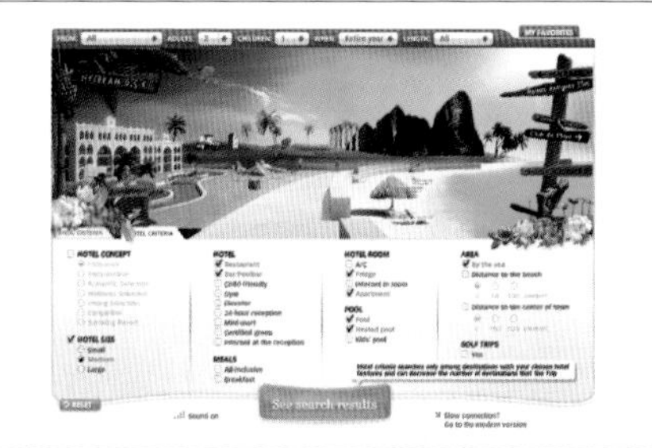

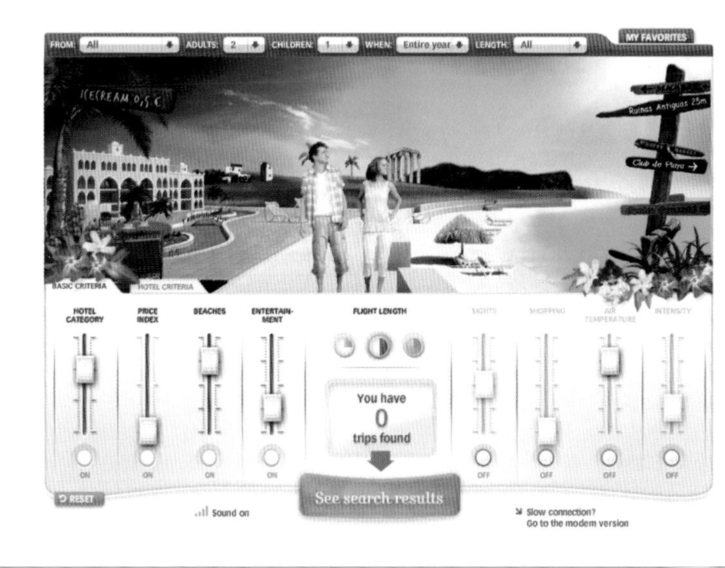
FROM: All
ADULTS: 2
CHILDREN: 1
WHEN: Entire year
LENGTH: All
MY FAVORITES
ICECREAM 0,5 €
Ruinas Antiguas 25m
Club de Playa →
BASIC CRITERIA
HOTEL CRITERIA
HOTEL CATEGORY
PRICE INDEX
BEACHES
ENTERTAIN-MENT
FLIGHT LENGTH
SIGHTS
SHOPPING
AIR TEMPERATURE
INTENSITY
You have
0
trips found
ON
ON
ON
ON
OFF
OFF
OFF
OFF
RESET
Sound on
See search results
Slow connection?
Go to the modem version

TRUST THE MAN

USA

www.foxsearchlight.com/trusttheman

2006

Concept

As part of the *Trust the Man* movie website, a game was created with a "scroll over" navigation over an aerial view of Manhattan. Players need to choose a pair of characters and match them according to their likes and dislikes. /// Als Bestandteil der Website für den Film *Trust the Man* wurde dieses Spiel mit Scroll-over-Navigation und einer Luftansicht von Manhattan entwickelt. Spieler müssen Figuren anhand ihrer Vorlieben und Abneigungen zu Paaren zusammenfügen. /// Le site Web du film *Trust the Man* inclut un jeu avec une navigation par « défilement » sur une vue aérienne de Manhattan. Les joueurs doivent choisir deux personnages et les associer en fonction de leurs points communs et leurs différences.

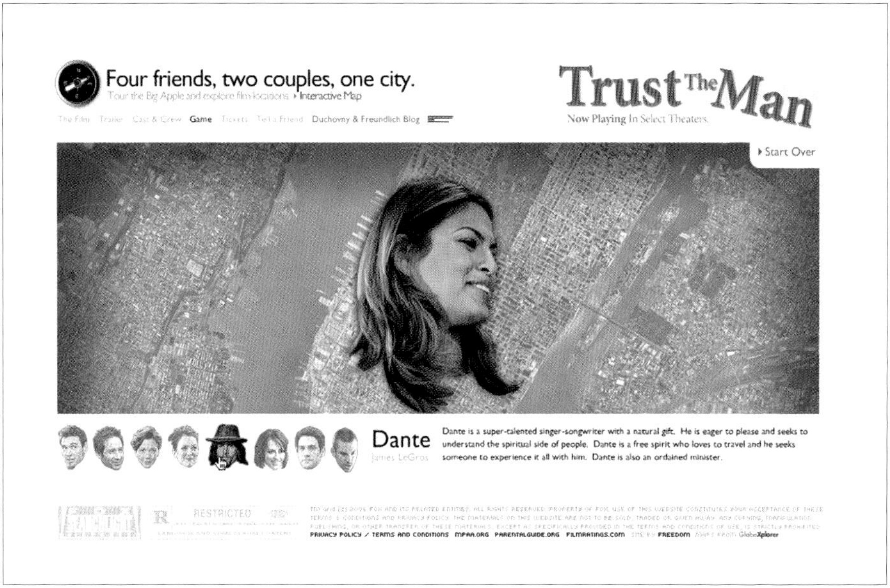

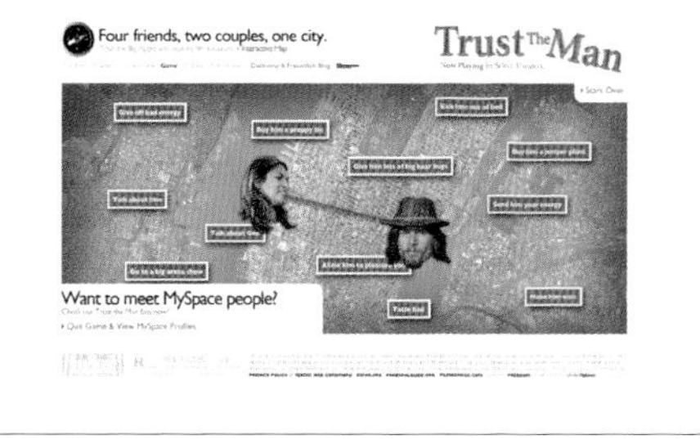

Info

Design: Freedom Interactive Design <www.freedominteractivedesign.com>. /// **Programming:** Freedom Interactive Design. /// **Tools:** Flash. /// **Awards:** FWA (Site of the Day).

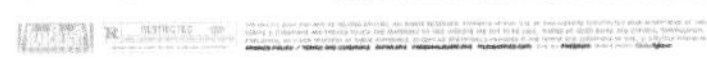

FOX SEARCHLIGHT

R RESTRICTED
LANGUAGE AND SOME SEXUAL CONTENT

TURNER ROAD SHOW

BRAZIL

www.w3haus.com/temp

2007

Concept

Created to release the media opportunities from Turner channels, the project uses the theme of cookery, showing each channel as a menu (related to its segment purpose). /// Das Projekt dient dazu, die TV-Sender von Turner zu präsentieren. Es greift die Kochthematik auf und zeigt jeden Sender als Menü (passend zur jeweiligen Ausrichtung). /// Créé pour expliquer les possibilités offertes par les chaînes Turner, le projet se sert du thème culinaire pour présenter chaque chaîne sous forme de menu (en fonction du segment correspondant).

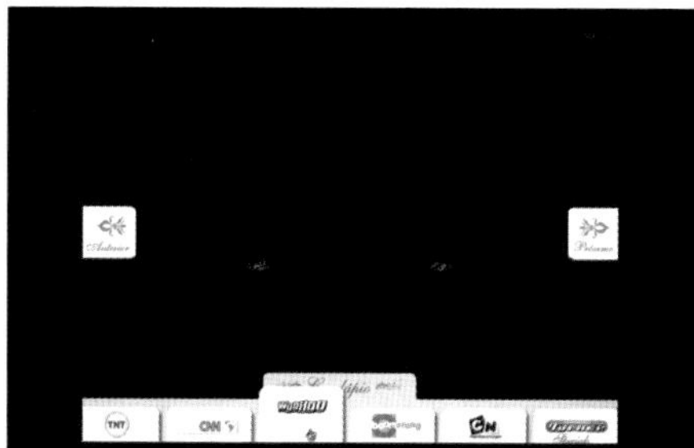

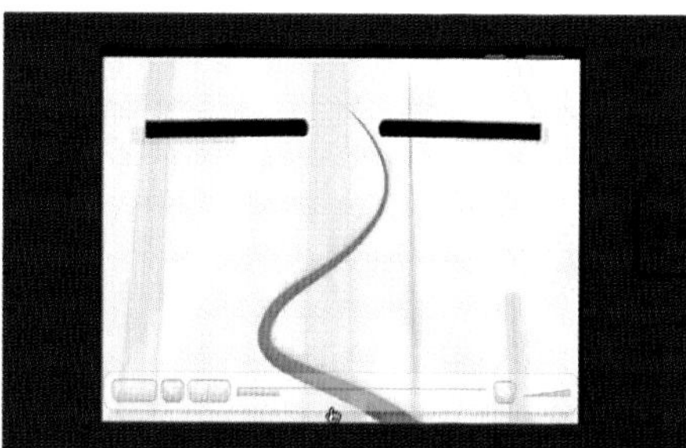

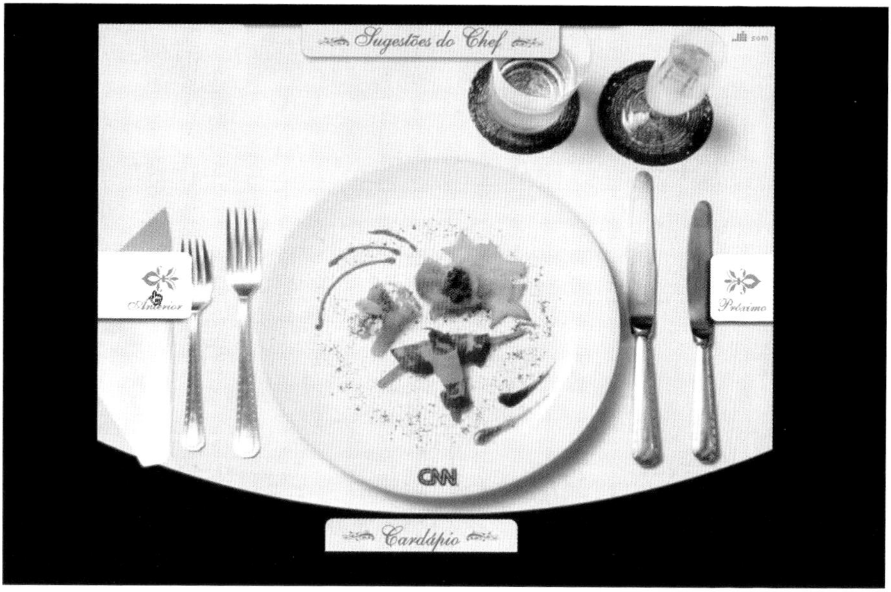

Info

Design: W3Haus <www.w3haus.com.br>, Chico Baldini, Pablo de la Rocha, Matias Causa. /// **Programming:** Matias Causa. /// **Tools:** Adobe Photoshop, Flash, HTML, XML. /// **Cost:** 300 hours. /// **Others:** Tiago Ritter (Account Manager).

Sugestões do Chef
Anterior
Próximo
TNT
Cardápio

Sugestões do Chef
Anterior
Próximo
Cardápio
TNT

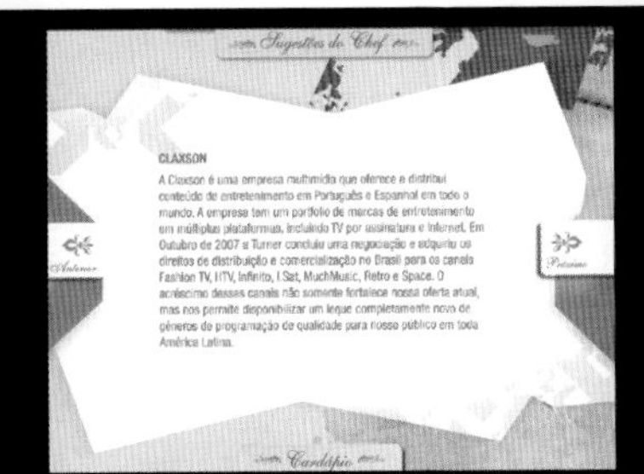
Sugestões do Chef
CLAXSON
A Claxson é uma empresa multimídia que oferece e distribui conteúdo de entretenimento em Português e Espanhol em todo o mundo. A empresa tem um portfolio de marcas de entretenimento em múltiplas plataformas, incluindo TV por assinatura e Internet. Em Outubro de 2007 a Turner concluiu uma negociação e adquiriu os direitos de distribuição e comercialização no Brasil para os canais Fashion TV, HTV, Infinito, I.Sat, MuchMusic, Retro e Space. O acréscimo desses canais não somente fortalece nossa oferta atual, mas nos permite disponibilizar um leque completamente novo de gêneros de programação de qualidade para nosso público em toda América Latina.
Anterior
Próximo
Cardápio

Sugestões do Chef
Anterior
Próximo
Cardápio

Sugestões do Chef
Anterior
Próximo
Cardápio

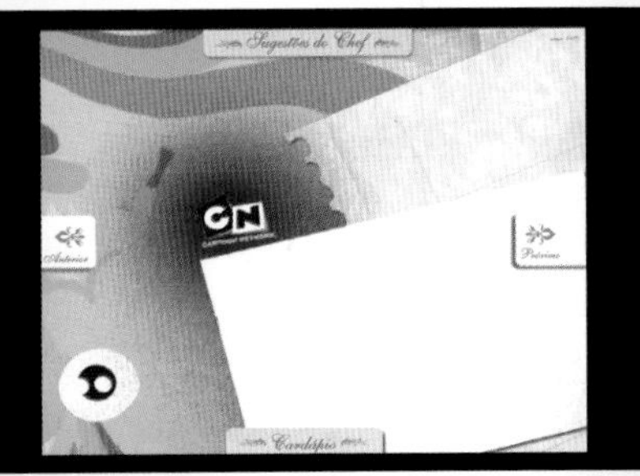
Sugestões do Chef
CN
Anterior
Próximo
Cardápio

Sugestões do Chef
CN
PROJETOS CUSTOMIZADOS
SPOTS CUSTOMIZADOS DE KAPO
Kapo, a marca de sucos da Coca-cola, queria trabalhar o lançamento do achocolatado Kapolate. Para divulgar o produto produzimos 3 comerciais de 30" em animação, mostrando os desafios do personagem Kapolate e sua turminha.
VÍDEO 1
Anterior
Próximo
Cardápio

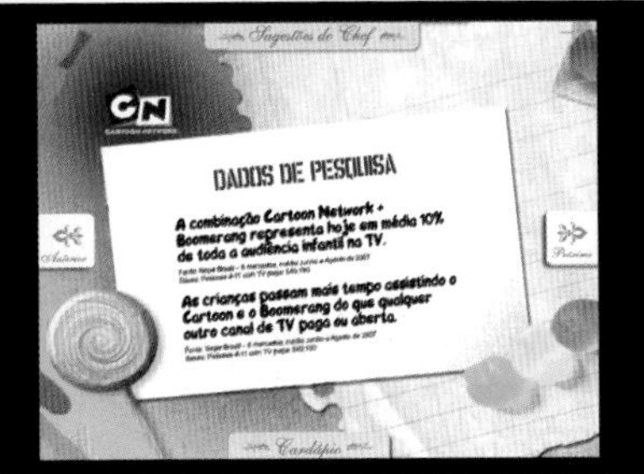
Sugestões do Chef
CN
DADOS DE PESQUISA
A combinação Cartoon Network + Boomerang representa hoje em média 10% de toda a audiência infantil na TV.
As crianças passam mais tempo assistindo o Cartoon e o Boomerang do que qualquer outro canal de TV paga ou aberta.
Anterior
Próximo
Cardápio

VF INSIDER

USA

http://siitemail.com/vanityfair

2007

Concept

The gift finder gives holiday shoppers a unique way to find just the right gift for friends and family. With its slider-based interface, users can narrow down the perfect gift by selecting from categories. The site also features a custom widget. /// Der Geschenkesucher hilft dabei, genau das richtige Geschenk für Freunde und Verwandte zu finden. Benutzer können anhand eines Schiebereglers die Kategorien eingrenzen. Die Website enthält auch ein eigenes Widget. /// Ce conseiller en cadeaux offre aux acheteurs une façon unique de trouver le cadeau parfait pour des amis et la famille. Grâce à une interface dotée de curseurs, les utilisateurs peuvent affiner la recherche du cadeau idéal en choisissant des catégories. Le site fournit aussi un widget personnalisé.

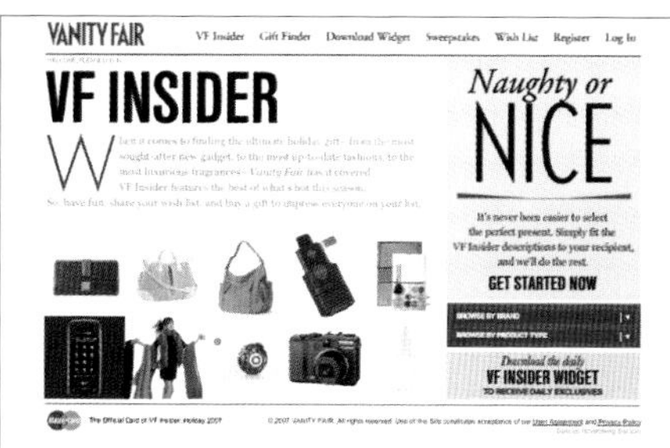

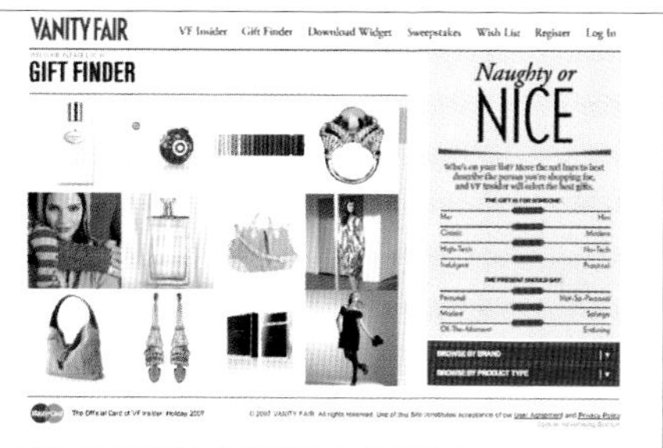

VANITY FAIR
VF Insider Gift Finder Download Widget Sweepstakes Wish List Register Log In
VF INSIDER
Naughty or
NICE
It's never been easier to select the perfect present. Simply fit the VF Insider descriptions to your recipient, and we'll do the rest.
GET STARTED NOW
VF INSIDER WIDGET

VANITY FAIR
VF Insider Gift Finder Download Widget Sweepstakes Wish List Register Log In
GIFT FINDER
Naughty or
NICE

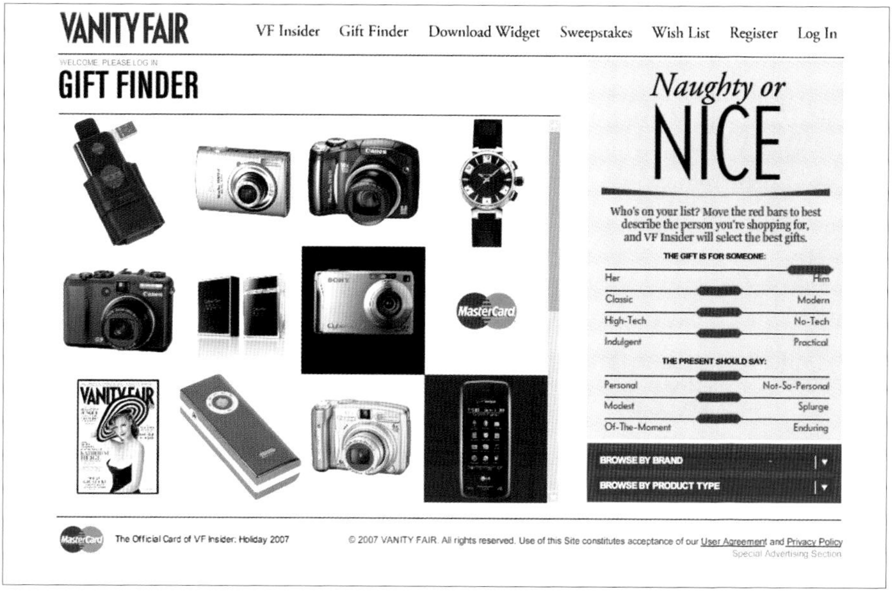

VANITY FAIR
VF Insider
Gift Finder
Download Widget
Sweepstakes
Wish List
Register
Log In
WELCOME. PLEASE LOG IN
GIFT FINDER
Naughty or
NICE
Who's on your list? Move the red bars to best describe the person you're shopping for, and VF Insider will select the best gifts.
THE GIFT IS FOR SOMEONE:
Her
Him
Classic
Modern
High-Tech
No-Tech
Indulgent
Practical
THE PRESENT SHOULD SAY:
Personal
Not-So-Personal
Modest
Splurge
Of-The-Moment
Enduring
BROWSE BY BRAND
BROWSE BY PRODUCT TYPE
MasterCard
The Official Card of VF Insider: Holiday 2007
© 2007 VANITY FAIR. All rights reserved. Use of this Site constitutes acceptance of our User Agreement and Privacy Policy
Special Advertising Section

Info

Design: SiiTE Interactive <www.SiiTE.com>. /// **Programming:** SiiTE Interactive. /// **Tools:** Adobe Photoshop, Flash, ASP.net. /// **Awards:** Adobe (Site of the Day).

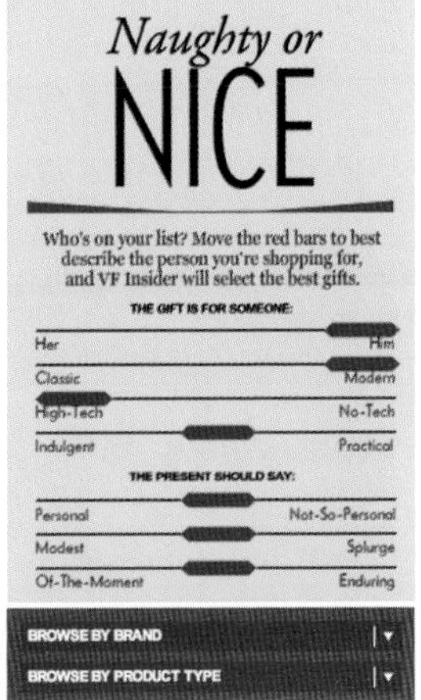

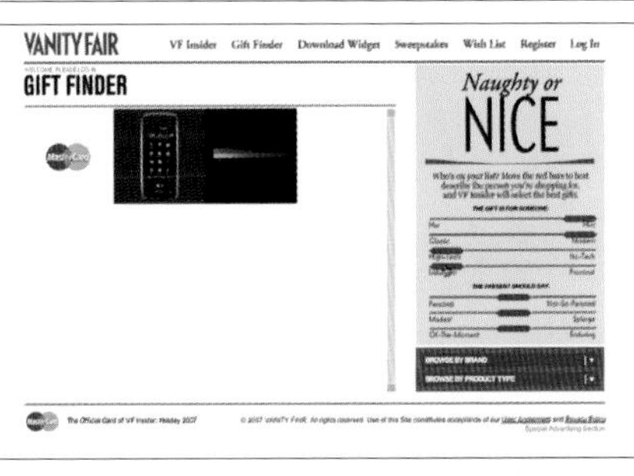

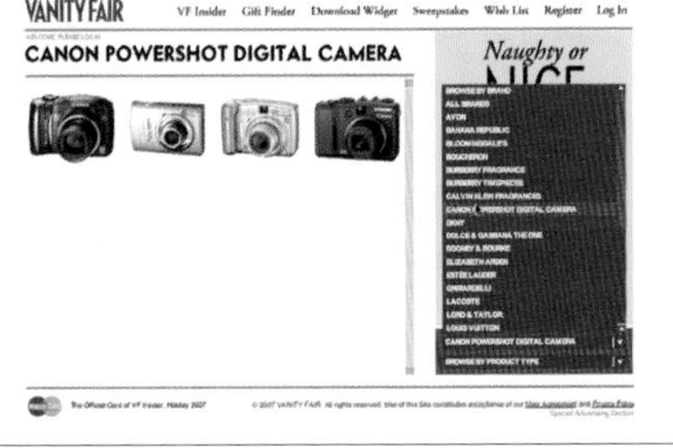

Results

Vanity Fair was able to get great advertiser buy-in. /// Vanity Fair konnte viele Werbekunden akquirieren. /// Vanity Fair a obtenu une grande adhésion des annonceurs.

WAS AUCH KOMMT: HDI

GERMANY

www.wasauchkommt.de

2007

Concept

A microsite for one of Germany's biggest insurance companies. The concept for the TV spots was to show possible tragedies without really showing the ending. The microsite goes a step further and shows the user why he might need a good insurance policy. /// Eine Microsite für eine der größten deutschen Versicherungsgesellschaften. Das Konzept der TV-Spots bestand darin, potenzielle Unglücke zu zeigen, ohne dass man das Ende sieht. Die Microsite geht einen Schritt weiter und führt dem Benutzer vor Augen, warum er oder sie möglicherweise eine gute Versicherung braucht. /// Mini-site pour l'une des plus importantes compagnies d'assurance d'Allemagne. Dans les spots télévisés, le concept était de montrer des catastrophes possibles sans vraiment expliquer la fin. Le mini-site va plus loin et montre à l'utilisateur pourquoi il a besoin d'une bonne assurance.

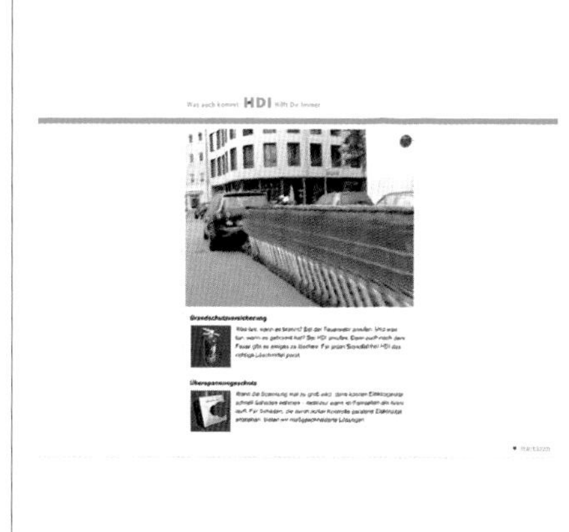

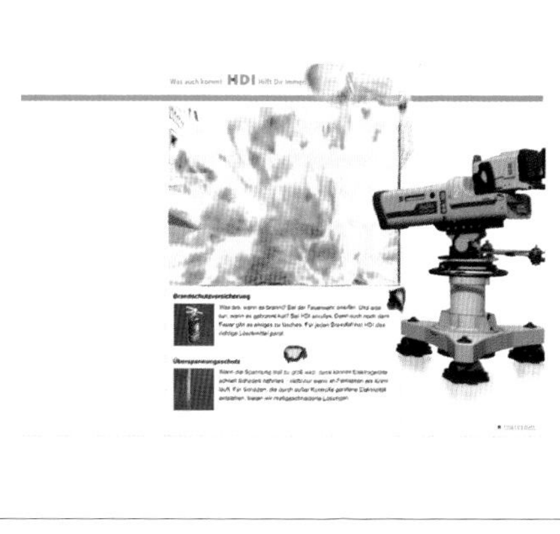

Info

Design: blackbeltmonkey <www.blackbeltmonkey.com>, Creative Director/Art Direction: Mike John Otto; Concept: Mike John Otto, Oliver Bentz and GudellaBarche (TV-Spot). /// **Programming:** Robert Menzel. /// **Tools:** Adobe Photoshop, Flash, Cinema 4D, Combustion, CMS, XML, PHP. /// **Cost:** 1,5 month. /// **Others:** Silbersee Film/Silberlink (Film production); DeliPictures (Post Production); Andre Haupt (3D).

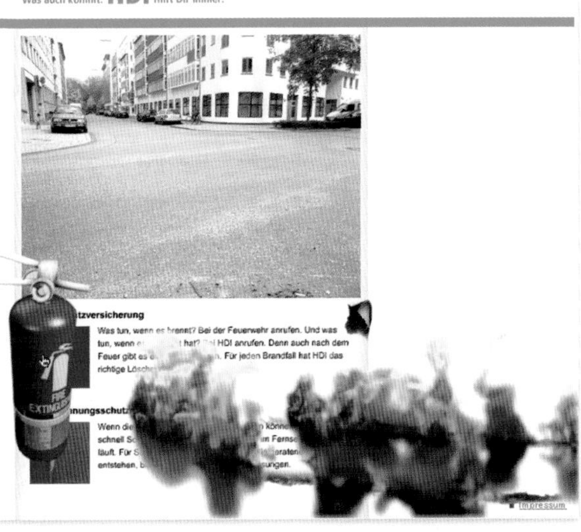
Was auch kommt: HDI Hilft Dir Immer.
Impressum

Was auch kommt: HDI Hilft Dir Immer.
Nanu? Riechen Sie das auch? Hat es hier gebrannt? Naja. Wenn Sie sich trauen, dann klicken Sie auf Kamera 3!
Brandschutzversicherung
Was tun, wenn es brennt? Bei der Feuerwehr anrufen. Und was tun, wenn es gebrannt hat? Bei HDI anrufen. Denn auch nach dem Feuer gibt es einiges zu löschen. Für jeden Brandfall hat HDI das richtige Löschmittel parat.
Überspannungsschutz
Impressum

WHO IS DOCTOR WHO?

UK

www.whoisdoctorwho.co.uk

2006

Concept

A game with multiple stand-alone games centred around the concept of having "online adventures with a friend." The aim was to enable the audience to act as an able assistant to the Doctor, helping him save the universe. /// Ein aus vielen Einzelspielen zusammengesetztes Projekt, die sich alle um die Idee drehen, dass man „mit einem Freund Online-Abenteuer besteht". Die Benutzer sollten dem Doktor als fähige Assistenten zur Seite stehen und ihm dabei helfen, das Universum zu retten. /// Ensemble de plusieurs jeux indépendants tournant autour du concept d'« aventures en ligne avec un ami ». L'objectif était de permettre au public de servir d'assistant compétent au Doctor pour l'aider à sauver la planète.

Info

Design: Sequence <www.sequence.co.uk>, Mark Johnson, Leo Yeung, James O'Dwyer, James Goss, Rob Francis. /// **Programming:** Mick McNicholas, Gavin Davies, Reuben Whitehouse. /// **Tools:** Adobe Photoshop, Flash, Illustrator, Fireworks, Soundbooth, XML, HTML, CSS. /// **Awards:** BAFTA (Shortlist), Y Design Awards. /// **Cost:** £150,000.

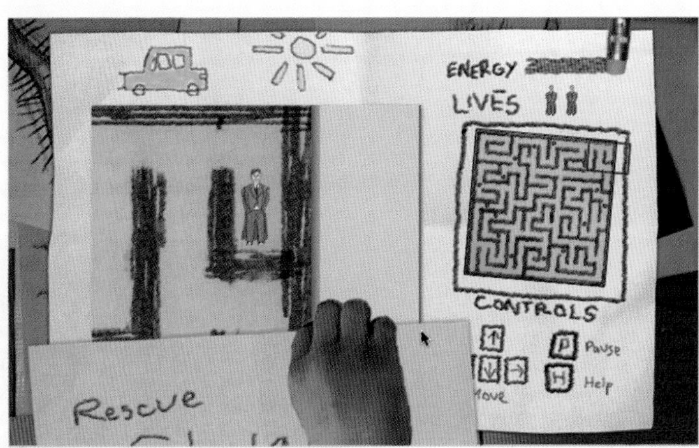

Results

The overall projects and stand-alone games were massively successful with online audience take-up in the hundreds of thousands. Rave reviews on fan boards, almost every week, greatly accelerated the site's viral campaign. /// Das übergeordnete Projekt und die Einzelspiele waren unglaublich erfolgreich und erreichten Hunderttausende. Enthusiastische Besprechungen auf Fanboards gaben der viralen Kampagne enormen Auftrieb. /// Tous les projets et les jeux indépendants ont remporté un immense succès, avec l'accroche de centaines de milliers d'utilisateurs en ligne. Les commentaires élogieux sur les forums de fans quasiment toutes les semaines ont nettement accéléré la campagne virale du site.

XM WILD RIDE

USA

www.driftlab.com/xm

2007

Concept

As part of a viral campaign, this game gets the user to fling animals from the hood of a car, with the goal of having them land on another. /// Als Teil einer viralen Werbekampagne soll der Benutzer bei diesem Spiel Tiere von einem Autodach werfen und erreichen, dass sie übereinander landen. /// Dans le cadre d'une campagne virale, ce jeu permet à l'utilisateur de lancer des animaux depuis le capot d'une voiture afin qu'ils atterrissent sur un autre.

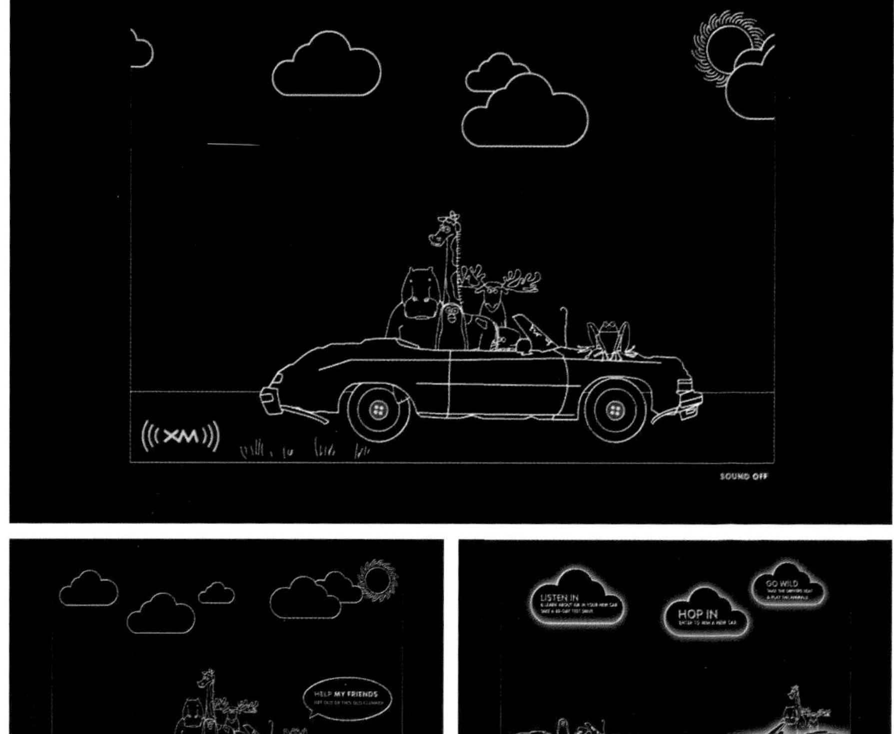

Info

DESIGN: driftlab <www.driftlab.com>. /// PROGRAMMING: driftlab. /// TOOLS: Flash, Actionscript, XML, Dreamweaver, Illustrator. /// COST: 80 hours. /// OTHERS: Anselm Yew.

Results

This game created substantial viral activity through people sending the link to a friend. /// Das Spiel erzielte eine virale Verbreitung, weil viele Menschen den Link an Freunde schickten. /// Ce jeu a entraîné une activité virale importante grâce aux personnes qui ont envoyé le lien à des amis.

YARIS VS. YARIS

USA

www.radassembly.com/work/yaris-vs-yaris/500x250/left_index.html

2006

Concept

The Yaris is known for its humourous and satirical campaigns. The online game continues this mood by allowing the user to drive around a city, paying extra care to pedestrians and other obstacles. /// Der Yaris ist für seine humorvollen Werbekampagnen bekannt. Das Online-Spiel greift diese Stimmung auf. Der Benutzer darf in einer Stadt herumfahren und muss besonders auf Fußgänger und andere Hindernisse achten. /// Le modèle Yaris est célèbre pour ses campagnes humoristiques et satiriques. Le jeu en ligne est fidèle à cet état d'esprit et permet à l'utilisateur de conduire dans une ville, en faisant notamment attention aux piétons et à d'autres obstacles.

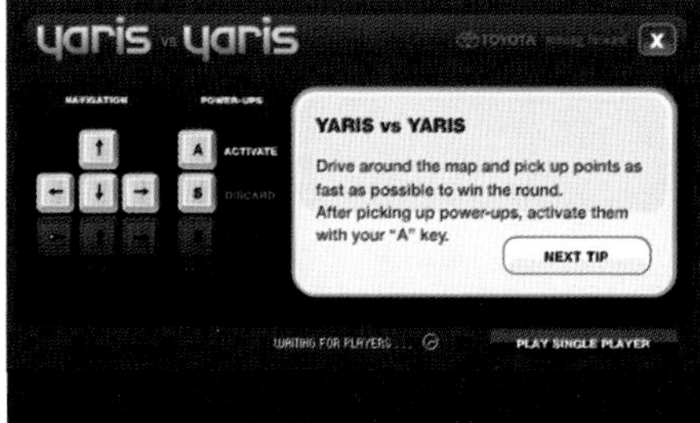

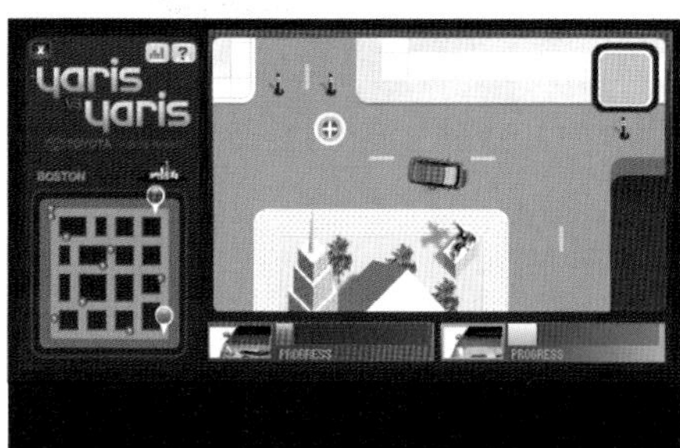

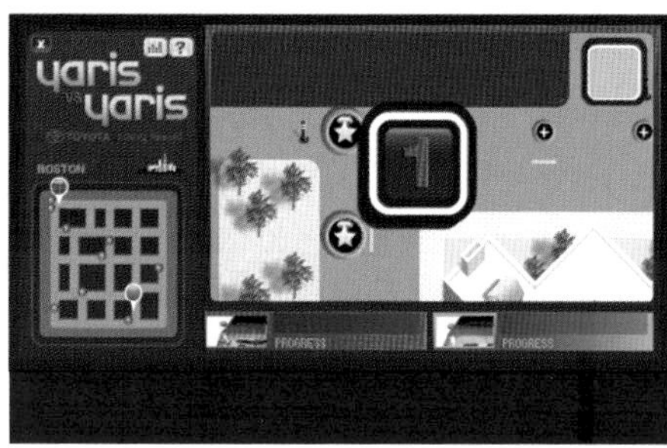

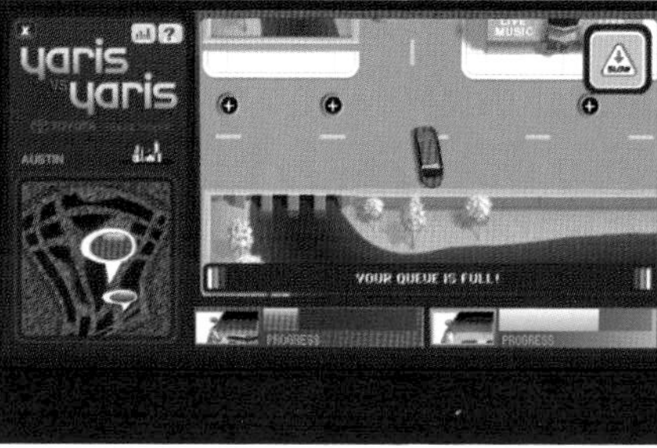

Info

Design: Bad Assembly <www.badassembly.com>, Jimmy Walker, Scott Baggett. /// **Programming:** Nathan Holloway. /// **Tools:** Adobe Photoshop, Flash, After Effects, Maya, Illustrator, Ableton Live, Logic Audio. /// **Awards:** Adobe [Site of the Day], Webby [Advertising, Game/Application]. /// **Cost:** 400 Hours. /// **Client:** Saatchi & Saatchi.

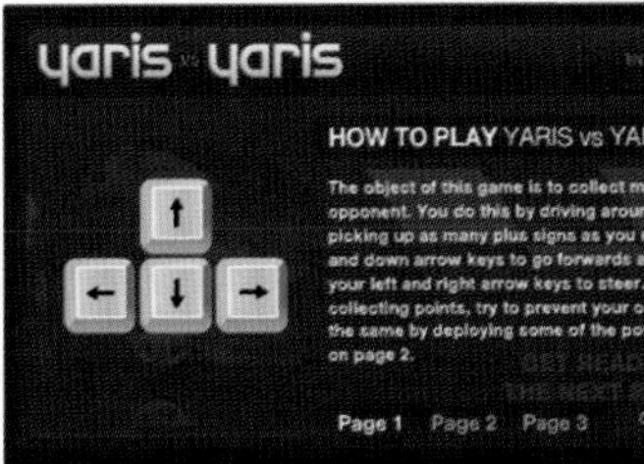
yaris vs yaris
HOW TO PLAY YARIS vs YARIS
The object of this game is to collect more points than your opponent. You do this by driving around the city and picking up as many plus signs as you can. Use your up and down arrow keys to go forwards and backwards, and your left and right arrow keys to steer. While you're collecting points, try to prevent your opponent from doing the same by deploying some of the power-ups described on page 2.
Page 1 Page 2 Page 3

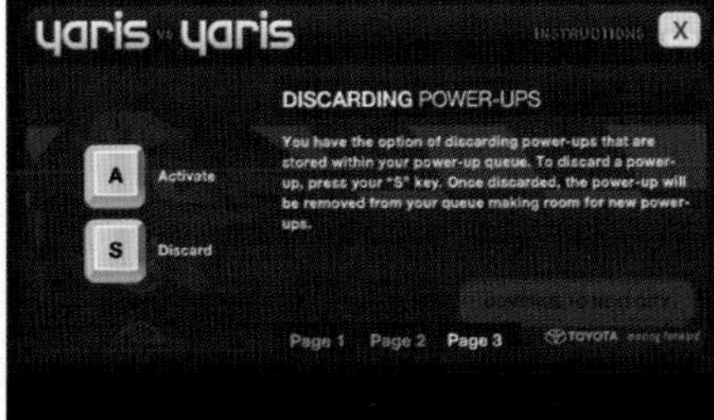
yaris vs yaris
DISCARDING POWER-UPS
A Activate
S Discard
You have the option of discarding power-ups that are stored within your power-up queue. To discard a power-up, press your "S" key. Once discarded, the power-up will be removed from your queue making room for new power-ups.
Page 1 Page 2 Page 3

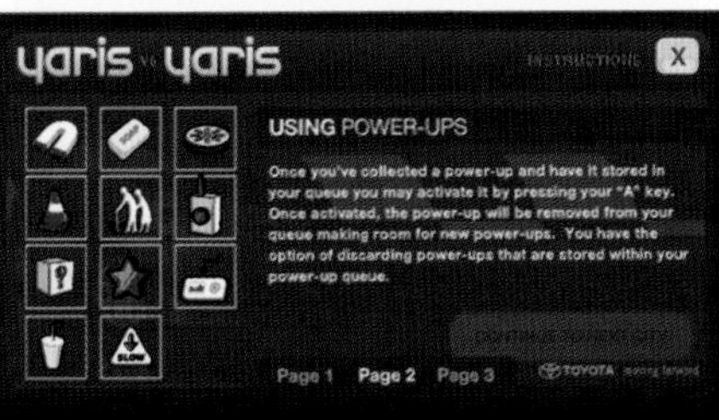
yaris vs yaris
USING POWER-UPS
Once you've collected a power-up and have it stored in your queue you may activate it by pressing your "A" key. Once activated, the power-up will be removed from your queue making room for new power-ups. You have the option of discarding power-ups that are stored within your power-up queue.
Page 1 Page 2 Page 3

yaris vs yaris
SEATTLE
READY!
READY!

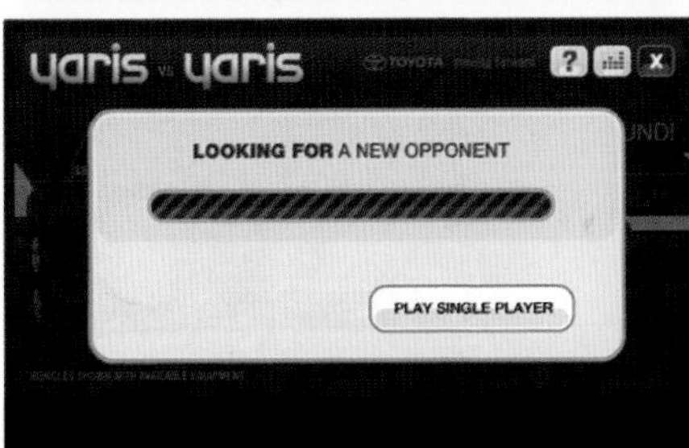
yaris vs yaris
LOOKING FOR A NEW OPPONENT
PLAY SINGLE PLAYER

yaris vs yaris
HOW ABOUT THE REAL THING?
Single player is fun but multiplayer is where the real action is at! Challenge others online by clicking on "Find a New Opponent" or stick with single player by clicking on "Play Single Player."
FIND A NEW OPPONENT
PLAY SINGLE PLAYER

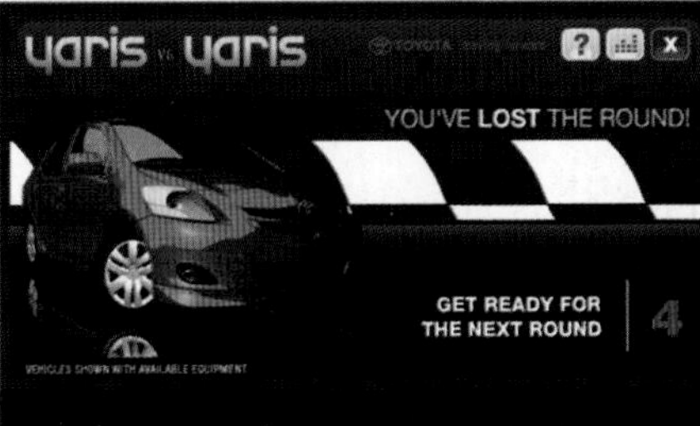
yaris vs yaris
YOU'VE LOST THE ROUND!
GET READY FOR THE NEXT ROUND
4
VEHICLES SHOWN WITH AVAILABLE EQUIPMENT

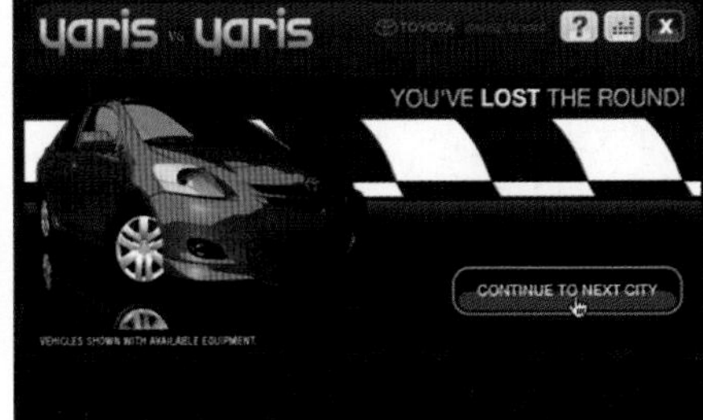
yaris vs yaris
YOU'VE LOST THE ROUND!
CONTINUE TO NEXT CITY
VEHICLES SHOWN WITH AVAILABLE EQUIPMENT

CREDITS

Doing a book on interactivity online can sound redundant. At last, it is all about interacting and taking action to go to the next step. But there are designers and programmers that have taken that concept to another dimension, and they keep pushing the technological boundaries to create user experience never imagined before. Having said that, I would like to thank these professionals that have given their invaluable collaboration for this publication, including the introduction and the three case studies in the beginning of this book, from Mike John Otto from Hamburg, Sergio Mugnaini from Sao Paulo, Jonathan Hills from New York, and Patrick Gardner from Stockholm. These army of creative directors, art directors, planners, animators, programmers, illustrators, and so much more are reinventing the world. The credit is all theirs.

I have also to hugely thank Daniel Siciliano Brêtas, that has created the design of the series, and also has pushed the boundaries to improve every book of the series. It is now the seventh title, and we have been so happy to see how readers have been enjoying the diversity of the subjects we have touched on.

Have a good read!

Julius Wiedemann

IMPRINT

Web Design: Interactive & Games

To stay informed about upcoming TASCHEN titles, please request our magazine at www.taschen.com/magazine or write to TASCHEN, Hohenzollernring 53, D-50672 Cologne, Germany, contact@taschen.com, Fax: +49-221-254919. We will be happy to send you a free copy of our magazine which is filled with information about all of our books.

Design & layout: Daniel Siciliano Brêtas
Production: Stefan Klatte
Editor: Julius Wiedemann
Editorial coordination: Daniel Siciliano Brêtas

German translation: Ronit Jariv
French translation: Valérie Lavoyer

Printed in Italy
ISBN 978-3-8228-4053-5

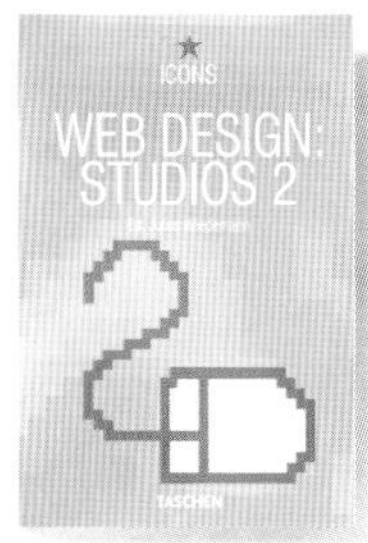

Web Design: Studios 2
Ed. Julius Wiedemann / Flexi-cover, 192 pp. / € 6.99 / $ 9.99 / £ 5.99 / ¥ 1.500

Web Design: Flash Sites
Ed. Julius Wiedemann / Flexi-cover, 192 pp. / € 6.99 / $ 9.99 / £ 5.99 / ¥ 1.500

Web Design: Music Sites
Ed. Julius Wiedemann / Flexi-cover, 192 pp. / € 6.99 / $ 9.99 / £ 5.99 / ¥ 1.500

"These books are beautiful objects, well-designed and lucid." —*Le Monde*, Paris, on the ICONS series

" Buy them all and add some pleasure to your life."

60s Fashion
Ed. Jim Heimann

70s Fashion
Ed. Jim Heimann

African Style
Ed. Angelika Taschen

Alchemy & Mysticism
Alexander Roob

Architecture Now!
Ed. Philip Jodidio

Art Now
Eds. Burkhard Riemschneider, Uta Grosenick

Atget's Paris
Ed. Hans Christian Adam

Bamboo Style
Ed. Angelika Taschen

Barcelona, Restaurants & More
Ed. Angelika Taschen

Barcelona, Shops & More
Ed. Angelika Taschen

Ingrid Bergman
Ed. Paul Duncan, Scott Eyman

Berlin Style
Ed. Angelika Taschen

Humphrey Bogart
Ed. Paul Duncan, James Ursini

Marlon Brando
Ed. Paul Duncan, F.X. Feeney

Brussels Style
Ed. Angelika Taschen

Cars of the 70s
Ed. Jim Heimann, Tony Thacker

Charlie Chaplin
Ed. Paul Duncan, David Robinson

China Style
Ed. Angelika Taschen

Christmas
Ed. Jim Heimann, Steven Heller

James Dean
Ed. Paul Duncan, F.X. Feeney

Design Handbook
Charlotte & Peter Fiell

Design for the 21st Century
Eds. Charlotte & Peter Fiell

Design of the 20th Century
Eds. Charlotte & Peter Fiell

Devils
Gilles Néret

Marlene Dietrich
Ed. Paul Duncan, James Ursini

Robert Doisneau
Jean-Claude Gautrand

East German Design
Ralf Ulrich/Photos: Ernst Hedler

Clint Eastwood
Ed. Paul Duncan, Douglas Keesey

Egypt Style
Ed. Angelika Taschen

Encyclopaedia Anatomica
Ed. Museo La Specola Florence

M.C. Escher

Fashion
Ed. The Kyoto Costume Institute

Fashion Now!
Eds. Terry Jones, Susie Rushton

Fruit
Ed. George Brookshaw, Uta Pellgrü-Gagel

Greta Garbo
Ed. Paul Duncan, David Robinson

HR Giger
HR Giger

Grand Tour
Harry Seidler

Cary Grant
Ed. Paul Duncan, F.X. Feeney

Graphic Design
Eds. Charlotte & Peter Fiell

Greece Style
Ed. Angelika Taschen

Halloween
Ed. Jim Heimann, Steven Heller

Havana Style
Ed. Angelika Taschen

Audrey Hepburn
Ed. Paul Duncan, F.X. Feeney

Katharine Hepburn
Ed. Paul Duncan, Alain Silver

Homo Art
Gilles Néret

Hot Rods
Ed. Coco Shinomiya, Tony Thacker

Grace Kelly
Ed. Paul Duncan, Glenn Hopp

London, Restaurants & More
Ed. Angelika Taschen

London, Shops & More
Ed. Angelika Taschen

London Style
Ed. Angelika Taschen

Marx Brothers
Ed. Paul Duncan, Douglas Keesey

Steve McQueen
Ed. Paul Duncan, Alain Silver

Mexico Style
Ed. Angelika Taschen

Miami Style
Ed. Angelika Taschen

Minimal Style
Ed. Angelika Taschen

Marilyn Monroe
Ed. Paul Duncan, F.X. Feeney

Morocco Style
Ed. Angelika Taschen

New York Style
Ed. Angelika Taschen

Paris Style
Ed. Angelika Taschen

Penguin
Frans Lanting

Pierre et Gilles
Eric Troncy

Provence Style
Ed. Angelika Taschen

Safari Style
Ed. Angelika Taschen

Seaside Style
Ed. Angelika Taschen

Signs
Ed. Julius Wiedeman

South African Style
Ed. Angelika Taschen

Starck
Philippe Starck

Surfing
Ed. Jim Heimann

Sweden Style
Ed. Angelika Taschen

Tattoos
Ed. Henk Schiffmacher

Tokyo Style
Ed. Angelika Taschen

Tuscany Style
Ed. Angelika Taschen

Valentines
Ed. Jim Heimann, Steven Heller

Web Design: Best Studios
Ed. Julius Wiedemann

Web Design: Best Studios 2
Ed. Julius Wiedemann

Web Design: E-Commerce
Ed. Julius Wiedemann

Web Design: Flash Sites
Ed. Julius Wiedemann

Web Design: Music Sites
Ed. Julius Wiedemann

Web Design: Portfolios
Ed. Julius Wiedemann

Orson Welles
Ed. Paul Duncan, F.X. Feeney

Women Artists in the 20th and 21st Century
Ed. Uta Grosenick

ICONS